The
BEADING BIBLE

A COMPREHENSIVE GUIDE TO BEADING TECHNIQUES

The
BEADING BIBLE

A COMPREHENSIVE GUIDE TO BEADING TECHNIQUES

DOROTHY WOOD

DAVID & CHARLES

www.davidandcharles.com

A DAVID AND CHARLES BOOK
© David and Charles, Ltd 2008

David and Charles is an imprint of David and Charles, Ltd
Suite A, Tourism House, Pynes Hill, Exeter, EX2 5WS

First published in the UK & US in 2008 as "The Beader's Bible"

Text and designs © Dorothy Wood 2008
Photography and illustrations © David and Charles, Ltd 2008

A catalogue record for this book is available from the
British Library.

ISBN-13: 9781446308868 paperback

This book has been printed on paper from approved
suppliers and made from pulp from sustainable sources.

Printed in the UK by Pureprint for
David and Charles, Ltd
Suite A, Tourism House, Pynes Hill, Exeter, EX2 5WS

10 9 8 7 6 5 4 3 2 1

Senior Commissioning Editor: Cheryl Brown
Desk Editor: Bethany Dymond
Art Editor: Sarah Underhill
Designer: Sue Cleave
Project Editor: Natasha Reed
Technical Editor: Jean Power
Production Controller: Bev Richardson
Photography: Kim Sayer and Karl Adamson
Illustrators: Ethan Danielson and Mia Farrant

David and Charles publishes high-quality books on
a wide range of subjects. For more information visit
www.davidandcharles.com.

Layout of the digital edition of this book may vary
depending on reader hardware and display settings.

Contents

Introduction

*B*eads are the oldest and most widespread art form, having been used in virtually every culture since ancient times. Originally beads were worn to give an indication of social status or religious beliefs and were widely used as a currency, talisman or healing token. These early beads, made from organic materials such as bone, horn, teeth, ivory, stones, nuts, seeds, shell, wood and various plant and insect resins, are still popular today. Over the years new materials and methods of making beads have been introduced and now bead workers have a vast array of stunning beads to work with.

This stunning selection of semi-precious beads shown opposite gives you just some idea of the huge selection available in shops and from online retailers.

Beading has also developed over the years and, even though many traditional techniques are still popular, the craft is constantly evolving and so there has never been a more exciting time to work with beads. With so many techniques, and such a vast array of beads and materials available for the contemporary bead worker, there is definitely a need for a comprehensive guide.

The Beading Bible is just that – an encyclopedia of beads and beading techniques that aims to educate and inspire anyone who loves working with beads. It is designed, in the first instance, to be a workbook with step instructions on all the basic techniques and, secondly, to be a source of ideas and inspirations giving you the opportunity to advance your skills.

Because people generally focus on one type of beading at a time the book is divided into eight chapters that cover all the traditional techniques such as bead loom weaving, jewellery and bead embroidery, as well as introducing newer techniques such as knitting and crochet with beads. Each chapter gives a good grounding in the basic techniques and shows ways to develop these skills to a more advanced level. There are inspiration pages giving you interesting ideas using the different techniques in each chapter and fabulous projects dotted throughout so that if you have the urge to 'Bead Something Now' you will have all the necessary skills. Illustrated with step-by-step photography and diagrams to make everything as clear and easy to follow as possible, this will be the only bead book you ever need.

Beads

Walk into any bead shop and you will find a wonderful array of beads in all shapes, sizes and colours. It is worth having a good look around first to see what is available as many shops specialise in particular types of beading; if jewellery is the main focus the shop will stock mainly large decorative beads, whereas another shop may have a wide range of smaller beads such as seed beads and bugles for loom work and off-loom bead stitches.

Choosing Beads

With such a variety of beads it can be overwhelming deciding what to buy but it is easy to narrow down your choice to make the task less daunting. As different beading techniques often use specific types of beads, once you decide what you are going to bead then the task becomes much easier. Seed beads are ideal for techniques such as bead loom weaving, off-loom weaving or ropes and cords, whereas larger beads are more suitable for wirework and threading and stringing. Learning a little about the different types of beads, how they are measured and different finishes will help you make an informed choice next time you visit the bead shop.

Beads Direct!

Although it is always a pleasure actually handpicking your beads, internet shopping is becoming increasingly popular and you will be able to find any bead you need online. The internet makes it easy to buy beads from around the world and these will be delivered to your door in a few days. Although postage is added, it is often still more economical.

LARGE BEADS

Glass

Glass is the most versatile of all the materials from which beads are made. Not only can it be made into a wide range of sizes and shapes but the variety of finishes, described on page 11, make for endless possibilities. **Pressed glass** beads are made in moulds to create lots of different shapes, from leaves and flowers to discs, cylinders and drops. **Powder glass** beads, from Ghana and Nigeria, are made from recycled glass, which is ground and then fused in moulds to create beads with striped layers. **Millefiori** beads are made from canes of glass, in the same way as seaside rock, and then cut into slices to reveal the decorative cross section. **Metallic-lined** beads are transparent beads with the holes lined in gold, silver or another metallic colour to create a beautiful sparkly effect that shines through the glass surround. The metallic lining looks a little like leaf metal and can be flecked or plain.

Lampwork

These exquisite glass beads are handmade on a workbench using a blowtorch with rods or canes of plain or patterned glass. The beads are formed around a mandrel, a revolving metal rod that determines the size of the hole. The winding process creates distinctive lines of glass wound around the outside. Whilst still soft, glass can be pressed with a ribbed tool or crumbs of glass can be sprinkled on the surface to create texture.

Crystals

The term 'crystal' describes a faceted bead ranging from the finest quality cut glass, such as Swarovski crystals, to inexpensive faceted glass or even moulded plastic beads. There is a huge difference in price but, as always, you get what you pay for and the more expensive crystals have a far superior shine and sparkle. Crystals are available in a wide range of colours and shapes.

Pearls

The lustre on pearls takes them into the luxury look even though the beads themselves can be inexpensive. It is easy to distinguish between real and fake pearls because if you rub a real pearl gently against your tooth it produces a grating sensation whereas the surface of imitation pearls is completely smooth. Real pearls, which fall into the organic group, see page 9, can either be cultured (from a pearl farm) or from the wild. Like every other type of bead the price varies with quality. The most valuable pearls have an iridescent lustre and are not too wrinkled. Pearls can be dyed almost any colour but are most often white, cream or pastel shades.

Metal

Metal beads are available in a wide range of materials such as brass, copper, aluminium and different alloys. Some silver and gold beads are plated over a base metal but you can buy precious metal beads in sterling silver. As gold is so expensive, 'gold' beads are generally a cheaper substitute known as rolled or gold-filled. Metal beads can be moulded, modelled or shaped from sheet metal and often have a distinctive textured surface.

Modelled Beads

Modelling materials for beads include resin, gesso, lacquer, pâpier maché, ceramic, polymer clay and cinnabar. Although many are mass-produced these beads are still in the main handmade and have a quaintness and individuality that is lost with manufactured beads.

Plastic

These beads range from the cheap and cheerful to highly collectable early plastic beads such as bakelite and vulcanite. More recent plastics include perspex, acetate and coloured cast resins. Plastic beads can be dyed or coated, with metallic coatings looking surprisingly authentic, although much lighter than metal beads.

Gemstones

Gemstones or semi-precious beads are pieces of mineral, which have been cut and polished to make extremely attractive and valuable beads. Some rocks, such as lapis lazuli, and organic materials like amber or jet are considered to be gemstones too. Often sold in strings the price varies considerably depending on the aesthetic value and rarity of the mineral. Transparent gemstones are sometimes faceted to add sparkle and opaque gemstones, like opal, are often made into cabochons. Some semi-precious stones, such as jade, are dyed to produce a more varied range of colours. Inexpensive chips are small rough pieces of mineral, ideal for jewellery and crochet.

Organic

Organic beads, made from a huge variety of natural materials, were the first beads made by our ancestors for artistic ornamentation. Seeds, nuts, shells, bones and horn were all fashioned into beads then and are still popular now. Some organic materials like ivory, amber, tortoiseshell and jet are now rare but can be found in antique jewellery. Painted wood beads are colourful and cheap but there are also lots of really attractive beads made from unusual woods from around the world.

SMALL BEADS

Seed Beads

These are round doughnut-shaped beads ranging from size 3 to 15. Larger seed beads are known as pebble or pony beads and the smaller ones as petites. The most common size of seed bead is size 11.

Cylinder Beads

Cylinder beads, also known by their trade names delicas, antiques or magnificas, are precision-milled tubular beads. They are ideal for off-loom and bead loom weaving as the beads sit so neatly side by side to make an even bead fabric. Cylinder beads have a large hole, enabling you to pass the thread through each bead several times.

Hex Beads

These are cylindrical beads made from a six-sided glass cane. They are like a squat bugle bead and useful for creating texture. Twisted hex beads are also called two-cuts.

Drop Beads

Drop beads, such as Magatamas™, are beads with an off-centre hole that adds interest and texture to many bead projects. They are available in the same colours and finishes as ordinary seed beads.

Triangle Beads

These beads have three sides and add an interesting texture to bead fabric, especially herringbone stitch. There are two main styles, both from Japan; the geometric sharp-sided Toho triangle and the more rounded Miyuki triangle.

Bugle Beads

Bugle beads are glass canes cut to a variety of lengths. The most common sizes are 3–4mm, 6–7mm, 9m and 15mm. Twisted bugles are five- or six-sided tubes that have been twisted while the glass is still hot.

Bead Sizes

When you handpick beads it isn't so essential to know the exact size as you can mix and match on the spot. However, if you are buying online or from a catalogue the beads may not be shown actual size and it is useful to know how different beads are measured. Beads are generally measured in millimetres but some, especially seed beads and bugles, can also have bead sizes. Beads are measured across the widest point. So if the bead is round it is the diameter, on a square bead it is the width and if oval, cylindrical or rectangular, the beads are measured by length and width.

SEED BEADS

Many beading techniques use small beads known collectively as seed beads which range in size from the tiny size 15, known as petite beads, to large size 3 pebble beads. Seed bead sizes relate to the number of beads that fit into 2.5cm (1in) when laid out like rows of doughnuts. It is not always accurate but, as shown below, there is an obvious scale of sizes.

Size 15 = 1.3mm
Size 11 = 1.8mm
Size 10 = 2.0mm
Size 9 = 2.2mm
Size 8 = 2.5mm
Size 6 = 3.3mm

BUGLE BEADS

These tubes of glass are measured in millimetres or by size, depending on where you buy them. To make matters more confusing, Czech and Japanese bugles are measured differently so check before you buy. If you want to match bugles with seed beads, a size 1 bugle is about the same diameter as a size 12 seed bead; other bugles are about the same diameter as a size 11 bead.

Czech
Size 1 = 2mm (³⁄₃₂in)
Size 2 = 4mm (³⁄₁₆in)
Size 3 = 7mm (¼in)
Size 4 = 9mm (³⁄₈in)
Size 5 = 11mm (⁷⁄₁₆in)

Japanese
Size 1 = 3mm (¹⁄₁₀in)
Size 2 = 6mm (¼in)
Size 3 = 9mm (³⁄₈in)

Bead Quantities

Beads are either sold individually, in a packet of some sort or on a string. Larger beads are more often sold individually although bead strings have become quite popular, especially for semi-precious beads. These strings are generally a standard 40cm (16in) long and so the number of beads varies depending on the size of the individual beads. The chart below gives you an idea of the quantities for one string.

Size	No. of beads	Size	No. of beads	Size	No. of beads
2mm (³⁄₃₂in)	200	6mm (¼in)	67	10mm (⁴⁄₁₀in)	40
3mm (¹⁄₁₀in)	133	7mm (¼in)	57	12mm (⁵⁄₁₀in)	33
4mm (³⁄₁₆in)	100	8mm (³⁄₈in)	50	15mm (⁶⁄₁₀in)	27
5mm (²⁄₁₀in)	80	9mm (³⁄₈in)	44	20mm (¾in)	20

With seed beads the strings are 51cm (20in) long and generally sold as hanks of 12 strings. The quantity varies depending on the size of the beads. Use the chart below as a guide.

Size	Beads per 2.5cm (1in)	51cm (20in) string	Size	Beads per 2.5cm (1in)	51cm (20in) string
15	24	480	9	15	300
11	17	340	8	13	260
10	16	320	6	10	200

Seed beads, cylinder beads and bugles are sold in a variety of packets, bags and tubes with no standard bead packet sizes. Packets or containers usually have the weight marked, making it easier to determine how many you require. Some beads are sold in round weights such as 5g or 100g; others are sold with a particular number of beads so have an odd weight like 4.54g. Do check the weight of each different bead – some companies keep the bead quantity the same in each packet and vary the price whereas others keep the price the same and alter the quantity. Many small beads are sold in standard tubes and sold by length of tube usually either 3in (8cm) or 6in (16cm). To give you a rough idea of quantity and weight here are a few examples, but bear in mind that different manufacturers beads vary.

SEED BEADS			
Size 15	8cm (3in) tube	3800 beads	13g
Size 11	8cm (3in) tube	1650 beads	15g
Size 8	8cm (3in) tube	600 beads	15g
Size 6	8cm (3in) tube	150 beads	13g
DELICAS			
Size 11	2.5cm (1in) tube	1000 beads	5g
Size 8	2.5cm (1in) tube	150 beads	5g
TOHO TRIANGLES			
Size 11	8cm (3in) tube	1020 beads	12g
MAGATAMAS™			
4 x 6 mm	8cm (3in) tube	150 beads	14g
CUBE BEADS			
3mm	8cm (3in) tubes	240 beads	12g
4mm	8cm (3in) tube	140 beads	12g

Bead Finishes

Beads, especially small beads like seed beads and bugles, have several descriptive words that explain exactly what the bead looks like. For example, 'SL purple AB' is a silver-lined purple bead with an iridescent, rainbow effect on the surface (AB meaning Aurora Borealis). This information can be extremely useful when you are ordering from a catalogue or on the internet where you can see lots of different purple beads that all look fairly similar.

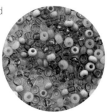

Transparent beads made from clear or coloured glass are see-through and allow light to pass through. **Opaque** beads are a solid colour that don't allow any light to pass through, whereas **translucent** beads are between transparent and opaque and sometimes referred to as **greasy**, **opal** or **satin** beads.

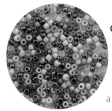

Gloss beads are very shiny glass and **matt** beads are opaque beads that have been tumbled or dipped in acid to give them a dull, flat surface. **Frosted** beads are transparent or translucent beads, which have been treated in a similar way.

Lustre beads are opaque beads with a coating that gives the bead a pearl finish. **Ceylon** beads are transparent beads with a milky lustre. **Gold** or **silver lustre** beads have been treated with a gold or silver pearl finish.

Colour-lined or **inside colour** beads are transparent beads with the hole lined in another opaque colour. **Silver-lined (rocailles)** beads have the hole lined with silver and look really sparkly. Sometimes the hole is square to enhance the shine. They are also available with a matt finish that has a frosted appearance.

Iris, **iridescent**, **rainbow** or **AB** beads have been treated with metal salts while the glass is hot to create a coating that resembles an oil slick. Matt beads have an appearance like raku, or pottery-fired clay.

Dyed beads have been painted with a dye or paint on the surface. They often have bright or unusual colours but the dye or paint can wear off in use.

Metallic beads have been heated and sprayed with oxidised tin. **Higher metallic** beads are surface coated with gold and then sprayed with oxidised titanium. The gold gives a brighter finish. **Galvanised** beads are electroplated with zinc for a more durable finish.

Choosing Colours

Monochromatic colour schemes look clean and elegant and are very easy on the eyes, especially in blues and greens. Choose one colour and then paler tints and darker shades of the same colour. This colour scheme always looks balanced and visually appealing but is rarely vibrant.

Analogous colour schemes are often referred to as 'cool colours' or 'warm colours' as they use adjacent colours on the wheel. They have a richer appearance than monochromatic schemes. Choose one colour as the dominant colour and the other one or two to enrich the scheme.

Complementary colour schemes use two colours opposite one another on a colour wheel for a strong contrast and work best when you put a cool colour such as green/blue against a warm red for example. Choose one of the colours as the main colour and use the other as an accent.

Split complementary colour schemes use one colour and two colours that sit either side of its complementary colour. It is a subtler scheme than straight complementary colours and works really well if you use a single warm colour and two cool colours or vice versa.

Tetradic colour schemes use two colours and their complementary colours. It is one of the most vibrant schemes using more variety of colours but as a result can be difficult to balance harmoniously. It works better if you choose one colour as the dominant colour or tone down the colours.

Triadic colour schemes use three colours equally spaced around a colour wheel. It is a popular scheme because it offers strong contrasts and richness, while still retaining a balanced effect. Use more of one colour than the others and if the beads look gaudy, tone down the colours slightly.

Tools and Equipment

When beginning bead work it is quite possible to make lots of beautiful beaded items without buying any specialist tools. The variety of beading techniques covered in this book use a wide range of tools and equipment but, to begin, basic equipment from your workbox will be fine and then as you progress you can invest in one or two particular tools as required. Bead work tools are readily available from craft and bead shops or from one of the many online suppliers, some of which are listed on page 175.

Tools

Essential Tool Kits

Almost any tool you might need for bead work is shown here to give an overview of what is available. Don't be daunted – each chapter has an essential tool kit, showing specific tools that will make your life easier for the techniques covered.

Cup Bur

The tool is useful for rounding off the end of wires, especially when making earring wires and other fastenings.

Bead Reamer

Most bead reamer tools have several different heads, encrusted with fine diamond powder, so that you can open out bead holes. It is ideal for using on the occasional small hole in strings of pearls or other semi-precious stones.

Thread Conditioners

Thread conditioners strengthen and protect thread and make it less prone to tangling. Conditioner reduces the amount of friction as the thread is pulled through beads and will help prolong the life of bead fabric.

Needles

There are a wide variety of different needles suitable for different types of bead work. To make it easier for you, each project lists the type of needle best suited to the technique used.

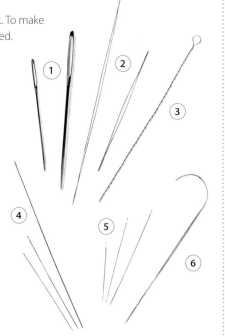

Tapestry ①
These large eye needles have a relatively blunt tip and are generally used for embroidery on evenweave fabric. When knitting or crocheting, use a tapestry needle for threading large hole beads with yarn or for sewing in the ends.

Big Eye ②
Two very fine needles are soldered together at each end to make a needle with a long eye. These needles are ideal for threading thicker yarns and are available in several sizes.

Twisted Wire ③
Twisted wire needles are available in several sizes and are ideal for threading through beads with very small holes. The round eye is easy to thread but collapses as it is pulled through the beads.

Bead Loom ④
These fine extra long needles are designed to go through the small holes in seed beads when working on a loom. The length of the needle enables you to go through all the beads at once but do make the needles fragile – keep a stock in case they break.

Bead Embroidery ⑤
You can buy special bead embroidery needles in short or long lengths but regular quilting needles, or sharps, are also ideal. The eyes are small and round so fairly easy to thread with sewing cotton. These needles are ideal for embroidery and off-loom (needle) weaving. Choose a size to suit the thread that will also go through the beads.

Big Eye Curved ⑥
These specialist needles are ideal for threading beads using a bead spinner. The curved shape follows the flow of beads so that they thread onto the needle quickly.

Crimping Pliers

If you plan to use crimps regularly for spacing beads and fastening thread, crimping pliers (shown below) will produce a more professional finish than flat-nose pliers. The pliers come in three sizes to suit different sizes of crimps.

Nylon Jaw Pliers

Available either as flat- or round-nose (shown below), these specialist tools are useful for straightening wire and for working with very soft aluminium wires so that they don't get damaged.

Tweezers

Fine pointed tweezers are useful if you need to untie knots and also for picking up individual small beads from the bead mat or a dish of beads.

Wire Cutters

Also known as flush cutters, this tool has a flat side so that you can cut wire with a straight end. Use a small pair with fine tips to get in close when making jewellery.

Flat-Nose Pliers

Jewellery pliers, both round- and flat-nose, are used to attach findings and fastenings. Some flat-nose pliers, also called snipe- or chain-nose pliers (directly above), taper towards the tip and others have a blunt end (blunt-nose, above right). Flat-nose pliers have flat jaws with a slightly rough surface to grip wire or findings.

Round-Nose Pliers

These pliers have tubular tapered jaws and are used for coiling, bending wire and making jump rings. Work near the tip of the jaws for tiny loops and further towards the base for larger rings.

Split-Ring Pliers

Split rings are notoriously difficult to open. If you use them regularly consider buying split-ring pliers, which have a special tip to open the ring so that you can attach a finding.

Equipment

Bead Loom

Bead looms come in all shapes and sizes and can be made in a variety of materials. The three looms shown here are all suitable for beginners but if you progress to larger more advanced pieces, adjustable professional looms are available from specialist suppliers.

The **basic metal loom** is ideal for making longer pieces as there are rollers at both ends.

Wood frames allow you to make wider, more advanced pieces. It can be adjusted using longer dowels.

To work bead loom pieces as a tube, look out for a **small acrylic loom**.

Tube Looms

These round plastic looms are ideal for making small pieces of beadwork without side seams. You can use the tubes for loom work or off-loom stitches. Place a chart or design behind the clear plastic so that you can work a pattern as you go.

Mandrels

Mandrels are used to support bead work and vary in size from fine rods to large tubes. Often used with off-loom bead weaving stitches to make ropes, cords, amulet purses and other 3-D forms.

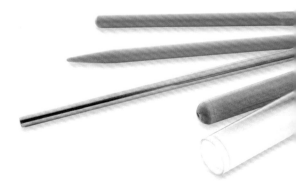

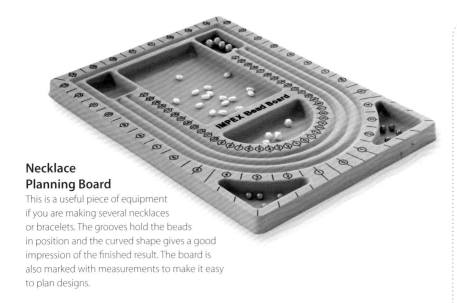

Necklace Planning Board

This is a useful piece of equipment if you are making several necklaces or bracelets. The grooves hold the beads in position and the curved shape gives a good impression of the finished result. The board is also marked with measurements to make it easy to plan designs.

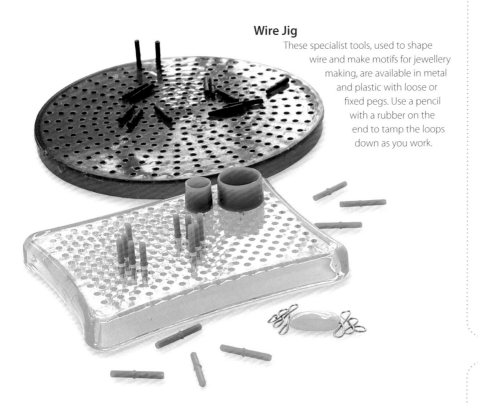

Wire Jig

These specialist tools, used to shape wire and make motifs for jewellery making, are available in metal and plastic with loose or fixed pegs. Use a pencil with a rubber on the end to tamp the loops down as you work.

Bead Mat

Textured mats are inexpensive and indispensable for all beading work. The fine pile stops the bead rolling about and lets you pick up directly onto the needle. Once finished it is easy to fold the mat and tip the beads back into their container.

Bead Pots and Containers

It is important to store beads carefully so that they are easy to access, don't spill out and can be returned to the container quickly once the work is done.

Beads are sold in a variety of containers, from plastic bags to tubes and boxes. In general, these are adequate for point of sale but once opened it is often better to transfer the beads to stronger containers. Beads sold in tubes should be fine so long as the lid is a good fit. Once the beads are finished, hold on to empty tubes to store other beads.

You can buy a variety of containers with secure screw tops that are ideal for seed beads. Larger beads can be stored in small polythene boxes. Look for inexpensive storage boxes sold at bead and craft fairs. Boxes with a lid the same size are particularly useful as you can tip half the beads into the lid to make it easier to handpick a few.

TIP REMEMBER TO LABEL BEADS CAREFULLY WHEN TRANSFERRING TO A NEW CONTAINER. SIZE, COLOUR AND FINISH, AS WELL AS WHERE YOU BOUGHT THEM, IS ESSENTIAL INFORMATION.

Lighting

Good lighting is essential for most bead work, especially if you are working with small beads. Even if you do not need to wear spectacles, poor light makes it difficult to see the small holes in the beads, making it harder to pass the needles under threads when off-loom weaving and working on a loom. Lamps that direct the light and are fitted with a daylight bulb are the most suitable. A magnifying lamp can be useful for very close work and is indispensable when working tubular crochet or brick stitch with tiny seed beads.

Techniques

You will find each beading technique explained in detail throughout the chapters. However, before you begin, it is good to have a basic knowledge of essential techniques, such as working from a chart and knotting, which are explained below.

Bead Stitch Charts

Bead stitches are often simply worked with one colour of bead or in a repeat pattern where different beads or rows of beads alternate to make basic striped patterns. For pictorial work or more ornate patterns, a chart is essential. Stitches that are closely packed, such as bead loom work, square stitch, brick stitch and peyote stitch are ideal for pictorial designs, whereas looser stitches like right-angle weave and netting work better with geometric patterns.

Some stitches, such as square stitch and bead loom weaving, can share a chart because they look exactly the same; brick stitch and peyote stitch look similar if one is turned 90 degrees so you can use the same chart oriented in different directions. You can use the basic square stitch grid for herringbone stitch but the chevron grid lets you see where the stacks lie. Bead graphs have been printed at the back of the book so that you can have a go at designing your own patterns from the stitches.

CHART PROPORTIONS

Beads are not exactly the same size or shape as the graphs and so, with some pictorial designs, a little adjustment may be required. Most seed beads are slightly longer in one direction and even the most regular sized cylinder beads are not square.

If you are looking for an accurate design, perhaps for a flower, heart or other shape, work a small section and adjust the chart accordingly. When working on a tube loom you can simply position the drawing or pattern behind the acrylic and add beads as required to build up the design.

When working with a tube loom the chart can be a simple sketch or even a picture cut from a magazine.

Working from a Chart

You can work from the top down on a chart or the bottom up, just make sure that bead stitches which are not square, such as peyote stitch and three-bead netting, begin in the same way as the chart. For example with peyote stitch you need a corner bead on the first row. If in doubt work a small sample up to the first two or three rows to check that the beads are following exactly the same formation as the charts.

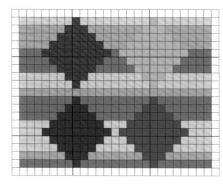

KEY

- pale aqua
- blue rainbow
- green/blue iris
- deep blue
- blue/green
- dark olive green
- pink

Using Knots

There are several simple knots used in beading to anchor threads or for tying off ends securely. The knots ensure that your bead work remains intact and fastenings firmly attached. For extra security add a drop of beading glue on the knots and then allow to dry before snipping tails close to the bead work.

HALF HITCH

When beginning or finishing a thread in beaded fabric or ropes, work a single or double half hitch over another thread within the beading to secure. To work, take the needle behind a thread in the beadwork to leave a loop. Pass the needle back through the loop and pull up to make the first half hitch. Repeat to make a second half hitch for extra security. Feed the tail through several more beads before trimming.

Double half hitch knot

REEF (SQUARE)

This is the basic knot for joining two threads of equal thickness. It is fairly secure but can be loosened if required by tugging one end back over the knot. This is always worked by passing the left thread over the right and tucking it under. Then pass the right thread over the left and take it under the left thread and out through the gap in the middle.

Reef (square) knot

SURGEON'S

This knot is similar to a reef knot but each thread end is taken over and under twice to begin. This double twist prevents the threads loosening again while you complete the knot. Like a reef knot, you pass the left thread over the right and under it, then pass the left thread over and under again to make a double twist. Pull taut, then pass right over left and take it under to complete the knot.

Surgeon's knot

OVERHAND

Use this knot to tie a bundle of threads together before setting up on a bead loom or to join two threads at the edge of beadwork. An overhand knot is the easiest to tie. Simply cross the tail over the main thread to make a small loop then pass the tail under the thread and back through the loop. You can manoeuvre the knot into position with a needle.

Overhand knot

FIGURE OF EIGHT

This knot is used to secure a thread in a calotte or other knot cover. It makes a fairly large knot that is unlikely to unravel and pull through the hole. Cross the tail in front of the main thread and hold between your finger and thumb so that the loop is facing towards you. Take the tail behind the main thread and pass through the loop from the front. Pull both ends to tighten. Add a drop of glue for extra security.

Figure of eight knot

SLIP

Knitting and crochet both begin with a slip knot. When it is tied the working thread is the end that can be pulled through to make the loop larger or smaller (see page 139). Cross the tail behind the main thread and hold between finger and thumb so that the loop is facing towards you. Take the main thread behind the loop and pull through. Pull the tail to tighten and the main thread to adjust the size of loop.

CHAPTER 1:
Bead Loom Weaving

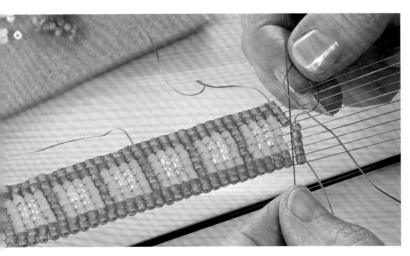

Bead Inspirations

One of the most popular projects for bead loom weaving is a bracelet. It's quick to complete and you can experiment to create different textures and patterns. Based on the Bead Something Now Bugle Bracelet on page 25, these four pretty bracelet ideas should just be a starting point for you.

Pretty Plaits

A little forward planning is required when making a bracelet with inset plaiting, as you need to set up the loom with double warp threads along the slit lines. Work the main body of the bracelet and then complete the fastening at either end. The toggle is simply a square of loom work folded in half. Once the bracelet is off the loom, carefully sew in all the thread ends.

Prickly Pink

This funky bracelet makes up quickly using size 8 (2.6mm) beads. The bright pink fringing stands out against the silver-lined beads and a pretty pink border pulls both elements together. Make the fringing slightly longer towards the middle of each bundle for a slight dome effect and finish the bracelet with a simple loop, adding a large pebble bead for the toggle.

Chunky Charm

Picot edging adds an elegant touch to a simple bracelet made with triangle beads. These beads have a crinkly texture that contrasts with the metal beads added after the bracelet has been woven. As the beads are heavy, make sure you sew them securely using two strands of thread. Finish the bracelet with a woven thread panel at each end and attach bar ends and a clasp.

Sparkly Stripes

Mixing larger beads and smaller beads appears to be impossible but you simply choose small beads that fit in twos or threes across the width of the larger bead. In this design two small beads are woven between each warp thread. Create an interesting texture with matt cube beads and colour-lined triangle beads, then finish the bracelet with a blackberry toggle and loop fastening.

Loom work is one of the easiest bead techniques to learn. It is used primarily to make simple bead bands for bracelets or pretty decorative borders that can be embellished to become quite ornate and intricate. Looms hold a number of tensioned warp threads so that beads threaded on to a weft thread can be 'woven' across them. In reality the beads are held in place by two horizontal threads going above and below the vertical threads. Bead loom pieces look best with evenly sized beads, although you can achieve interesting textures by using a variety of bead types of similar size. This chapter covers various techniques when using a bead loom, including setting up a loom, various warp methods, weaving on a loom, finishing off loom work, edging, fringing and netting, and other techniques.

Basic Tool Kit

In this chapter you won't need much to get started, apart from a bead loom and some basic materials. There is a wealth of beads available for you to try, so you can really experiment and have some fun!

■ Bead Looms

Looms are usually made from metal or wood. Some looms have a roller at each end and others have extending side sections so that you can work a bead panel longer than the loom length. There are also small curved acrylic (Perspex) bead looms, known as tube looms (see page 25), that can be set up to work beading in a complete circle.

See page 14 for other types of loom that you can use.

■ Threads

Warp threads need to be quite strong so that they don't snap under tension or when the beadwork is complete. Nymo™ thread is a strong multifilament thread available in various sizes from 00 through 'B' and 'D' to 'G', the thickest. Fishing line monofilament threads such as PowerPro™ and Fireline™ are also popular, especially for the continuous warp method. You can experiment with different materials for warp threads: elastic to create stretch cuff-style jewellery; craft wire, which allows the piece to be shaped once woven, or decorative yarns for a completely different look. However, if using a thicker material for the warp, you may need to use a finer thread or wire for the weft as it must pass through the beads several times.

■ Needles

Beading needles need to go through the beads many times and so the size you choose will depend on the thickness of the threads and size of the bead hole. You can buy very long beading needles specially made for loom work or try a big eye needle, as it is less likely to break than a long beading needle. Use a tapestry needle, 'T' pin or embossing tool to arrange the warp threads across the spring or coil.

■ Beads

Evenly-sized beads work best for bead loom work as the beads sit snugly side by side. For fine work cylinder beads, also known as delicas or antiques, are ideal. These beads are very uniform and have a large hole that allows you to pass threads through several times. High quality seed beads are also suitable if you discard uneven beads. Bugles and square beads add interesting textures or you can use more decorative beads such as bicone crystals and round beads, using more advanced techniques.

Getting Started

Once you have learnt the basic methods of bead loom work you can begin to start weaving your own projects. There are several ways to set up a loom, depending on the style of loom and the finished project. See below for advice on both flat and tubular techniques.

◼ SETTING UP A LOOM

Bead work can be done on any firm structure that will hold the warp thread parallel and taut. You can use a purpose-made loom or a simple homemade structure. On traditional looms you can separate a bundle of warp threads along a coil or spring, or set up the loom with a single thread. Tubular looms use a single thread technique that allows you to bead all the way round or you can set up a loom with an innovative method that eliminates the need for sewing in thread ends. The number of beads widthways varies, depending on the design, but it is often easier to create a pattern with an odd number of beads because there is usually a centre bead with an even number of beads on either side.

INDIVIDUAL WARP METHOD
Cut warp threads long enough to fit the piece of bead work, plus at least 20cm (8in) at each end to attach to the loom. Once the bead work is completed the extra thread is used for finishing off. Cut one more warp thread than the number of beads across the width of your work. For extra strength use a thicker thread for the two outer warps or you can add a double-length of your regular thread instead. Metal looms are sprung and help to keep the threads at an even tension.

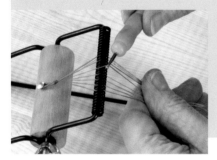  

1 Tie all the threads together with an overhand knot (see page 17) at one end and loop over a peg at the end of the loom. Hold the threads taut and separate them into the springs or coil. Separate the warps enough so that the beads you are using will fit between the threads.

2 Position the threads over the spring or coil at the other end of the loom so that the threads are parallel and equally spaced. Holding the threads taut, tie an overhand knot at the end and hook over the peg. Use a strip of low tack tape to prevent the threads jumping out of the springs while setting up the loom.

3 Turn the roller to take up the slack and then rotate the rollers at each end until there is an equal quantity of thread at each end. Tighten one roller then tension the threads by turning the other roller before tightening the screws.

SINGLE WARP
This method is similar to the individual warp method except you use one thread only. It is quick to set up, simple enough for children and ideal for small projects where there will be enough thread for finishing off at each end of the finished beading.

1 Tie the warp thread, straight off the reel, to the peg at one end of the loom. Insert the thread in one of the grooves on the nearest end and then take it over the corresponding groove at the other end.

TIP THIS METHOD IS SUITABLE FOR METAL LOOMS AS WELL.

2 Loop the thread around the peg at the other end and take it back across the grooves. Continue wrapping the thread around the pegs, fitting it into the grooves so they are spaced as wide as the beads. Once you have one more thread than the number of beads across the width, tie the end to the last peg. The threads should be taut but not too tight.

WEAVING ON A LOOM

The thread used for the weft can be lighter in weight to that used for the warp. Check that you can pass the needle and thread through the beads several times. Cylinder beads are ideal as they are even in size and have large holes, but if you don't mind a slightly uneven finish you can use seed beads. Begin at either end of the loom – whichever is more comfortable for you.

1 Tie a length of thread to the outside warp on the side you have your bead mat and beads, leaving a 20cm (8in) tail. Use a simple overhand knot (see page 17) and as long a thread as you are comfortable with as it means fewer joins. Then thread the end into a long beading needle.

TIP WEAVING A FEW ROWS WITH THE WEFT THREAD BEFORE YOU BEGIN WILL STABILISE THE WARP THREADS, BY HELPING TO SPACE THE THREADS AND MAKING IT EASIER TO POSITION AND SLOT THE FIRST ROW OF BEADS INTO THE THREADS.

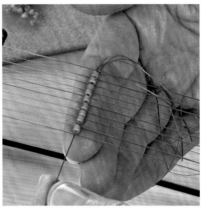

2 Pick up the beads for the first row on the needle and position under the warp threads so that there is one bead between each pair of threads. Hold the beads in place with your finger and pull the needle with the weft thread through the beads with your other hand.

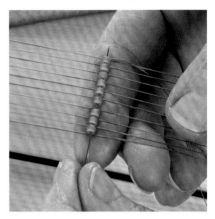

3 Keeping the beads in position with your finger, feed the needle back through the beads, making sure that it goes above the warp threads this time. For the continuous warp method, in particular, it is essential not to split the warp threads with the needle (see page 24).

TIP TO PREVENT THE NEEDLE SPLITTING THE THREAD, RUB THE TIP OF THE NEEDLE ON EMERY PAPER TO BLUNT IT OR USE A FINE TWISTED WIRE NEEDLE INSTEAD.

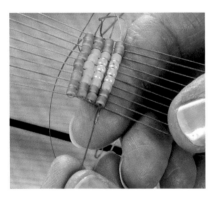

4 Pick up the beads for the second row and repeat steps 2 and 3. It becomes easier to weave as more beads are added. If you have a chart pick the beads up in the order required and push the beads rows together snugly.

5 When you get near the end of the working thread join on a new thread. Feed the needle between two beads near the opposite edge and pass through several beads. Work a half hitch (see page 17) and then pass the needle through the remaining beads out to the edge where the other tail has been left. Sew the tail in later.

TIP BEGINNING OR FINISHING A THREAD BETWEEN TWO BEADS IN THE BODY OF THE WORK IS NEATER AS THE TAIL END IS INVISIBLE WHEN TRIMMED.

6 If you are working on a loom with rollers, loosen the rollers and wind the work further along until there is enough length of warp thread to complete the beading. On long pieces tuck a piece of card in between the peg and beadwork to prevent it getting damaged.

FINISHING OFF BEAD LOOM WORK

There are lots of different ways to finish off loom work, depending on how you are going to use the bead panel. You can either sew in the ends or weave the ends, as explained below.

SEWING IN THE ENDS

Tails on the side edges are sewn back through the beads and secured with a half hitch knot (see page 17). You can also sew warp threads into the loom work in the same way. To keep the work looking neat avoid trimming threads, making knots or oversewing on the outer edges.

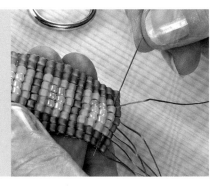

Thread the tail on a needle. Take the thread over the warp thread at the edge then go back through a few beads. Work a half hitch (see page 17) between the beads, taking the needle under the warp thread, pass through a few more beads then trim the thread ends close to the beadwork. With warp threads, weave down one or two rows between the beads first and then secure in the same way as the side tails.

WEAVING THE ENDS

You can simply fold the warp threads to the reverse side and attach to a backing but a tightly woven thread panel holds the beads in position. Although it takes a little time to weave, the beadwork is more secure. Fold the panel to the reverse to hide.

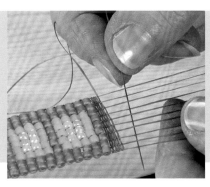

1 Weave the tail end of the weft thread through the warp threads until it is 6mm (¼in) deep. Weave a similar panel at the other end. Loosen the roller screws and lift the bead panel off the loom, releasing the threads from the pegs at both ends.

2 Tie the warp threads together in pairs or groups of four, using a surgeon's knot (see page 17), and then trim the ends close to the knots. This woven panel can be folded back and the beading attached to a backing or you could attach a crimp style of bar fastener to make a bracelet or belt.

CORRECTING MISTAKES

If you make a mistake in the pattern and have noticed fairly quickly, unpick several rows and replace the wrong bead. If the bead is further into the work it is fairly easy to crush the bead with pliers and sew in a replacement, although this is risky as you can snap the thread.

CRUSHING A BEAD

- Carefully crush the bead with snipe or chain-nose pliers from end to end, avoiding the thread altogether.
- Before you crush the glass bead put a needle in the hole to prevent the thread from snapping.
- For beads further in you can also insert the needle through the row of beads and carefully crush the offending bead with a metal punch and hammer.

Missing a Bead

The most common error when bead weaving is to pass the needle under some of the warp threads rather than over them in a row. This isn't always obvious while the beadwork is on the loom but if you notice soon enough unpick a few rows and rework. Once the beadwork is off the loom and not tensioned it can be quite noticeable as the beads tend to drop below the surface of the beadwork.

To correct the mistake, weave a thread through the offending beads with the needle above the warp threads and then sew in the ends.

CONTINUOUS WARP METHOD

This new innovative technique allows you to pull the warp thread through the bead fabric so that there are only two ends to sew in. It is essential the warp threads are not pierced with the needle as you work otherwise it will not pull through freely. Use a monofilament thread to set up the loom and a blunt needle to add the beads.

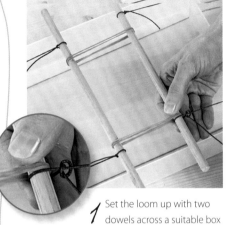

1 Set the loom up with two dowels across a suitable box or structure. The elastic bands provide the tension to create the bead work. To attach the cords that support the dowels, use a slip knot or wrap the cord around the dowel twice and tie a couple of half hitches (see page 17) to secure the cord. The distance between the dowels should be slightly longer than the finished piece.

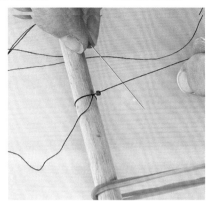

2 Tie a 2m (2yd) length of strong thread around the dowel at one end of the loom with a surgeon's knot (see page 17) and thread the other end in a needle. Pick up a seed bead and drop it down to the dowel. Take the thread behind the dowel. Bring it over the front and through the loop next to the bead. Pull taut.

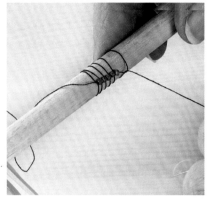

3 Work along the dowel, adding enough beads to complete the design and then add two extra beads. Attach the same number of beads along the dowel at the other end of the loom in the same way.

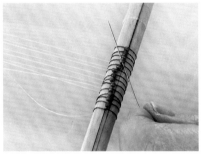

4 Using the thread straight off the reel without cutting, thread a needle onto a monofilament thread such as PowerPro™ or Fireline™ and sew through the first bead at the top of the loom. Take the needle through the second bead at the bottom of the loom. Miss the second bead at the top and go through the third. Continue along the bead rows, taking the needle through alternate beads. Pull the thread through as you go until you reach the end.

5 You should have one more thread than the beads across the design. Leave about 60cm (24in) at each end and tape out of the way. Then attach a new thread and weave the beads, taking care not to catch the warp thread with the needle as it passes back and through the beads.

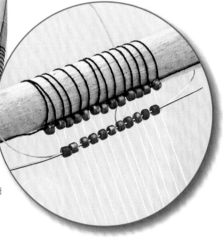

To prevent the needle piercing the warp threads you can rub the tip of the needle on fine sandpaper to blunt it slightly. Make sure the needle passes above each warp thread as it passes back through the beads.

Bead Something Now
Bugle Bracelet

In most bead loom pieces the beads are all the same size but this pretty bracelet mixes short bugles and hex beads to create a delightful texture. This is a great project to experiment with the bead loom weaving technique as there is no chart to follow. The beads have different diameters but are both the same width so can be woven in different rows. Depending on which beads you choose you can create a whole selection of bracelets that all look totally different. Once the bead band is complete, a panel of thread weaving secures the beads at each end (see page 23), so that you can attach the simple elegant bar end fastenings. Full instructions on how to make the bracelet are on page 152

■ TAKING THE BEAD PANEL OFF THE LOOM

This technique for bead loom weaving is finished in a different way to traditional methods. Its success depends on the weft threads being separate and not going through any of the warp threads – as a result it is often known as the 'pull and pray' technique.

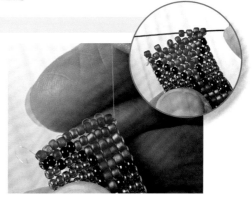

1 Once the bead panel is complete snip the loops of thread going over the dowels to release it from the loom, alternate beads on the top will drop out. Remove any cut threads and then tape the bead panel on to the work surface going across the beads.

2 Beginning in the centre, begin to pull the warp threads through the beads, one column at a time. Work to the edge then begin in the centre again and pull the threads out to the other edge. Sew in the replacement beads on the end rows then sew in the two ends.

■ TUBE LOOM

These small acrylic looms are ideal for making amulet purses, bags and bracelets. The looms are available in a range of sizes and allow you to bead all the way round to make a piece of tubular beading. The threads are secured in a similar way to the continuous warp method but without the beads. Weave until the gap is filled and then move the beading round to the next section. Once complete, squeeze the sides of the tube gently to release the loom work. Full instructions come with the looms.

1 Tie the end of the thread to the anchor hole at one side of the loom. Wrap the thread around the loom and bring the bobbin under the thread again to form a half hitch (see page 17). Work several half hitches to secure this first loop. Position the loom by holding it with your index finger extended and pass the thread over your extended finger and around loom.

2 Pass the bobbin through the loop formed by finger and pull thread taut. Add threads until you have one more than the number of beads and secure with half hitches. Weave beads in the gap until filled. Snip the thread tied through anchor hole and rotate the beadwork to bring the next section of threads into the gap.

Bead On

When you have learnt the basics, you can move on to more advanced bead loom weaving techniques, such as making a loop and toggle, embellishing your projects and increasing and decreasing.

■ MAKING A LOOP AND TOGGLE

Bracelets and choker style necklaces are one of the most popular ways to use bead loom work. Use the warp threads at each end to make a simple loop and toggle fastening with seed or accent beads. You can make one or more loops, depending on the width of the band, and use large beads or peyote stitch tubes for the toggle fastening instead.

1 Sew in the warp threads leaving a pair of threads in the middle. Thread these onto a beading needle and pick up five seed beads. Take the needle back through the last three beads to make a circle.

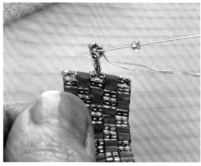

2 Pick up a bead and take the needle through the centre of the circle. Keep adding beads in this way, one at a time, until you create a beaded toggle that looks like a little blackberry.

3 Feed the threads back through the first two beads and then weave into the beadwork, working a half hitch (see page 17) to secure.

TIP PICK UP BEADS ON A SPARE PIECE OF THREAD AND FORM INTO A LOOP TO FIND THE NUMBER REQUIRED TO FIT OVER THE TOGGLE FASTENING.

4 At the other end sew in the warp threads to leave a pair of threads in the middle again. Thread these separately onto two beading needles. Pick up half the beads required to make the loop on each thread.

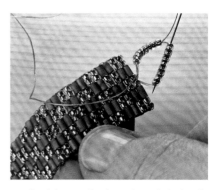

5 Feed the needles down through the beads on the opposite threads. For extra strength, go back through the bead loop with one of the needles and then weave the tails into the beadwork, working a half hitch knot to secure.

When making a loop and toggle it is always better to make the toggle or choose a large bead first so that you know how large to make the loop. It should be quite a snug fit so that the toggle doesn't easily slip through the loop.

■ EMBELLISHMENT

Bead loom work creates a simple flat band that can be embellished by adding extra beads while the panel is on the loom or once it has been taken off. It is easy to customise the bead band with a few accent beads to create a unique design.

Basic techniques described here can be used to add edgings such as picot stitch, fringing or netting but there are literally infinite ways to embellish a plain band, the only limit is your imagination.

WORKING INTO THE WARP THREADS (BRICK STITCH EDGING)
Beads added onto the warp threads along the edge of the beaded band are effectively added using brick stitch (see brick stitch, page 41). If you use the same beads, the added beads will look exactly the same as bead loom work – this can be useful if you work a pattern on a bead loom that has a limited width and you need one or two more rows to complete the design. For a more decorative edge use more ornate beads or create a fringe by adding more beads (see fringes, on page 29).

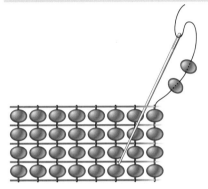

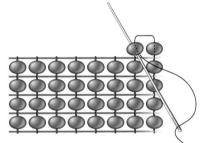

1 Take the bead work off the loom, finish the ends and sew in the side threads. Secure another thread in the work. Bring the thread out at the end row of beads. Pick up two beads and take the needle under the outside warp thread between the first two rows of beads.

2 Take the needle back up through the second bead added. Continue along the edge, picking up only one bead and taking the needle back through that bead each time.

Brick stitch edging can be used to add additional rows of beads to a piece of loom work if you find the design is slightly too narrow once it is off the loom.

WORKING INTO THE BEADS (PICOT EDGING)
With this technique the needle is passed through the beaded band itself. You can simply work along one edge, bringing the needle back through the next bead along the edge, or sew right through the bead band from side to side. This simple technique can be used to add three beads at a time for a traditional picot edge or to make more ornate loops (see loop edging, page 28) or fringing for a really decorative edge. Make the loops interlinked, side-by-side or spaced out.

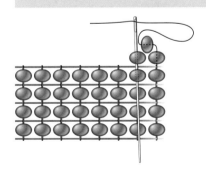

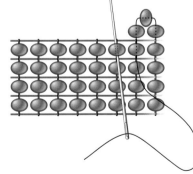

1 Take the bead work off the loom, finish the ends and sew in the side threads. Bring a new thread out at the end of the bead work. Pick up three beads and take the needle through the next bead on the band.

2 Bring the needle back through the next bead along and pick up another three beads. For a continuous picot edging bring the needle up through the last bead added before adding another two beads only each time.

The simple three-bead picot edging matches the pairs of beads in this pretty chequered panel and really pulls the two different bead types together.

LOOP EDGING

Beads can be added on top of the beaded band rather than out from the edge. You can add large accent beads using this technique or simply add loops of the same or a contrast seed bead. The loops or beads can be worked straight, as shown here, or at an angle.

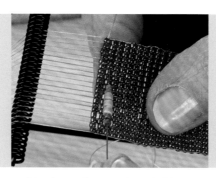

TIP If you want to add loops at more of an angle, space the loops evenly right down to the end and then go back and fill the gaps with the next and subsequent rows of loops.

1 Bring the needle out at the end of the beadwork and pick up sufficient beads to make the loop, in this example seven beads. Insert the needle into the loom work on the next row down, six beads from the edge.

2 Feed the needle back through the beads to the edge. Pass the needle under the warp thread ready to add the next loop. Continue picking up seven beads and passing the needle through six beads in the next row down.

Bead Something Now

Beaded Candle Border with Loop Edging

Plain candles can be dressed up with this fabulous beaded border that is tied around the candle and then removed once the candle has been used. The plain loom band is embellished with a loop edging. You can keep the band plain or sew on some delightful painted metal flower beads. Full instructions are on page 153, but if you are not fond of candles, this design makes a stunning cuff style bracelet too. Make the band to fit your wrist and add loop and toggle fastenings (see page 26).

Create interesting texture to loop edging by adding chunky cube beads to every second loop. Larger beads will need longer loops and wider spacing.

Follow the check pattern on the bead loom panel with the loop edging to draw the two elements together. You could use contrasting beads for a bolder effect.

■ FRINGING AND NETTING

Fringing can be added to loom work while you are working the beading or once the band is complete. Netting or looped fringes are added at the end of a piece of beadwork using the warp threads, or added to the side edges using one of the techniques shown here. Fringes and netting can be as simple or ornate as you want – see Chapter 4, page 76 for more ideas.

VERTICAL FRINGING

This technique adds a third dimension to a piece of loom work. Rows of beaded fringe are added to the basic bead loom panel. You can add the beads as you go, as shown here, or add the fringing once the panel is complete.

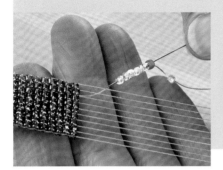 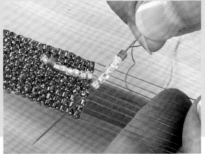 

1 Bring the thread out between two beads. Pick up the fringe strand beads and a pivot bead. Miss the pivot bead and take the needle back up the remaining beads.

2 Take the needle between the next two beads so that the fringe strand straddles a bead. Continue adding bead strands in rows so that each strand straddles a bead.

3 At the end of the row take the needle back through the bead loom work ready to work the next row of beading. Repeat rows of fringing to create a textured surface.

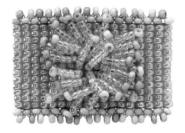

Add a little 'oomph' to vertical fringing by using the same bright pastel beads at the end of delicately coloured fringe strands to make a pretty picot edge.

INCORPORATING AN EDGING AS YOU WEAVE (INTEGRATED EDGING)

Either work a fringe on one side only or add a fringe to both sides. Alternatively add a smaller quantity of beads to make a picot edging instead (see page 27).

1 Work the beading up to the point where you want to begin adding the edging. Pick up the usual number of beads and then pick up the additional beads, including a pivot bead.

2 Hold the beads in position in the usual way with the extra beads in line along your finger. Miss the small end bead and pass the needle back through the other beads, passing the needle above the warp threads as usual.

Swarovski crystals add a luxurious touch to a simple band. Match the colour of the crystals to one of the triangle bead colours for a truly co-ordinated look.

Add just two or three beads to create an interesting edging rather than a longer fringe. Pick up a single bead on each row to finish the opposite edge.

To make a simple choker, graduate the length of the strands so that the fringe forms a 'v' shape. Add a simple picot edge (see page 27) to complete the design.

■ INCREASING AND DECREASING

Rather than simply working a straight panel you can change the shape of the loom work by increasing or decreasing the number of beads in each row. You can only increase by the number of warp threads on the loom so this has to be taken into consideration when setting up, although you can add extra warps later (see Evening Bag, opposite).

TO INCREASE
You can simply pick up one or two extra beads at the end of every row, but to increase at both ends in the same row use the technique below.

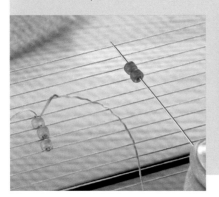 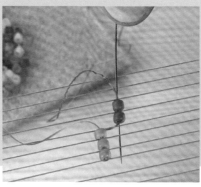 

1 At the end of a row pass the weft thread under the warp thread at the end of the bead row and bring it out above the beads. Pick up the number of beads you want to increase by, in this case, two.

2 Lay the beads in position on top of the warp threads. Push the beads down and pass the needle through the beads under the warp threads.

3 Pick up the remaining beads for this row, including the beads you need to increase by at the other side, and slot into position. Take the needle back through all the beads including those added at the other end.

TO DECREASE
To decrease the amount of beads used at both ends in the same row, simply reverse the technique used for increasing beads, so use fewer beads instead of picking up more at each end.

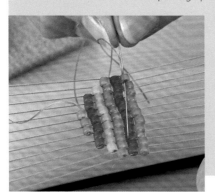  

1 At the end of the last full row, take the needle over the outer warp thread and through the number of beads to be decreased. Bring the needle out on the upper side and wrap around the new outer warp to the underside.

2 Pick up the beads for the next shorter row, press up between the warp threads and weave these in place as usual.

3 Continue decreasing beads at each end, to create the shaping.

The decreasing technique looks particularly effective when used at each end of a bracelet. Here the shaping narrows the bracelet in an attractive 'v' shape, creating a more elegant finish, ready for the bead and loop fastening.

Evening Bag

One of the delights of designing is marrying different textures together so that each component looks even more stunning than before. I was immediately inspired when I found this pretty buckle at a craft fair. The gorgeous beaded bag flap and strap is worked on a loom using a bead 'soup' mix of similar sized beads and shaped following the increasing technique on page 30. To add texture and body to the edge of the bag flap, larger triangle beads are added using the picot technique on page 27. Make a simple knitted bag following the instructions on page 153 and then choose your own bead mix to weave the beaded bag flap and strap.

CREATING A SLIT OR SLOT

To create a slot for a buttonhole, or divide the bead panel into two or more panels, you need to plan ahead. For example, a buttonhole usually has an odd number of beads so that there is a single bead in the middle and a single slit requires an even number of beads. When working a slit add a double thread between the beads on the slit when you set up the loom because you weave around one thread to finish the left side and the other to finish the right. Otherwise the technique is the same – just complete the beading on both sides then bead across the full width to close.

1 When you reach the point where you want to split the bead panel pick up half the beads on the needle and push up into position, taking the tip of the needle over the top of the unused warp threads. Pull the needle through over the unused warp threads. Take the needle back through only the beads that have just been added.

2 Continue working on these warp threads to complete one side to the required length. Attach a new thread and work the loom work on the other side.

3 Whether you are making a slit or buttonhole simply work across the full width once you have made a slot long enough for your toggle or other fastening to fit through.

■ BEADING THE WARP

Bead loom work can be as simple or as complicated as you like. One of the most exciting ways to create a different look is by adding beads on the warp threads. This is especially effective if using shaped beads such as bicones. When woven on the loom these pretty crystals leave large gaps between the rows because of their shape which can be filled with small round beads.

ADDING BEADS TO THE WARP

You can thread all the beads required at the beginning or take the beadwork off the loom to add more beads on the warp threads once a panel has been worked and then put it back on to finish.

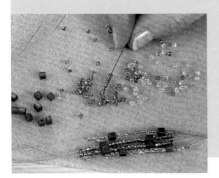

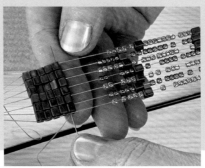

1 Cut the warp threads as described on page 21 and attach to the loom at one end. Then pick up the required number of beads on each warp thread.

2 Separate the threads on to the top spring so that they are spaced to fit the beads that will be woven across on the weft thread. Secure the threads over the end spring and finish setting up the loom as described on page 21. Weave a panel of beads.

3 Slide the required number of beads up the warp threads. Pass the weft thread down through all the beads on the outer warp thread ready to weave the next bead panel. Repeat the process of adding more beads to the weft threads as required.

WEAVING TWO TYPES OF BEADS

You can fill in the holes left between more unusual bead shapes, such as bicones, with smaller beads pre-threaded on to the warp.

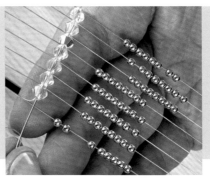

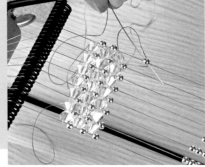

1 Tie the weft thread on the outside warp above. Pick up crystals required on the weft thread and position under the warp threads. Pull the needle through and go back through the crystals.

2 Slide a round bead up each warp thread then feed the needle down through the round bead on the outside warp thread. Pick up another row of crystals. Repeat the process until the panel is the required size.

■ VARYING BEAD SIZES

If you intend to create a plain panel of loom work, with a pattern or pictorial element, it does generally look better if the beads are of equal size and shape but, with a little forward planning, you can mix beads to create different effects.

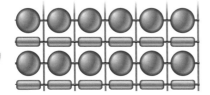

Beads that are the same width, but a different shape, can be woven in different rows to create a textured effect.

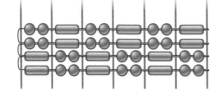

Use more than one bead between the warp threads. Mix several narrow beads with a wide bead or bugle and alternate on subsequent rows.

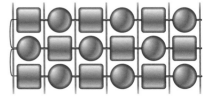

Mix cubes and round beads of the same size to create an interesting texture.

Taking It Further

Most bead loom work is created using small beads of the same size and woven on strong fine threads that are almost invisible once the panel is complete, but you can create completely different effects using a variety of threads. The thickness of the weft threads is always determined by the size of the bead holes but you can use thicker materials for the warp threads. Wire is also an alternative; the resulting bead work can be bent in a curve or folded to create 3-D shapes.

■ WORKING WITH WIRE

If you want a piece of bead loom work to hold its shape, to make a coiled decoration or a container, you can set up the loom using craft wire for the warp threads. Use a slightly thicker wire for the outer warp threads for more control. You can use fine wire or thread for the weft threads, the thickness of the wire will depend on the size of the bead holes as you need to be able to pass the needle through the beads twice. Coloured thread that will show at the edges can be particularly effective.

Using Decorative Yarn

Using decorative yarns for the warp threads, set up the loom in the same way as usual and add beads using a strong, fine thread for the weft threads. As you add the beads, take care to make sure the thread passes on both sides of the warp threads.

Bead Something Now
Medallion Belt

The style of the '60s is very distinctive and definitely inspired this funky hipster belt. With its large polka dot medallions and long fringing the belt will look equally fabulous with your favourite jeans or a pretty dress. Usually with bead loom weaving the warp threads are insignificant and almost completely hidden between the beads but it doesn't have to be the case. Using more decorative threads gives the bead work a completely different appearance as the wonderful textures come to the fore. You can simply weave square or rectangular panels across the threads or use your increasing and decreasing skills (shown on page 30) to create the circular bead motifs. Full instructions are on page 154.

CHAPTER 2:

Off Loom Bead Stitches

Often called needle weaving these stitches, worked with needle and thread, are generally used to make flat pieces of beaded fabric with even-sized beads although the techniques are versatile and can be worked in a circular (medallion) or tubular format to create 3-D structures. Each stitch has different properties that determine the way they are used. For example brick stitch is flexible horizontally, peyote stitch vertically and herringbone has a strong structure that allows you to make little bowls or containers. Some of the tubular stitches are ideal for making the ropes and cords; shown in Chapter 3 (page 62). The tubular version of these stitches can be used to make amulet purses or tiny bags without side seams. Look at the inspiration pages for some ideas or check out 'Taking it Further' on page 61 to learn how to use a tube loom.

Bead Inspirations

Bead stitches are often worked as flat pieces of fabric for bracelets and other items of jewellery but it can be an interesting challenge to try out three-dimensional designs. Amulet purses have always been popular but you can try making some of these little handbags using the different techniques. See page 155–6 for the instructions to these bags.

Zigzag Bag

Although at first glance this bag looks like it is worked in brick stitch, it is actually odd-count peyote stitch worked from side to side.

Shopping Bag

This pretty little shopping basket is worked in brick stitch, starting with a ladder stitch band. The top border and handles are added last.

Polka Dot Bag

Worked in two-drop square stitch, the subtle shaping on this delightful little bag is achieved by adding one extra bead on each edge.

Bucket Bag

Herringbone stitch is instantly recognisable because of the distinctive chevron effect, which shows up, particularly, when using short bugle beads.

Clutch Bag

Peyote stitch folds easily horizontally and so is ideal for making bags with a flap. Use the short bugles to make the side panels too.

Classic Handbag

Brick stitch has a really firm texture that holds its shape well. If you want a bag with dimension sew bugle beads across the gap to create a flat bottom.

Net Flap Bag

Three-bead netting makes a supple bead fabric that is ideal for a simple bag. Create the flap easily by using different coloured beads.

Shoulder Bag

Right angle weave makes a very soft, floppy bead fabric and so is more suited to simple shapes like this rectangular shoulder bag.

Basic Tool Kit

In this chapter all you will need is needles, threads and a couple of beading gadgets, such as a bead mat and bead stop spring for keeping beads on the thread.

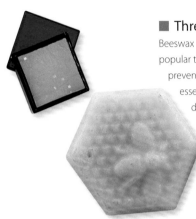

■ Thread Conditioner

Beeswax and Thread Heaven™ are the most popular thread conditioners. They help prevent tangling and fraying but are not essential and beaders are definitely divided into do's and don'ts on this issue. Using conditioner only on the end of the thread helps to keep the tail from tangling around the main thread as you work.

■ Beading Needles

When working beading stitches a long needle isn't necessary as you are only going through a few beads at a time. Short beading needles are ideal or use sewing needles that have a small eye such as betweens. As a guide the size of the bead should be a larger number than the needle size, for example thread size 11 beads with a size 10 needle. When working square stitch or right angle weave you may need to use a size 13 needle as the thread passes through each bead several times.

■ Threads

Strong threads such as Nymo™ or Superlon™ are ideal threads for bead stitches. Size D is the most popular thickness but you can use size B, which is finer and ideal when working stitches where the thread goes through each bead several times. PowerPro™ and Fireline™ are also suitable. When making jewellery with chain stitch or bead weaving, nylon monofilament threads such as illusion cord are ideal.

■ Bead Mat

Use a pile surface bead mat when working bead stitches. The mat makes it easy to pick beads up and prevents them from rolling about. Hold the needle almost horizontal to pick up beads straight off the mat.

■ Bead Stop Spring

This little gadget is ideal for stopping beads falling of the end of the tail when you are working beads stitches such as peyote stitch. There are several sizes but the small springs are less clumsy to work around.

Getting Started

Bead stitches are all worked in a different way but there are some basic techniques that are relevant to most of the stitches. As each bead stitch has a different arrangement of beads it isn't possible to show every stitch for each technique but the methods can be adapted accordingly.

■ JOINING OR SEWING IN A THREAD

You can join a new thread or sew in the tail by weaving back and forwards through the beads. Doubling back helps to secure the thread. It is much more secure to work a half hitch at some point (see page 17).

1 When joining a new thread, begin a short distance away from where the old thread emerges. Take the needle with the new thread through several beads, following the route of the threads that are already there. Work a half hitch by passing the needle under threads between two beads and pull it out through the loop of thread (see page 17).

2 To sew in the old thread, take the needle and thread back down through several beads. Pass the needle under threads between two beads and pull it out through the loop of thread to work a half hitch (see page 17). Take the needle through another few beads and either trim the tail or work a second half hitch for extra security.

Using a Stop Bead

When working some bead stitches it is essential to stop the beads falling off the end of the thread.

Pick up a spare bead on the needle and drop it down to about 15cm (6in) from the end of the thread. Pass the needle through the bead two or three times to secure.

Squeeze the levers on the spring and slot the thread in between the coils. Adjust the tension as you work by moving the spring up and down the thread as required.

■ WORKING WITH DIAGRAMS

Diagrams have been included with many of the bead stitches so that you can see the actual path of the thread through the beads. When trying out a technique for the first time it is easier to follow the diagram and make a small sample, repeating the process several times if necessary until you feel you really know how the stitch works. Then you will be much more comfortable and will enjoy creating the Bead Something Now project that the diagram and technique relates to. Although most of the diagrams are easy to follow whether you are right or left-handed, it is sometimes better, especially if it is a tricky technique like herringbone stitch three-row start, to flip the diagram so that the needle and thread are going in the opposite direction.

TIP You can also use a small mirror perpendicular to the page to see the reverse image.

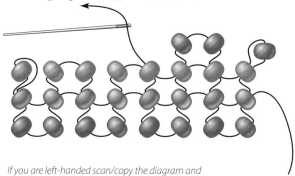

If you are left-handed scan/copy the diagram and using a photo program flip them vertically.

Thread Direction

When working bead stitches you can take the needle and thread through the needle in two different directions. To clarify two phrases are used – 'go through' and 'go back through'.

• **'Go through'** the bead means that both threads pass through the bead in the same direction.

• **'Go back through'**, means that the needle goes through the bead in the opposite direction to the previous thread.

SQUARE STITCH

Square stitch is very similar in appearance to bead loom work as the beads are stitched together in the same regular grid. Loom work is more practical for larger pieces of beading but the advantage of square stitch is that there are no thread ends to sew in. Square stitch is one of the strongest bead stitches as the thread passes through each bead several times though you do need to use uniformly sized beads that have a fairly large hole, such as delicas or toho seed beads. Cross-stitch and needlepoint charts work well for square stitch designs.

As with many stitches you can speed the beading process by adding two beads at a time, making it easy to introduce bugles and other longer beads into the design.

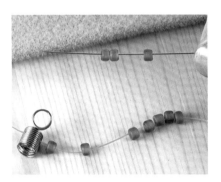

1 Use a long beading needle with about 1.5m (1½yd) of thread and attach a stop bead or stop spring (see page 37) 15cm (6in) from the end. Pick up the beads for the first row.

2 *Pick up the first bead of the next row and pass the needle through the last bead on the previous row. Pass the needle through the bead just added again.

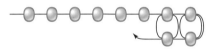

Each bead in the second and subsequent rows is suspended under the beads of the previous row.

3 Continue adding beads one at time in the same way until you get to the end of the row. Pass the needle all the way through the previous row and the one just worked. Repeat from *.

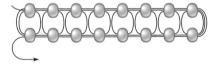

To stabilise the beads at the end of each row, take the needle back through all the beads in the previous row and the row just added.

EMBELLISHING WITH A PICOT EDGE

As square stitch is such a plain stitch you can embellish the edge with additional beads using the same techniques as for loom work (see page 27). Embellishing covers the multiple threads on the edge of the beadwork.

1 Start where the thread is emerging from the last bead. Pick up three beads and take the needle through the first thread loop.

2 *Pass the needle through the last bead added and pull taut.

3 Pick up two beads. Take the needle through the next loop along. Repeat from *.

INCREASING

When working in square stitch the beads are usually increased on the edge but you can pick up an extra bead at any point along the row if it suits the design better.

• Step Increasing

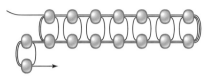
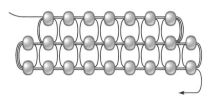

1 Pick up the number of beads you want to increase by, in this diagram, one. Pick up another bead and add it below the last bead as normal. Continue adding beads along the row.

2 At the other end of the row pick up the number of beads you want to increase by at this side. Pick up a bead and work the square stitch on top of the end bead instead of below. Pass the needle through the remaining beads on that row and the one below.

DECREASING

You can reduce the number of beads in a row by stopping short at each end or going from two beads to one at any point along the row.

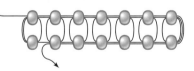

1 Pass the needle through the previous row as usual and then, when passing through the row just added, bring the needle out between two beads where you want the decrease to begin.

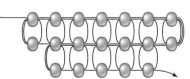

2 Work square stitch along the row as usual, stopping where you want before the end of the row. Take the needle between beads to pass the thread through the previous row and the one just worked.

Gradual Increasing

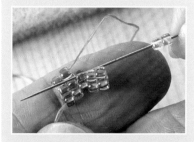

To increase within the row pick up two beads instead of one and work square stitch through a single bead in the row below. On the next row work into each bead as usual.

TIP THE INCREASE WILL BE SMOOTHER IF YOU SELECT NARROWER BEADS FOR THE TWO BEADS AND THEN REVERT TO THE USUAL SIZE IN THE NEXT ROW.

Bead Something Now
Square Stitch Bracelet

If you ever wondered what the advantage is to using square stitch instead of bead loom weaving then this stunning bracelet shows you why. The beauty of square stitch is that there is only one thread left at each end but, worked in bead loom weaving, there would be fifteen threads to sew in across the diagonal shaping. For a contemporary look link the square stitch pieces with gorgeous high gloss beads and finish with a gold-plated bar clasp. Full instructions on how to make the bracelet are on page 156.

LADDER STITCH

This stitch can be used in its own right to create bands of beading but it is more often used as a foundation row for brick stitch and herringbone stitch. There are several ways to work ladder stitch, such as the single needle method and the twin needle method, so try them all to see which you find easiest. It is easier to learn using bugles or other fairly large beads.

SINGLE NEEDLE

Ladder stitch worked with a single needle is the most popular technique. It is also used for increasing off-loom bead stitches using the step technique.

1 Pick up two bugles and drop down the thread to about 15cm (6in) from the end. Pass the needle through both bugles again. Pull the thread so that the two bugles sit together.

2 *Pick up another bugle. Pass the needle though the previous bugle and the one just added. Repeat from *.

TWIN NEEDLE

Twin needle ladder stitch uses the least amount of thread and has a reasonable amount of elasticity, making it ideal for bands and borders.

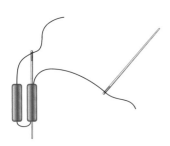

1 Thread a needle onto each end of a long thread. Pick up two bugles and let them drop down to the middle. Pass the other needle through one bugle again.

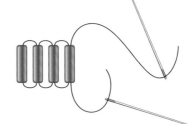

2 Pick up another bugle on one needle and pass the other needle through it in the opposite direction. Continue adding bugles, one at a time, until the band is the length required.

Joining the Ends

It is easy to join the ends of a ladder stitch band to create a circle or to make the base row for tubular brick stitch.

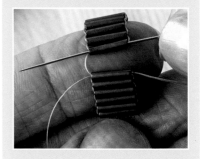

Bring the two ends together. Pass the needle through the first bead and then through the last bead. Pass through the first bead again.

TWO-DROP LADDER STITCH

You can use either of the other methods for two-drop ladder stitch and this method for adding one bugle or bead at time.

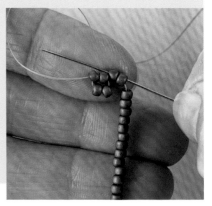

1 Pick up the number of beads required to complete the ladder stitch and drop down near the end of a 1.5m (1½yd) length of thread. Use a stop bead or spring to stop them falling off.

2 Pass the needle through the fourth and third last beads again. Pull thread taut so that the beads lie next to each other.

3 Go through the next pair (sixth and fifth beads) and then pull up. Continue bringing up one pair at a time and at the end tie the two tails together.

BRICK STITCH

Sometimes known as comanche or cheyenne stitch, brick stitch is different from many other stitches as the beads are added by looping through thread rather than the previous row. The fabric, which resembles a brick wall, is fairly stiff so it is often used to make amulet purses and other three-dimensional containers. Brick stitch can be worked onto ladder stitch, see ladder stitch start below, or try the double row base technique, also shown below.

4mm cube beads really show the brick wall effect. This bead fabric is quite firm because of the flat sides on the beads.

DOUBLE ROW BASE

This quick start technique for brick stitch creates the first two rows of brick stitch without the need for ladder stitch base. Ladder stitch is the most popular way to begin brick stitch but there is an obvious change of texture from one stitch to the next. This can be made into a feature but if you'd rather it all looks the same, use this quick start technique.

1 Thread a needle with a long thread. Pick up three beads and drop down to about 15cm (6in) from the end. Pass the needle back through the first bead in the opposite direction.

2 Pull the beads up so that they form a 'T' shape and tie the ends together. Pick up another bead and go back through the third bead added.

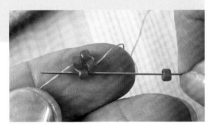

3 *Pick up another bead and go back through the previous bead again. Repeat from * until the base row is the length required (see step 1, below).

WORKING BRICK STITCH

Begin with a double row base, shown here, or ladder stitch (below). Brick stitch amulet purses often have a base row of bugles, then the brick stitch is worked with beads. You can work from side to side, left to right or vice versa.

1 Begin with the thread coming out of the top of the last bead in the base row. You may need to flip the ladder stitch over. Pick up two beads. *Pass the needle under the loop of thread between two end beads in the previous row.

2 Take the needle back through the second bead added and pull the thread taut. Pick up another bead. Take the needle under the next loop of thread and back through the bead just added. Pull thread taut.

3 Continue to the end of the row adding one bead at a time. To begin the next row pick up two beads and repeat from * working back and forwards until the piece is complete.

LADDER STITCH START

Brick stitch is worked in the same way into ladder stitch. Begin with the thread coming out of the top of the end bead in the ladder stitch band.

Bugle beads can be used for the ladder stitch base row and the brick stitch fabric. It is extremely pliable down the length.

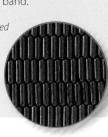

1 *Pick up two beads and pass the needle under the thread loop between the first two beads. Take the needle back through the second bead.

2 Pick up one bead and pass the needle under the next thread loop and back through the bead just added. Continue adding beads, one at a time, until you reach the end of the row. Turn the work and repeat from *.

TWO- AND THREE-DROP BRICK STITCH

Brick stitch can be worked as a two- or three-drop stitch instead. This creates an elongated brick wall effect and makes it easy to mix bugles and other long beads with seed beads.

• Two-Drop Brick Stitch

Make a ladder stitch base row with two-bead stacks. Pick up four beads in sequence to create the first two stacks of the second row. Pass the needle under the first loop and back through the second set of two beads just added. *Pick up two beads and pass through the next thread loop. Go back through the two beads and pull taut. Repeat from * to the end. Begin each row by picking up four beads.

DECREASING

Shape brick stitch by decreasing in the middle or at either end of a row. At the end of the row simply stop short and go back in the other direction. There are different ways to decrease in the middle, depending on whether you are working basic brick stitch or adding stacks of beads.

• At the Beginning of a Row

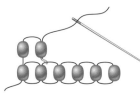

The method is the same regardless of the number of beads in each stack. The diagram shows one bead but you can decrease with two or more in each stack. At the beginning of the row add two beads as normal but take the needle through the second loop rather than the first. To make the beads just added sit straight, lock them into position by taking the needle back through the first bead and up through the second bead again.

• Miss a Loop

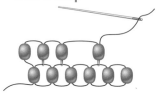

Pick up a bead then miss a loop and take the needle through the next loop along. Pass the needle back through the bead just added.

• Share a Bead

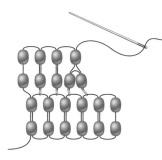

If you are working two or three-bead brick stitch, missing a loop can leave a large hole so decrease by sharing a bead instead.

TIP WHEN WORKING TWO- OR THREE-BEAD BRICK STITCH YOU CAN GO THROUGH TWO STACKS OF BEADS IN THE ROW BELOW TO LOCK THE BEADS MORE SECURELY.

INCREASING

Increase at the end or in the middle of a row. If you increase gradually the bead fabric will remain flat and if you increase rapidly the bead fabric will ruffle up.

• Share a Loop

Use this technique to increase in the middle or at the end of a row. The method works for two- or three-drop brick stitch as well.

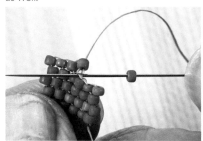

Work two beads, one at a time, into the same loop. It can help if you leave the previous row slightly loose to accommodate the extra beads.

• Share a Bead

This technique is ideal for two- or three-drop brick stitch.

Pick up one less bead on a second stack and take the needle down through the bottom bead of the previous stack. Then take the needle back up through all the beads in the last stack.

• Extend the End

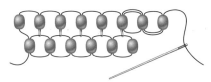

Add an even number of beads using ladder stitch and the thread comes out at the top of the second bead ready for the next row.

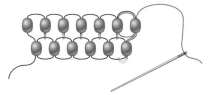

When adding one bead the thread comes out at the bottom of the bead. To change the thread direction, take the needle down through the last bead on the previous row. Pass the needle under the loop and back up through the same two beads.

■ CIRCULAR AND TUBULAR BRICK STITCH

Both circular and tubular brick stitch are worked in the same way as regular brick stitch and use a similar 'step up' technique at the end of each round. With tubular brick stitch there are no increases so you form an upright tube. Circular brick stitch stays flat or can be shaped like a bowl depending in the number of beads added in each round.

TUBULAR BRICK STITCH

This stitch is featured here rather than with the other tubular bead stitches in Chapter 3 because it is more suited to making small pouches and amulet purses rather than a rope or cord. Use bugles for the ladder stitch start to create an attractive border.

1 To make a tube, work a length of ladder stitch and join the ends (see page 40) by going through the end beads to form a ring finishing with the thread coming out of the top of the bugle or bead. *Begin the brick stitch round by picking up two beads, passing the needle under the first loop and back through the last bead added.

2 Work brick stitch all the way round, adding one bead at a time. At the end take the thread through the first and last beads to join them so that the thread comes out at the top again. Repeat from *.

CIRCULAR BRICK STITCH

A flat circle with a solid centre is ideal for the base of a round container or a mat. Begin with a bead or bugle, a large bead or a row of beads. You can add larger beads rather than increasing in subsequent rows. This technique is used for the rosette embellishment shown below.

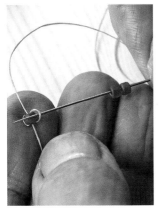

1 Thread a needle and pick up a bead. Drop down to about 15cm (6in) from the tail. Pass the needle back through the bead twice so that there is a thread on both sides. Pick up two beads and pass the needle under the thread loop on one side. Take the needle back through the second bead added, as in regular brick stitch. Continue around the bead, working brick stitch into the loops on both sides.

2 Loop the thread through the first and last beads at the end of the round so that the thread finishes on the outside. Begin each new round with the two-bead start. If you are working single bead brick stitch increase by sharing a loop. For stacked brick stitch use the shared bead increase, unless you want to use the holes left with the shared loop technique to create a lace effect.

Bead Something Now
Brick Stitch Rosettes

Brick stitch worked in a circular shape makes a super bead medallion that can be worn as a brooch or attached to a bag. Genuine Swarovski crystals elevate this brick stitch embellishment into the luxury class and will transform a pair of plain pumps into the perfect party shoes ideal for any special occasion. Instructions on how to make the rosettes are on page 157.

HERRINGBONE STITCH

This is the most instantly recognisable beading stitch as the beads sit in a distinctive fish bone pattern. It's quick to work as the beads are added in pairs and form stacks of tiny 'v's. The stitch can be worked on to a ladder stitch base in a similar way to brick stitch. This is an easy way to learn the technique but aficionados prefer the traditional triple row start as there is no visible join.

LADDER STITCH START
You can work the herringbone stitch onto a single row of ladder stitch but many beaders prefer the two-drop technique, shown on page 40. Either method creates a border along the bottom of the herringbone panel that can be used as a feature.

TIP As the beads sit in a 'v' shape, once you have mastered the technique you can take the needle down through one bead and up through the next in one movement.

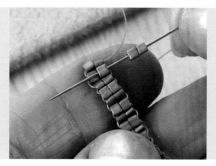
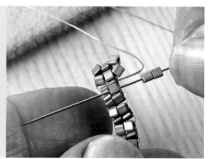

1 Work the ladder stitch base following one of the techniques on page 40. If necessary, flip the ladder stitch so that the thread is coming out of the top of an end bead. Pick up two beads and take the needle down through the next bead along.

2 *Bring the needle up through the next bead on the ladder stitch base. Pick up two beads and take the needle down through the next bead. Repeat from * to the end of the row.

Ladder stitch has a different appearance to herringbone stitch and can be used as a feature at the top and bottom of a piece of work. Toho triangles give the stitches an interesting texture (far left). Even-sized seed beads show the distinctive 'v' shape of herringbone stitch extremely well. The diagrams below show how to work the triple row start that creates herringbone stitch with no join visible between the base rows and the fabric (left).

TRIPLE ROW START
This is the best way to start as the bead fabric looks like herringbone stitch from row one. It is tricky to master but if you follow the diagrams closely using three similar coloured beads you will soon learn the technique. Left-handed beaders are advised to copy the diagrams and flip horizontally using a computer (see page 37). For your first attempt string the exact beads in the diagram but once the technique is familiar you can string any quantity in multiples of four between the two end beads.

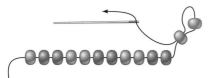

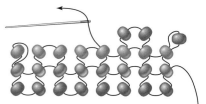

1 Use a stop bead or spring on the end of a long thread, leaving a 15cm (6in) tail. Pick up one pink, two brown, two pink, two brown, two pink, two brown and a pink bead. These beads form the first two rows. Pick up one olive, which is the first bead of row three. Take the needle through the last pink bead added.

2 Miss two brown beads (row one) and pass through the next pink bead. Pick up two olive beads and pass through the next pink bead. Continue adding olive beads between the pairs of pink beads and missing the brown beads to the end of the row. Pick up the last olive bead and then turn the work ready for the next row.

3 Pick up a brown bead and pass the needle back through the next two olive beads. Pick up two brown and pass through the next two olive beads. You are now working a more obvious herringbone stitch. Once you have worked a few rows pull the beads on the first row away from the tail until they are lined up snugly together.

TURNING
There are several ways to turn in herringbone stitch – weaving through the beads or looping through threads. So long as you come back up through the end bead it doesn't really matter how you get there!

• On a Ladder Stitch Base

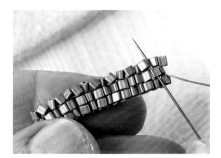

• On a Triple Row Start

1 To turn on the ladder stitch base, pick up the last two beads and take the needle down through the last bead of the ladder stitch row. Go across and up through the second bead in, then back across again to emerge through the last bead added.

2 Once on herringbone stitch, pick up the last two beads, take the needle down through the end bead of the previous row. Pass the needle under the loop between the beads in the row below then take the needle back up through the two end beads again ready to start the next row.

When turning triple row start herringbone stitch, pick up the last bead of the row you're on and the first bead of the next row. Pass the needle back through the first bead added and then go through the bead on the next stack.

TIP FOR A MORE SECURE TURN, WORK A HALF HITCH THROUGH THE LOOP BEFORE GOING BACK UP READY TO START THE NEW ROW.

TIP THE THREAD SHOWS ON EVERY SECOND BEAD DOWN THE SIDE EDGES SO USE A THREAD THAT MATCHES THE BEADS.

DECREASING
Reducing the number of beads in herringbone stitch is quite easy. At the edge of the work you simply stop early and turn to begin the new row. In the middle of the row decrease quickly by missing out a complete stitch or add only one bead instead of two.

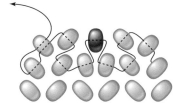

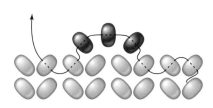

• Between Stacks
For a gradual decrease between stacks, pick up one bead instead of the usual two. On the next row pass the thread through the single bead and then in the third row work across the gap and pull the stitches tight. To decrease quickly simply pass the needle through two beads without picking up any beads. On the next row work across the gap and then pull the stitches tight.

• Within Stacks
Pick up three beads, skip a stack (pair of beads) and take the needle back through the next bead. Work herringbone as normal to the end of the row. On the next row go through the first bead of the three, pick up two beads and pass the needle through the last bead of the three. On the next row work herringbone stitch into the two beads just added.

To keep a stripe pattern going when decreasing, alternate techniques changing from between to within stacks every other row.

INCREASING

With herringbone stitch you can increase rapidly by fitting an extra stitch between stacks but usually beads are added gradually one in the first row, then two on the next row: these beads are simply strung and can appear to float. Generally only one or two beads float but you can add more in subsequent rows to create designs such as dragon wings or flowers (right). Alternatively you can work herringbone stitch into two floating beads, see between stacks below (far right)

• On the Edge
Use single needle ladder stitch to add beads to the edge of herringbone stitch.

1 At the end of a row, add beads one at a time using ladder stitch until there is the required number of pairs.

2 Turn and pick up two beads. Work herringbone stitch through these beads on the next row. Take needle down through second bead from the edge and back up through the next bead ready to work herringbone stitch to the end.

3 To increase at the same level on both sides work ladder stitch at the other end. Add one or more herringbone stitches above the beads just added and then turn ready to work the next row.

• Between Stacks
Use the same or different beads to create an increase between stacks of herringbone stitch.

1 After completing a herringbone stitch, pick up a bead and pass through the first bead of the next stack ready to work another herringbone stitch.

2 On the next row pick up two beads instead of just one between the stacks.

3 Work a herringbone stitch into these two floating beads in the next row.

TIP To increase rapidly pick up two beads instead of one.

• Increasing by Bead Size
Herringbone stitch can be worked with different sizes of beads to create a fan shape. It is easier to work with pairs of beads of the same size although they can be different colours, shapes or finishes.

1 Line up an even number of beads so that they gradually increase in size – it is the height that is important. Use ladder stitch (see page 40) to stitch the beads together in a line.

2 Work subsequent rows in herringbone stitch keeping the beads in order on each line. The graduated size of the beads will cause the beading to curve.

Herringbone stitch worked with graduated beads can be used to make curved panels or even a complete circle.

Bead Something Now
Herringbone Tealight

Triangle beads and herringbone stitch is a marriage made in heaven and this gorgeous tealight dish shows just how divine it can be. It is a perfect design as the facets on the beads sparkle in the flickering candlelight and as it is made to measure you can easily replace the tealight ready for the next occasion. The delightful frilled edge is created using the floating bead technique where beads are added between the stacks (see opposite page). Full instructions on how to make the tealight are on page 157.

CIRCULAR HERRINGBONE STITCH

Some people find circular herringbone stitch is easier to work than flat herringbone stitch. It is ideal for making coasters or the base for containers. To create the sides of the container simply stop adding increasing beads and continue working rounds of plain herringbone and the sides will automatically stand up straight (see page 61 – tubular herringbone).

1 Pick up seven brown beads and pass through the first two beads again to make a circle. Pick up one pink bead between each bead in the base circle.

2 Step up to the next round by going through the last brown bead and the first pink bead added in the last round.

3 Pick up two khaki beads between each of the beads you added in the last round.

4 Step up again, this time going through one pink and one khaki bead, added in previous round. Work a round of herringbone into each pair of beads.

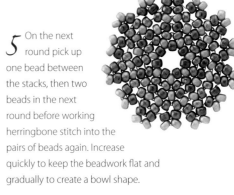

5 On the next round pick up one bead between the stacks, then two beads in the next round before working herringbone stitch into the pairs of beads again. Increase quickly to keep the beadwork flat and gradually to create a bowl shape.

PEYOTE STITCH

Peyote stitch is currently one of the most popular beading stitches possibly because it's so versatile and easy to work. It's an ancient stitch that creates a brick-paving pattern which looks similar to brick stitch when turned on its side. Peyote stitch is more pliable across the work and so is ideal for making flaps or horizontal folds in beadwork. Varying the thickness of the thread changes the handle of the bead fabric. A single thread creates a pliable fabric but a double thickness or thicker thread that fills the beads' holes makes it stiffer. Like all bead stitches, use even sized beads to make a flat smooth bead fabric.

EVEN COUNT PEYOTE STITCH

This is the basic peyote stitch that can be worked as a square, or a long narrow rectangle. It is easy to work back and forwards to create the bead fabric. To make it easier to work peyote stitch, attach a stop bead or end spring (see page 37) about 15cm (6in) from the end of the thread.

1 Pick up an even number of beads, the width of the finished piece; these will form the first two rows. Pick up the first bead of the next row and go through the second bead from the end. The first bead will sit above the second in a 'T' shape.

2 *Pick up a bead, miss a bead and go through the next bead. Repeat from * to the end.

3 *Turn the beadwork over. Pick up another bead and take the needle through the first 'up' bead. Work along the row going through every 'up' bead. Repeat from * until the piece is the length required.

At the end of the third row the working thread will come out of the same bead as the tail.

ODD COUNT PEYOTE STITCH

This stitch is worked in the same way as even count peyote stitch except that you need to make a different turn at the end because the last bead in each row is an 'up' bead. Use this technique when you need a pattern or shape to be centred exactly. If you prefer not to work the turns it is possible to add a row of brick stitch to a panel of even-count peyote stitch to make the panel with a centre line.

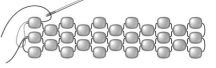

When you reach the end of the row pass the needle through the loop on the edge between the previous two beads and go back through the bead just added.

1 Pick up an odd number of beads, the width of the finished piece. Following the steps for even-count peyote stitch above, pick up a bead and work the third row. Then, after you add the last bead, tie the tail and working thread together.

2 *Turn the work and pass the needle through the last bead added then work back along the row adding beads between every 'up' bead. After you add the last bead, pass the needle through the outside thread on the previous row. Repeat from * until the piece is the length required.

Alternatively you can weave the thread through several beads and back out through the bead just added ready to start the new row.

TWO-DROP PEYOTE STITCH

Either even or odd count peyote stitch can be worked by picking up two or more beads instead of one at a time. This allows you to incorporate bugle beads into the work and to create a variety of textures by using a range of bead sizes. Begin in the same way for even or odd count peyote stitch and then treat each pair or group of beads as one.

1 Begin in the same way as for regular peyote stitch, picking up sufficient beads for the width required, in multiples of two. Pick up two beads and pass the needle through the third and fourth beads from the end.

2 *Pick up two beads, miss two beads and pass the needle through the next two beads. Repeat from * to the end. Depending on the number of beads added turn using the odd or even count techniques.

TIP FOR THREE-DROP PEYOTE STITCH PICK UP BEADS IN MULTIPLES OF THREE INSTEAD OF TWO.

DECREASING

You can decrease in the middle of the row or at the end. One of the attractive aspects of peyote stitch is that its diagonal lines make it easy to create triangle or diamond shapes.

• At the End of a Row

Choose one of these techniques depending on whether you want a step shape turn or a smooth diagonal line. Leaving or adding an 'up' bead creates a step, turning on a 'down' bead creates a smooth diagonal line. As techniques vary depending on which method of peyote stitch you are working remember that you will either be able to turn by adding a bead or by anchoring the thread between two beads.

Step Decrease

Work along to where you want to stop after taking the needle through a 'down' bead. Turn the work, pick up a bead and pass the needle back through the next 'up' bead.

The steps in peyote stitch create a decorative edge with the remaining 'up' beads.

Diagonal decreasing produces a much smoother line.

Diagonal Decrease

1 Pass the needle under the thread between the two beads at the edge of the work. Turn the work and take the needle back through the bead just added.

2 When you reach the decrease edge again pick up the last 'up' bead and take the needle under the thread between beads in the previous row. Turn the work, pass back through the 'up' bead and continue back along the row.

• In the Middle of a Row

1 Pass the needle through two 'up' beads without adding a bead in between. Pull the thread tight as you continue to the end of the row.

2 On the next row add one bead over the gap. On the next row work along as usual, passing the needle through the bead over the gap. You will have decreased by two beads.

TIP FOR A MORE GRADUAL DECREASE, ADD TWO BEADS INSTEAD OF ONE OVER THE GAP AND PASS BACK THROUGH THE TWO BEADS ON THE NEXT ROW. ON THE NEXT ROW ADD ONE BEAD OVER THE TWO.

The dark beads show where the single beads were added over the gap.

INCREASING

You can increase in the middle or at the end of the row. You can increase in the middle of the row gradually so that the bead fabric curves but stays flat or increase rapidly to force the bead fabric to ruffle up. Follow the steps on page 51 to increase at either or both ends.

• In the Middle of a Row

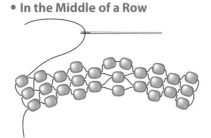

1 Pick up two beads instead of one where you want to increase. For a smoother increase choose beads that are slightly thinner than others.

The darker beads show where each increase occurred to create this arc-shaped piece of beading.

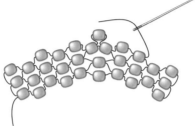

2 On the next row add a normal sized bead between the two slightly thinner beads.

If you increase frequently along the same row of peyote stitch you will create a ruffle effect. Work with contrast beads on the last row for a decorative edge.

Bead Something Now
Peyote Stitch Rings

If, like me, you doubt whether a ring made from beads can ever be comfortable to wear, have a go making one of these pretty rings and you'll be pleasantly surprised! They are quick to make and as you finish the band before joining it into a ring shape, it is easy to get it just the right size. Use small seed beads or bugles for the band so that it is not too bulky and sits comfortably between your fingers and then go to town embellishing the band to create a unique ring. Add semi-precious stones, Swarovski crystals or pearls for a luxury look or have fun using seed beads and some of the bead techniques you have learnt to make these funky designs. Full details are on page 158.
.

• Working a Step at the End of a Row

Although it is rarely necessary to increase at the end of a row as most designs can be worked so that you are decreasing instead which is an easier technique, it is useful to know how. These steps show the technique for even-count peyote stitch. Adapt for odd-count peyote by securing the thread on the turn as shown on page 48.

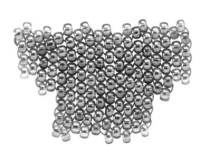

1 Pick up three beads and pass the needle back through the first bead just added.

TIP PULL THE THREAD TAUT SO THAT THE BEADS FROM A 'T' SHAPE BEFORE ADDING THE NEXT BEAD.

2 Pick up another bead and continue working peyote stitch to the end of the row. Work the next row along the increase beads as usual. If you want to increase further repeat step one.

Repeat the technique at the end of the following row to increase at both ends.

CIRCULAR PEYOTE STITCH

This technique creates a flat disc that can be used to create the base of a vessel or bowl. If you don't add enough beads in each round the disc will curve up to create a bowl shape. Once you have created a disc if you add one bead at a time in each round you will be working tubular peyote stitch and make a straight-sided vessel (see page 69).

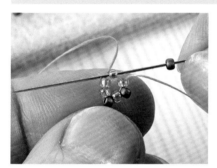

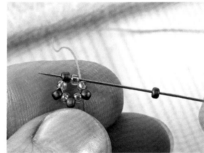

1 Pick up five beads and pass the needle through the first two beads again to make a circle. For the second round add a bead between each bead in the base circle.

2 'Step up' by passing the needle through the last bead of the base circle and the first bead added in the second round again.

Alternate between adding one and two beads in each round to create an even flat disc.

3 Pick up two beads between each bead added in the last round. 'Step up' by passing the needle through one of the two beads added again ready to begin the next round.

4 Add one bead between each 'up' bead in the next round then two beads between each of these beads in the following round. Step up through the first bead (or pair of beads) added in the previous round ready to start the new round.

TIP YOU CAN BEGIN WITH THREE BEADS IF YOU DON'T WANT A HOLE IN THE CENTRE AND MORE IF YOU WANT A LARGER HOLE TO CREATE A DOUGHNUT SHAPE.

■ NETTING STITCH ■

Netting is usually thought of as a loose lacy beaded mesh but netting stitch, also called three-bead netting, is actually a compact stitch that can be used to make a fairly firm bead fabric. Netting stitch is not as versatile as some of the other bead stitches but it has a unique texture and can be varied by using different beads such as bugles or by increasing the number of beads. Five-bead netting is a variation that has a much looser mesh. You can also work netting stitch in circular form and the tubular version is shown on page 61.

THREE-BEAD NETTING

Three-bead netting has a very close mesh so doesn't really look like netting at all. It is easier to learn using alternate contrast beads.

1 Pick up beads for the first row beginning with a shared bead and alternating between shared (red) and bridge (gold) beads in multiples of four. This sample has 20 beads.

2 Pick up four beads, keeping the pattern sequence, for the first turn. Turn the beadwork and pass back through the fourth shared bead from the needle.

3 *Pick up a bridge, a shared and a bridge bead. Miss three beads and pass through the next shared bead. Repeat to the end of the row.

4 Turn the beadwork, pick up five beads and pass through the second shared bead from the end. Repeat from * until the netting is the length required.

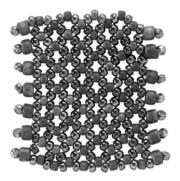

Three-bead netting worked in alternate contrasting beads has an attractive texture. Use the picot technique on page 53 to add an attractive edging.

FIVE-BEAD NETTING

This looser variation of three-bead netting has a more distinctive mesh effect and as a result doesn't hold its shape unless supported over an object such as a bead or bauble.

1 Pick up beads for the first row in multiples of six, following the sequence of one shared (gloss) bead, then two bridge (matt) beads. This sample has 18 beads. Pick up a further six beads for the turn and pass the needle through the fourth shared bead from the needle.

2 At the end of subsequent rows pick up eight beads in sequence for the turn, passing the needle through the second shared bead from the end.

PICOT EDGE

It is easy to add an attractive picot edge to netting. You can use the same size of bead or larger beads for a bolder effect. This technique can be used to add a fringe to the edge of netting. Simply add more beads in place of the size 6 bead to make a longer strand.

1 Pick up beads for the first row, there are 20 beads in this sample. Pick up a size 6 red seed bead and a size 10 gold seed bead. Pass the needle back through the size 6 seed bead. Work across the row as usual.

2 At the other end pick up a gold seed bead, a size 6 seed bead and a gold seed bead again. Pass the needle back through the size 6 seed bead again.

3 Pick up a gold, red and gold size 10 seed beads and pass through the second shared (red) seed bead along. Continue to the end of the row and add a picot at the other end to turn.

INCREASING AND DECREASING

Netting can be increased and decreased in the middle of a row by simply adding more or fewer beads on each loop. At the end of a row you can turn early and take the needle back through the previous bridge beads to come out at a shared bead. If you increase at each end of every row the netting increases rapidly in width.

• Increasing On the Edge

To create the turn, pick up nine beads in sequence instead of the usual five. Take the needle through the fourth shared bead from the needle and continue to the end of the row.

• Increasing In the Middle

Pick up more beads in each set to increase at any point along the row. You can either add more shared beads or more bridge beads or a mix of both.

At the last loop before the edge, pick up the extra beads before the shared bead and only one after so that you link into the right bead when you turn.

• Decreasing

When decreasing you simply pick up fewer beads between the shared beads. You can decrease evenly on both sides or by only one bead at a time in each loop.

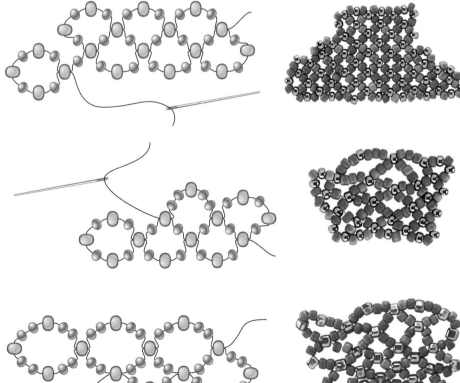

CIRCULAR NETTING

Begin with a circle of beads and use increasing techniques to create discs of netted beadwork. You can work in a regular pattern (**right**), increasing evenly on each loop or create a free-style piece using a more random pattern (**far right**). Depending on the number of beads added in each round, the bead fabric will either be a flat shape or can be adjusted to fit over a bead or bauble. Beaded buttons using circular netting are shown on page 89.

1 Choose two different colours of seed bead; one will be the shared bead and the other the bridge bead. Pick up beads in a multiple of four, alternating between the colours. This sample has 20 beads and is tied in a circle.

2 Bring the needle out through a shared bead. For the first round pick up two bridge beads, a shared bead and two bridge beads. Miss a shared bead and pass the needle through the next shared bead. Continue making this size of loop right round the circle.

3 To step up to the next round pass the needle through the first two bridge beads and the middle shared bead of the first loop again. On this round pick up three bridge beads between the shared beads, and four bridge beads on the next round and so on.

Bead Something Now
Beaded Bauble

Beaded baubles look absolutely stunning hung as an individual decoration from a length of beautiful organza ribbon or complementing the other decorations on a Christmas tree. The exquisite beaded netting can seem a daunting task but this stunning design makes it all quite easy as the beaded mesh is made up from individual netting motifs that are simply the first two rows of circular netting. These pretty motifs are then sewn together with sparkly accent beads and finished with a pretty fringe. Full details are on page 158–9.

RIGHT ANGLE WEAVE

This versatile stitch can be used to make a range of bead fabric from a close woven fabric to a loose and lacy mesh. All variations are based on the basic four-bead unit, so once you have learnt the basics you can try your hand at more advanced pieces. Right angle weave works well in 3-D too – four basic units can be worked as a cube or three for a triangular cross section. This is the basis of tubular right angle weave shown in detail on page 61.

BASIC STITCH

Simple right angle weave is worked with four beads that sit at right angles to each so that there are top, bottom and two side beads. For clarity in this example the top and bottom beads are matt and the side beads are gloss. You pick up four beads to start but thereafter you are using one or two beads from adjacent units to complete the right angle weave. As right angle weave is worked vertically the 'rows' are referred to as columns.

1 Pick up four seed beads, a gloss, a matt, a gloss and a matt, and tie in a circle. Take the needle back through the beads again to come out through the matt bead opposite the tail.

2 Pick up three seed beads; a gloss, a matt and a gloss then take the needle through the matt on the previous circle and through the beads just added to come out the top matt.

3 Continue adding three beads at a time, alternating between going around in a clockwise direction and anticlockwise depending on the direction the thread comes out of the last bead, until the column is the desired length.

CHANGING DIRECTION

When you complete a column, work a unit to the right or left ready to change direction and work downward to create the next column. At the end of that column you repeat the process to work upwards again.

4 To work the second column take the needle through the next side bead in the direction the thread is going. Pick up three beads in order (matt, gloss, matt) and pass the needle back through the side bead and the bottom bead in the new unit again.

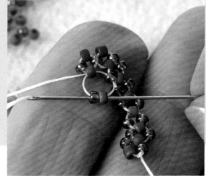

5 Pick up a gloss and a matt bead. Pass the needle through the gloss from the adjacent column and the matt from the unit above and then back through the other two beads to come out at the bottom matt bead again.

TIP To avoid snagging the thread when passing the needle through beads, you can blunt the tip with fine sandpaper.

6 Continue down the column adding two beads at a time, using the two beads from adjacent links to complete the circle. You will not always pass through the same number of beads to complete a unit each time – just remember to go round until you come out of the correct bead ready to add the next unit. Add further columns as required.

ADDING EXTRA BEADS

Right angle weave can be worked with more than four beads. This example keeps the square format with four size 6 beads and four size 11 seed beads in each unit.

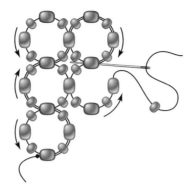

Begin with a large bead and then pick up alternate small and large beads to make the unit. Tie the beads in a circle and pass back through the beads to come out at the top large bead. Pick up beads for the next unit and take the needle back through the beads as shown. When adding the next column of beads, remember to add the small bead between the two large beads that you are 'borrowing' from the adjacent units to complete the new unit so that there are four small beads in total.

VARYING THE SHAPE

Units don't have to be square; they can be based on a rectangle too so that the basic 1 x 1 unit can be 1 x 2, 1 x 5 or any number of extra beads. The technique is still the same – there are just more beads to go through in one direction. These longer units create a lacy fabric or are ideal for making necklaces or bracelets.

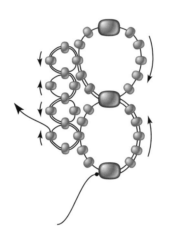

Begin with the larger right angle weave unit (1 x 5). Work enough units to get the first column the length required. Take the needle through the beads again until it emerges from the centre bead on one side. Add the first small unit and then add further small units until you are ready to link into the middle bead of the next large unit.

INCREASING AND DECREASING

Increasing and decreasing in right angle weave is quite easy once you are familiar with the basic stitch and the way the units join together. With the basic 1 x 1 unit you can increase and decrease by a whole unit or half a unit at time for a more gradual slope.

When increasing and decreasing right angle weave units with larger quantities of beads there is more flexibility. You can add or remove whole or half units or work in part units using more or fewer beads as required.

DECREASING

Right angle weave can be decreased in the middle of a row or at the end. To decrease at the end simply stop short and turn.

• In the Middle of a Row

It is easy to decrease in the middle of a row by working two beads together as though they were one. You can decrease quite rapidly using this technique. Whether you pick up the two beads for the right angle weave before or after the decrease will depend on whether you are on a clockwise or anticlockwise unit (see page 55).

1 To decrease in a clockwise direction simply take the needle through two adjacent side beads instead of just the one.

2 Pick up two beads as normal and pass the needle back through the unit to come out at the bottom bead again.

3 To decrease in an anticlockwise direction the two beads are picked up first before passing the needle through two adjacent side beads.

INCREASING

Right angle weave can be increased at the end of a column or in the middle instead. You can increase by one unit or half a unit at a time.

• At the End of a Row

In this example you would miss out the matt bead on the needle to make the half unit increase at the end of the row.

1 When you reach the end of the column take the needle through the beads in the last unit to come out at the top bead. Pick up three beads in sequence and pass back through the top bead.

2 You then have to take the needle through the beads in the last unit to come out at the side bead ready to begin the next column.

3 At the end of the row add an extra unit at the end. You will then need to go through the beads to come out at the inner side bead. Add a unit to match the increase at the other side.

• In the Middle of a Row

You can increase at any point along the column and as many times as you want although every other stitch is usually sufficient. Increasing more often will create a ruffle effect rather than a flat shape.

1 At the point where you want to increase pick up a bottom bead and two side beads instead of just one; then pass the needle through the beads in the unit to come out of the bottom bead again.

2 On the next column work a single unit into each of the side beads added to create the increase. To increase rapidly you need to add two beads to some units on this row and increase again in subsequent rows as required.

TIP DEPENDING ON WHICH UNIT YOU STOP ON YOU MAY NEED TO GO ROUND IN A FIGURE OF EIGHT OR SIMPLY PASS THE NEEDLE BACK THROUGH THE SIDE BEAD IN THE UNIT BELOW READY TO ADD THE NEXT UNIT.

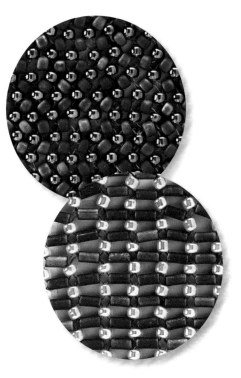

*The appearance of basic right angle weave can be varied using different beads. Matt and gloss beads give the stitch a lively appearance (*top*) and short bugle beads create a rectangular pattern and a more open mesh.*

CHAIN STITCH

Chain stitch, a variation of right angle weave, is generally used to make jewellery, belts, straps and cords. The stitch can be worked in the same way as a single column of right angle weave, as shown on page 55 or you can try this simple technique based on a figure of eight. Working with two thread ends makes it easier to create right angle weave units off to the side of the main strand. If you are using a firm thread, such as nylon cord or monofilament, you will not need to use needles.

WORKING A FIGURE OF EIGHT
This basic technique can be used to make a variety of chain shapes. Four is the minimum number of beads in each unit but you can increase the number to make different shapes. The basic unit of four is described as 1 x 1, a longer unit for example could be 1 x 4, which is one bead at each end and four down each side or 2 x 5, two beads at the ends and five down each side.

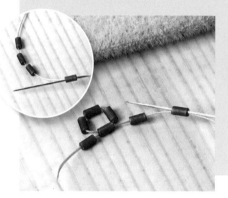

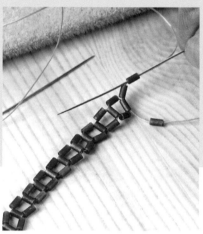

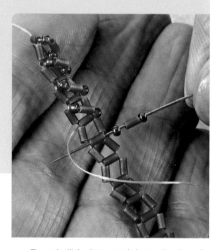

1 Add a needle to each end of a long length of beading thread and pick up four bugles. Take one needle and pass it through one of the end beads to create the right angle unit. Pick up two bugles on one thread and one bugle on the other. Pass needle with the single bugle through the last bugle on the other side. Pull the threads taut to make the figure of eight.

2 Continue adding more units to create the chain. Pick up two bugles on alternate needles each time.

TIP AVOID CATCHING THE THREAD WITH THE NEEDLE AS YOU GO BACK THROUGH THE BEADS.

3 To embellish chain stitch bring the thread out at the side of a top bead, pick up the embellish beads and take the thread through the bottom bead of the next unit in the opposite direction.

Chain Stitch Variations
These four samples show just how different chain stitch can look when you alter the beads and threads.

Bugles make each link in chain stitch a square shape. Longer bugles will make larger squares.

Add extra beads across each link to embellish a plain chain stitch band. Beads added on both sides will create a rope.

Bicone crystals work particularly well with chain stitch as the beads lock together so neatly.

Nylon monofilament (illusion cord) makes this 1 x 7 chain rounded rather than square as the stiffness of the thread holds the beads in a curve.

Bead On

Now you can combine the skills learnt in right angle weave and chain stitch to create beautiful bead weaving projects then learn how to use a large tubular mandrel to make quick and easy bags and purses.

■ BEAD WEAVING

The figure of eight technique is the basis of bead weaving where the beads are woven together to create motifs. These motifs can either stand alone, or be worked as part of a longer piece of jewellery. Generally right angle weave is symmetrical but with bead weaving you can increase the number of beads on one side or use larger beads to make asymmetrical links.

WORKING A BASIC MOTIF

Once you have made the base doughnut shape interesting features, such as picots, can be added.

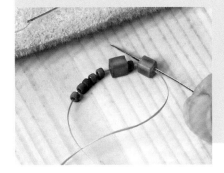

1 Begin with a needle on each end of a long thread. Pick up five seed beads, a cube, a seed bead and a cube on one needle. Drop the beads down to the centre of the thread. Pass the other needle back through the end cube bead.

2 Pull the threads through. *Pick up a seed bead and a cube on the needle that has just passed through the last cube and five seed beads on the other needle. Pass that needle back through the cube bead. Repeat from * until you have added seven cubes.

3 Pick up five seed beads on the thread emerging from the last bead added. Pass the needle through the first cube again to create the doughnut shape. Secure the thread with a half hitch (see page 17). This is the basic motif, which can be incorporated in a chain or band or used to embellish shoes and bags.

4 To make a more ornate motif, weave one thread to come out at a middle seed bead on an outer loop. *Pick up a short bugle, a seed bead, a short bugle, a seed bead, a cube, a seed bead and a short bugle. Take the needle back through the first seed bead added.

5 Pick up another bugle and pass the needle through the centre seed bead on the next loop. Repeat from * going right round the circle.

6 Weave the other thread through the beads to come out through the cube and a seed bead. *Pick up a short bugle, a seed bead and a short bugle and take the needle through the next seed bead, cube and seed bead. Repeat from * all the way round. Secure the thread ends.

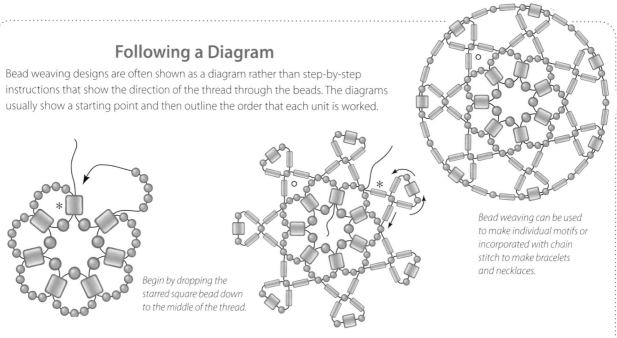

Following a Diagram

Bead weaving designs are often shown as a diagram rather than step-by-step instructions that show the direction of the thread through the beads. The diagrams usually show a starting point and then outline the order that each unit is worked.

Begin by dropping the starred square bead down to the middle of the thread.

Bead weaving can be used to make individual motifs or incorporated with chain stitch to make bracelets and necklaces.

Bead Something Now
Butterfly Necklace

Necklaces are often simply strings of beads but with right angle weave and bead weaving techniques you can create pretty motifs that can be incorporated into the design. Butterflies are perennial favourites as a design motif and look absolutely fabulous worked in a mix of faceted beads and Swarovski crystals. As the butterfly motif is finished before it is incorporated into the necklace it would make a beautiful brooch or stunning hair embellishment if attached to a comb accessory. Full details are given on page 159.

Taking It Further: Tubular Techniques

The tubular techniques used to make ropes and cords with off loom bead stitches can also be used to create wider pieces of tubing that can be used to make small bags or amulet purses.

■ USING WIDER TUBING

It is easier to work around a mandrel of some sort for support. You can simply use a large tube or similar object but purpose-made Perspex (acrylic) tubes are ideal as they have pre-drilled holes to secure the work. Once complete the tube is simply stitched along the bottom edge to create the pouch or bag shape.

MAKING TUBING
As well as the peyote stitch shown here, brick stitch, herringbone stitch, three-bead netting and right angle weave are all suitable to be made into larger tubes.

1 Tie the thread through one of the holes at the top of the tube and pick up sufficient seed beads to fill the gap round to the next hole. Pass the needle through the hole and out the other side. Pick up the same number of seed beads and pass the needle through the next hole round. Continue adding beads and criss crossing the tube until there are beads all the way round. Tie the thread ends together.

2 If you have an even number of beads you can work two-drop peyote stitch for speed. Attach a new thread and pass the thread through two beads on the base circle. Pick up two beads, miss two beads and pass the needle through the next two beads. Repeat all the way round. At the end of the round pass the needle through the first pair of beads added in the last round ready to begin the next round.

3 Cut a piece of paper to fit exactly inside the tube so that the edges butt together rather than overlapping. Draw the design on the paper and then slot it inside the tube. Tape the paper in place at the bottom edge.

4 Continue working rounds of peyote stitch changing colours of beads as required to create the design or pattern. If you draw or paint an accurate design, it is possible to create quite ornate patterns with this technique. Once the tube is complete untie the knotted threads at the top and pull the criss cross threads out. You will lose some beads from the first row as you pull the anchoring thread out.

CHAPTER 3:

Ropes and Cords

*B*eaded ropes and cords are a versatile way to work with beads. Although often associated with bracelets, you can use long ropes to make necklaces, lariats or handbag handles and short lengths for earrings. In this chapter, you will learn techniques such as creating spiral cords and tubular bead stitches. If you want to take things a little further try making some funky beaded beads shown on page 75. Many of the beading stitches such as peyote stitch and herringbone stitch, covered in Chapter 2, can be worked in a tubular form to make ropes but there are many other stitches for you to try that are only worked in a tubular or rope formation. Each stitch has two inspiring variation samples to show how the stitch works with different beads.

Bead Inspirations

These stunning bracelets are created using a variety of techniques explored in this chapter, including twisted herringbone stitch, dutch spiral and right angle weave. All you will need is a needle and thread to get started.

Simply Stunning

The glossy copper brown core of this spiral rope offsets pale coffee coloured pearls and satin beads to make a really elegant bracelet. Rather than simply attaching the rope to the fastenings, try adding a couple of pearls and a silver washer bead to each end first.

Do the Twist

A Dutch spiral rope looks completely different when you use an eclectic mix of beads rather than the traditional bugles. The rope is worked in the usual way but with a different bead at each point of the triangle. This example has a flat disc, size 6 seed bead and a 3mm pearl with two or three seed beads in place of the bugles. Finish with bell cone ends and a loop and bead fastening.

Silver Sparkles

Herringbone stitch always works well with triangle beads of any kind; flat-sided Toho triangle triangle beads create a particularly attractive mosaic appearance. In this twisted herringbone stitch bracelet, tiny seed beads are added between each pair of beads for extra interest (see embellishing ropes and cords on page 75). The rope is finished with ladder stitch and large metal beads then tied into a bracelet with several strands of elastic thread.

Striking Silk

These crusty tubular beads are made using right angle weave. Four Miyuki triangle beads with metallic seed beads in between make the basic unit for a three-sided tube then the tubes are embellished with another metallic seed bead added diagonally over each unit. Thread large beads and tubes onto three strands of silk ribbon and tie in a bow to finish.

Basic Tool Kit

For making ropes and cords, threads and conditioners are just as important as beading needles and mandrels.

■ Beading Needles

When working beading stitches to make ropes and cords you don't need a long needle as you are only going through a few beads at a time. Short beading needles are ideal or use between sewing needles that have a small eye. As a guide the size of the bead should be a larger number than the needle size, for example thread size 11 beads with a size 10 needle. When working spiral twist cord (see page 66) you may need to use a size 13 needle as the thread passes through each bead several times.

■ Threads and Thread Conditioner

Strong threads such as Nymo™ or Super-lon™ are ideal for making bead ropes and cords or use a fine twisted nylon beading thread. Quilting thread is also suitable but these will deteriorate over time, as the cotton fibres are susceptible to damp and mildew.

Thread conditioners are discussed on page 36.

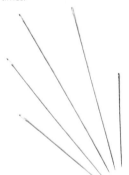

■ Mandrels

Some beaded ropes and cords, such as spiral twist, have a solid core and can simply be worked in the hand, but most are hollow and easier to work around a support of some sort. This support is called a mandrel – any rod, knitting needle, pencil or tube can be used so long as it fits snugly inside the beading.

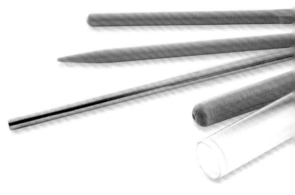

Getting Started

Ropes and cords are all worked in different ways, so you should carefully refer to the instructions for each stitch before you begin. There are, however, some techniques used for all ropes and cords, such as joining on another thread and adding clasps.

■ JOINING ON ANOTHER THREAD

It is possible to join a thread by weaving back and forwards through the beads. However, it is much more secure to work a half hitch or two and then hide the tail in the work, as described here.

1 When joining a new thread, select a column of beads directly below where the old thread emerges. Take the needle with the new thread in between two beads about eight or nine beads from where the old thread ends and out about four beads further up.

2 Pass the needle under threads between two beads and pull it out through the loop of thread to work a half hitch (see diagram, page 17). Go up through the next few beads to bring the needle out the same bead where the old thread emerges.

3 To sew in the old thread, take the needle and thread back down through several beads. Pass the needle under threads between two beads and pull it out through the loop of thread to work a half hitch (see diagram, page 17). Take the needle through another few beads and either trim the tail or work a second half hitch for extra security.

ADDING CLASPS

Ropes and cords are often used for making bracelets or necklaces. With solid ropes, such as the spiral twist, you can simply sew on a clasp using the tail thread but hollow ropes need a little more consideration. You can either reduce the beads in each round to make a cone shape, flatten the tube or use a bell cone end to finish.

SEWING ON A CLASP
Solid ropes such as spiral twist have a thread coming straight out of the centre core at each end.

You can simply sew a clasp onto the bead rope using the tail thread at each end. Go through the loop on the clasp several times and then sew in the tail using a half hitch (see step 2 on page 64) and trim.

FLATTENING THE ENDS
Tubular ropes can be finished neatly at each end by flattening the tube and working ladder stitch. The actual technique will vary depending on the stitch but this is a guide using peyote stitch to illustrate.

1 Pick up one bead between each pair of beads on the last round. Flatten the tube so that all the beads are in a row and take the needle through.

TIP IF THE BEADS ARE ALL THE SAME LEVEL SEW BACK AND FORWARDS TO JOIN THE TWO SIDES THEN ADD A SINGLE ROW OF BEADS ON TOP.

2 You can bring the thread through between the two middle beads to add the clasp or reduce the beads in each row to make a triangle shape. Pick up one less bead and pass the thread through the previous row and the one just added until you get to one bead.

MAKING A CONE SHAPE
Many tubular stitches such as peyote and herringbone stitch can be reduced to make a cone shape. This technique is illustrated here with peyote stitch; refer to the decreasing techniques in Chapter 2 for each particular bead stitch.

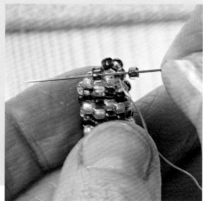

1 If it suits the design, reduce the size of the beads for the last few rows until you are using delicas or size 12 or 15 seed beads. You can then add a large round bead with some smaller beads before adding a clasp to finish.

2 To decrease the number of beads in each round miss picking up a bead for every second stitch, passing the needle through two beads instead. Work a round and then decrease again in the next round until you make a cone shape.

Using Bell Cone Ends
These attractive findings come in all shapes and sizes and are a simple and effective way to finish a rope or cord. Choose a bell cone end that fits the diameter of the rope or cord and, for best results, reduce the tubular end with one of the techniques (left) (see Chapter 5, page 90, for ways to add fastenings).

SPIRAL CORDS

Spiral ropes are delightful to work, as the cord twists around itself because of the way the beads are added. Beads are either added stepping up each time on one side only to create the twist, or loops of beads are added diagonally, also causing the spiral effect. The basic technique can be varied by altering the type of beads and the number of beads stepped up on the core. Using larger beads for the core creates a completely different effect.

SPIRAL TWIST

This is one of the easiest ropes to learn as you simply keep adding the same sequence of beads over and over again. Experiment with different beads on the outside, using a contrast colour for the core beads to create the most attractive effect. This style of spiral twist requires no additional finishing. There is a single thread at each end, which can be used to sew a fastening or add a bead loop.

1 Pick up four size 11 opaque seed beads, then a three bead sequence of a size 11 transparent seed bead, a size 8 bead and a size 11 transparent seed bead and tie into a circle. Pass the needle through the four opaque seed beads again.

2 Pick up one opaque and the three beads sequence. Take the needle through the last three opaque seed beads on the spiral. Pull the thread up and then take the needle through the last opaque seed bead added. Pull thread taut.

3 Repeat step two to add a second loop of beads. Continue repeating step two, making sure that the loops lie right next to each other. After four or five repeats the spiral effect will be obvious. Join new threads as required and secure the ends as shown on page 65.

Bead Something Now
Spiral Bag

Spiral twist is one of the strongest rope techniques as the thread goes back through each bead in the centre core several times as you progress. For this reason it is ideal for a bag handle, especially a pretty evening bag. Attach the spiral rope to a ready-made bag or make this delightful design following the instructions on page 160.

DOUBLE CORE SPIRAL

This variation of the basic spiral technique uses large beads for the core with bugles and loops of seed beads on the outside to create a delightful textural effect. The design can be varied with different textures of beads added around the core or longer loops worked over three or four beads.

1 Pick up two pink 6mm crystals and two 6mm plum crystals and tie in a circle. Take the needle back through the two pinks again and add another pink and plum crystal. Take the needle through the top three pinks ready to add another pair.

2 *Add a pink and plum crystal and take the needle down through the two plum crystals already added. Pick up a 7mm matt pink bugle and take the needle across and up through two pink crystals. Then turn the beading over.

3 Pick up eight size 8 seed beads. These will sit diagonally across a group of four crystals. Take the needle back down through the two plum crystals opposite. Take the thread across and pass the needle through the last pink crystal ready to add the next pair of crystals. Repeat from * until the bead rope is the length required, joining on new threads as required and securing the ends as shown on page 65.

DUTCH SPIRAL

Although worked in a similar way to tubular peyote stitch the Dutch spiral technique has a quite distinct look. The classic Dutch spiral, also known as triple helix, usually features bugle beads (see the variation on page 62), or try incorporating long loops of beads for a more ornate appearance. After the first few rounds it is easier to work this spiral around a mandrel. I've used a large plastic drinking straw that fits snugly inside the tube of beads.

1 Pick up one seed bead and one bugle; repeat until there are six beads. Pass the needle through all the beads again and tie in a circle. Go through the first seed bead again.

2 *Pick up one seed and one bugle and pass the needle through the next seed bead. Repeat from * until the rope is the length you require. As you progress the beads and bugles will form an obvious triangle cross-section and begin to spiral.

Spiral Variations

Like many beading techniques these spiral ropes can be varied using different beads or by altering the sequence slightly. These examples show how you can achieve completely different effects with the same techniques.

Spiral Twist

Bugle beads give a completely different look to the spiral twist. The core beads should measure slightly less than the outer beads when laid side by side.

If you increase the step up to two beads on a spiral twist the beads fall in a more open pattern.

Double Core Spiral

A combination of three quite different beads in toning colours makes an unusual chunky rope with a gentle spiral.

Dutch Spiral

Long bugles make a floppy tube that can be supported with organdy ribbon to make a stunning necklace.

Short bugles and size 10 seed beads make a much neater, more compact tube. Use a different colour of seed bead in each corner of the triangle to create lines of colour spiralling around the tube.

Usually bugles are the most prominent bead in Dutch spiral but when the bugles are smaller than the contrast bead you can a completely different look.

Bead On

Now you can try some more unusual and advanced stitches and beading techniques, such as variations of peyote stitch, herringbone stitch, netting and right angle weave, as well as tubular bead stitches.

◼ AFRICAN HELIX ◼

Use a variety of beads and bugles for African Helix to make different diameters and styles of tubular rope. If the resulting tube is floppy, thread with wide organza ribbon to make an attractive necklace or bracelet. Choose two beads of different colour or texture. One will form the spiral and the other will be the background.

1 In this example I've used size 8 and 10 seed beads. Pick up three background beads (size 10) and one spiral (size 8). Repeat three times until you have a total of 16 beads on the thread. Next, take the needle back through all the beads again to form a circle and then tie securely.

2 Slip the ring of beads on a pencil or similar rod shape so that it is a very snug fit. For the second round *pick up three background beads and two spiral beads. Take the needle down behind the thread of the bead ring **after** the next spiral bead. Repeat from * all the way round, keeping the thread taut.

After the first round always take the needle down the first spiral bead on the next loop.

3 For the third round *pick up three background beads and two spiral beads. Take the needle down behind the thread **before** the first spiral bead on the next loop. Repeat from * all the way round. Continue repeating the third round until the cord is the length required.

4 To finish the other end to match the beginning, pick up three background beads and one spiral bead and loop behind the thread before the spiral beads as usual. Take the needle through the last four beads to finish.

TIP To stabilise the rope once it is complete you can take the needle and thread through the spiral beads. This technique lines up the beads and makes the spirals smoother.

African Helix Variations

You can create some striking looks with the African Helix technique, by varying the number and types of beads that you use for the background.

Using opaque beads for the spiral and transparent beads for the background creates a bold effect.

Use four beads the same size and colour but different finishes to create a co-ordinated look. One is the background bead and the other three are on each corner and create toning spirals along the rope.

Alternatively, replace the three background beads with a long bugle. Size 8 beads and 7mm bugles work well together. This tube is neater if you pass a needle and thread down each of the seed bead lines at the end.

TUBULAR BUTTONHOLE STITCH

This simple method creates a straight tube that looks a little like square stitch but is quicker to work. As the beads form a grid pattern you can use different widths of beads in columns. Bugles and seeds work particularly well together.

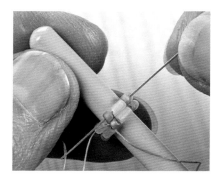

1 Pick up a seed bead and a bugle and repeat until there are enough beads to go around the mandrel and tie a knot. Pick up a seed bead and take the needle down between the next two beads. Loop the thread under the needle and pull the needle through so that the bead is sitting above the bead in the first round. Pick up a bugle and work another buttonhole stitch. Continue alternating beads all the way round.

2 When you reach the first seed bead again take the needle through all the beads and back through the first seed bead. Work each round in the same way, taking the needle one bead further on each time to begin the next round, to finish.

TIP As you pull the stitch tight make sure the bead is lying above the bead on the previous round.

Tubular Buttonhole Variations

This technique is ideal for short lengths of tubing and works particularly well for tubular beads.

Subtle colours create a really gorgeous tubular rope. Using short bugles you can fit four, or even five, around the mandrel (above left).

Create a tube with a triangular cross section using three long bugles and size 10 seed beads. As the thread is visible at each corner, use a colour that matches the beads (above right).

Triangle beads create a completely different look. This sample uses alternate rows of gloss and matt beads. The gloss show as squares and the matt as short lines in between.

TUBULAR PEYOTE STITCH

There are two methods of working peyote stitch depending on the number of beads in the base circle. With odd count peyote you can work round and round continuously, whereas even count peyote stitch requires a step up at the end of each round.

If worked in one colour of beads the two stitches look the same but by using different coloured beads, odd count peyote stitch creates a diagonal spiral whereas even count peyote is more suitable for horizontal or vertical stripes or check patterns.

EVEN COUNT PEYOTE STITCH

When tubular peyote stitch is worked with an even number of beads you need to do a 'step up' at the end of each round ready to begin the next. The beads threaded in base circle are rounds one and two.

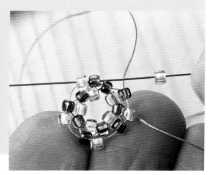

1 Pick up an even number of beads, say 10 beads in alternate colours beginning with a light bead makes the technique easier to follow. Take the needle back through all the beads and the first light and dark bead again. Third round: *Pick up a dark bead and take the needle through the next dark bead. Repeat from * three times to reach the tail thread again.

2 You are ready to complete the round and 'step up' to the next round. Pick up a dark bead and pass the needle through the next dark bead and the first bead added in that round.

3 Fourth round: Add light beads between the dark beads all the way round. Step up through the dark and then the first light added in the last round then pull the thread taut easing the beads into a tube shape. Add another round of light beads. Continue alternating two rounds of dark with two rounds of light to create the zigzag pattern.

ODD COUNT PEYOTE STITCH

This sample uses seven beads for the base circle but you can reduce or increase the quantity of beads so long as there is an odd number. The bead sequence makes the stitch easy to learn and creates the distinctive spiral (see page 71).

1 Pick up two light, two medium and two dark beads, and then one light bead again. Take the thread through all the beads again and back through the first light bead. These beads form the first two rounds.

2 Third round: Pick up a medium bead and go through the next medium, pick up a dark bead and go through the next dark, pick up a light bead and go through the next light.

3 Fourth round: Pick up a medium bead and go through the next medium added in the last round. Pick up a dark and go through the next dark added in last round then pick up a light and go through the next light added in the last round. Continue adding beads in sequence until the rope is as long as required.

TIP TO KEEP THE SPIRAL PATTERN GOING THE BEAD TO PICK UP IS THE SAME COLOUR AS THE ONE YOU ARE ABOUT TO GO THROUGH.

Bead Something Now
Cellini Spiral Beads

If you use beads of the same size you will make a peyote tube with an even surface. By varying the sizes of the beads you can create a more ornate rope or cord. This variation of even count tubular peyote stitch, known as the cellini spiral, makes really attractive beaded beads that can be strung with other beads to make a gorgeous necklace. If you prefer, work a longer length of cellini spiral and change over to ordinary peyote stitch using the smallest beads to make an unusual necklace. Full instructions for the beaded beads are on page 160–1.

Even Count Peyote Variations

When designing for even count tubular peyote stitch, it is easier to work if you base the pattern on horizontal or vertical stripes.

Miyuki triangle beads are even-sized and fit together snugly while giving the peyote stitch tube an interesting texture. This pattern is formed with two rows of dark beads and two rows of light beads.

As the beads in even count peyote stitch are worked in complete rounds you can make striped bands along the length of the tube. Work with one colour for several rows and then after the step up change to another colour.

Pick up a multiple of four beads in pairs of two colours to create a two-drop peyote stitch tube. The pairs of beads are worked together as if they were one bead. Keep the bead sequence going to create stripes or alternate every two rows to make a check pattern.

Odd Count Peyote Variations

Odd count tubular peyote stitch works extremely well with spiral patterns. Worked with the same size beads the tube is flat but you can vary the bead size to make a textured surface (see the Cellini Spiral Beads on page 70).

Plain opaque seed beads in toning colours make an attractive rope. You could add a little 'oomph' using a gold or silver bead in place of the white beads or use transparent beads with an interesting finish.

Pick up one contrast bead in the middle of an even number of main beads to make a tube that has a bold single spiral running down the length. Use a tubular satin bead and a round seed bead to create a distinct contrast.

Alternatively, vary the size of beads in odd count peyote to create a more textured effect. Although the beads are of different sizes, the beads spiral round, giving the closely packed appearance of normal peyote stitch.

HERRINGBONE STITCH

In herringbone stitch the beads are added two at a time, forming the distinctive 'stacks' that are much more obvious if you work with different colours of beads in adjacent pairs. Using different colours also makes it easier to learn the stitch.

TUBULAR HERRINGBONE STITCH

Herringbone stitch is, to my mind, easier to learn in tubular form rather than the flat version, even though the technique is the same! Use only six or eight beads to create a rope and 12 or more to create a tube. The angle of the beads gives the stitch a wonderful texture that is enhanced by using triangle or hex beads, as shown in the examples on page 72.

1 To work the ladder stitch base rows, pick up four dark beads and go back through all the beads and pull up. Pick up two light beads and take needle through the first two dark beads and then the light beads again. Continue adding two beads at a time, changing the colours every four beads to make a six-bead wide, two-bead high strip. Join the two ends together by taking the needle through the end beads twice.

2 To work the herringbone stitch * pick up two beads the same colour as the bead you've just gone through and take the needle back down through the next bead along. Bring the needle up through the first bead in the next stack. Repeat from* until you reach the first stack again.

3 To step up ready for the next round simply take the needle through the top two beads on the next stack. Repeat from * until the rope or tube is the length required.

Bead Something Now
Herringbone Earrings

Work tubular herringbone stitch with a variety of beads from the same colourway to create a pair of unusual loop earrings. Cylinders, twisted bugles and short bugles all have a similar diameter but different lengths and are added in rows to create bands of texture. Use the same design to work a longer rope to make a matching bracelet, adding attractive clasps to finish. Details of how to make these are on page 161.

Herringbone Variations

Herringbone is one of the most distinctive stitches and looks wonderful with a variety of beads. Use ordinary herringbone for horizontal or vertical patterns and twisted herringbone for spiral designs.

Tubular Herringbone Stitch

Using a different colour for each stack makes bold vertical lines. Rotate the colours every two rounds to create a check pattern.

Bugle beads of all lengths can be used although the tube becomes less flexible the longer the bugles. Short 3mm bugles create an attractive texture.

Try alternating two or more contrast beads in different rounds. The beads can be of different length but should have a similar diameter so that they stack neatly together. This example mixes size 11 triangle and pink seed beads.

Twisted Herringbone Stitch

Contrasting colours emphasise the spiral pattern created with twisted herringbone. Using silver-lined beads or another strong contrast emphases one line in particular.

Using tubular seed beads instead of the usual round seed beads gives twisted herringbone a completely different look. Three soft shades seem to merge into one another and the translucent quality of the beads creates a really delicate effect.

Triangle beads work well with herringbone stitch and the twisted version is no exception. Each bead sits with a slightly different surface facing forward to create an interesting texture and the petrol finish introduces a variety of colours.

TWISTED HERRINGBONE STITCH

This variation of tubular herringbone is created by a simple alteration in the way the thread is routed through the beads, which causes the bead stack to tilt to one side and then spiral round as you add further rows.

1 Beginning with four light beads, then adding medium and dark beads two at a time, make a six-bead wide, two-bead high strip of ladder stitch (see page 40) and join the ends together by going through the end pairs of beads twice. Work two rounds of straight tubular herringbone stitch, keeping the colour sequence the same as the ladder stitch base.

2 To begin the next round, rather than stepping up through two beads, take the needle through the top bead only. Pick up two beads and take the needle back down through the next two beads.

TIP PULL THE THREAD TAUT TO FORCE THE BEADS TO TWIST ROUND.

3 *Take the needle through the top bead on the next stack and pick up two beads. Take the needle back down through the next two beads. Repeat from *. As you are spiralling there is no step up – simply keep repeating the 'two down, one up' until the rope is the length you require.

NETTING

Netting worked as a tube makes a rather attractive tyre-like rope. The open lace effect allows the rope to stretch and so you can make a bracelet without a clasp – just sew the ends together to finish. Three- or five-bead netting can be worked in rounds with a step-up (see beaded tassels, page 86) or you can work this easy version that just spirals round. The thread passes through the shared beads in each round and these are usually slightly larger or a contrast to the bridge beads. You can vary the diameter of the tube so long as there are an odd number of five or more shared beads in the base circle.

1 Pick up one shared bead and two bridge beads. Repeat until there are 15 beads on the thread. Tie the thread in a circle, leaving a long tail, and pass the needle through the first bead again.

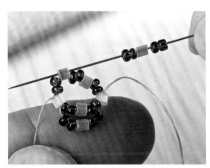

2 *Pick up two bridge beads, a shared bead and two bridge beads. Miss the next shared bead and pass the needle through the next one in the circle. Repeat from * once more so that there are two netting loops coming off the circle.

3 For the third loop, *pick up two bridge beads, a shared bead and two bridge beads. Pass the needle through the shared bead on the next loop. Repeat from * to add another two or three loops.

4 Choose a mandrel (see page 64) that fits snugly through the initial loop and insert through the tubular netting. Pull the thread up until the beads are taut and then continue adding loops as before until the rope is the length you require.

Avoid piercing the previous thread as you take the needle through the shared beads.

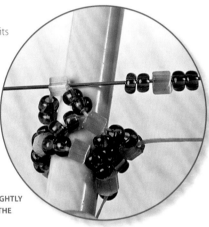

TIP CHOOSE A MANDREL THAT FITS FAIRLY TIGHTLY THROUGH THE BASE RING. HERE I HAVE USED THE HANDLE END OF A LARGE CROCHET HOOK.

Netting Variations

Tubular netting is a versatile stitch that can be worked with a wide variety of beads. Bugles work well as bridge beads or you can use quite distinctive beads, such as drop beads, for the shared beads to create ornate ropes. Increase the number of bridge beads to make an open mesh with plenty of stretch or work a more solid rope in three-bead netting.

Five-bead netting makes a more open mesh than three-bead netting and, as a result, has more stretch. Using a strong contrast for the shared bead gives the rope an attractive spotty appearance.

Rather than adding two or three bridge beads between the shared beads, add a short bugle to create a different effect. As they are solid tubes, bugles hold the cylindrical shape better than using all small beads.

Slide one tube inside another for a more substantial rope. Make one tube with seed beads and the outer tube with short bugles or more shared beads so that it has a larger diameter. Feed the tail through and pull one tube inside the other.

RIGHT ANGLE WEAVE

Although you can work in a circle to create a tube with right angle weave it is much easier to create a flat piece of beading the length required and then sew the long edges together as you complete the last row to form the tube. You can make either a three-sided tube or one with four sides. If you are new to right angle weave, read the detailed instructions on page 55 before beginning.

1 Pick up four beads and tie in a circle with a reef knot (see page 17), leaving a long tail. Pass the needle through three beads so that the thread emerges at the opposite side to the tail. Pick up three beads and pass the needle back through the top bead, taking the needle through the next two beads in a clockwise direction to the top bead again.

2 Pick up three beads, pass the needle through the top bead and pass the needle through the beads in an anticlockwise direction to again exit the top bead. Continue adding beads, alternating between a clockwise and anticlockwise direction, making sure you exit from the top bead each time.

3 Take the needle through the beads to a side bead. Pick up three beads and pass the needle through the side bead again and round through the bottom bead again. From then on, as you use the beads already on the panel to create each circle, add only two beads each time down to the bottom of the chain.

4 To form a three-sided tube, bring the thread out at a side bead. Pick up one bead, pass the needle through the side bead at the other edge and then pick up another bead. Go right round through the beads again and out at the top bead. Continue joining the two edges together, adding only one bead each time until the tube is complete.

Adding More Beads

Although right angle weave is based on a four-sided unit, more beads can be added to each unit to create a more ornate cord or rope.

Try using a larger number of beads (left). Pick up 12 beads, alternating colours and between opaque seed beads and silver lined seed beads, then tie into a circle. Work the right angle weave, treating three beads as one and picking up the beads in sequence each time. To add corner beads (centre), go back through each right angle weave circle to add a bead on each corner or simply take the needle down the length of the tube on each outer edge, adding a smaller bead in the gaps. To create more embellishment (right), bring the needle through a 'south' bead and pick up a seed bead, a crystal and a seed bead. Pass the needle through the 'north' bead in the opposite direction so that the beads lie diagonally across the right angle weave. Continue until the rope is covered with extra beads.

Right Angle Weave Variations

The basic four-bead unit of right angle weave can be varied using different beads and colours.

A three-sided rope worked in faceted beads has a rounded shape. The same rope worked in tubular or bugle beads would be more triangular in shape.

A four-sided tube is worked in the same way, except that you make three columns of right angle weave before joining the sides together with the fourth side.

Creating a Spiral Effect

Create a spiral effect by using different colours of beads in diagonal lines across the bead panel. Use the chart below to help you pick up the correct beads each time.

Colour the pattern on a right angle weave chart so that you can see which beads to add as you go along.

This sample with seven beads in a diagonal line allows the spiral pattern to continue round when it is stitched into a tube.

Taking It Further

Tubular bead stitches usually have a flat surface but any of the stitches can be embellished to create a more textured surface. The beads are simply stitched into the tube and different textures can be achieved by varying the type of beads and the way they are added. You can create textured areas on a rope or even embellish the whole length but an easy way to try out the different effects is by making a selection of beaded beads.

MAKING THE BASE TUBE

You can make the tubular base from any of the bead stitches. The tubes should be quite small in diameter and not too long. Use beads with a large hole such as cylinders or top quality Japanese seed beads for the tubes as the needle and thread has to go through the holes several times.

Peyote Stitch: Pick up seven or eight beads and work either odd or even count peyote stitch to make a short tube.

Herringbone Stitch: Make a six-bead ladder stitch base, work five rows of herringbone stitch and finish with a row of ladder stitch to form a solid ring .

Brick Stitch: Make a six-bead ladder stitch base and follow the instructions on page 43 to create a short tube.

LOOPS

You can make short or long loops to cover the tube surface. Work over one bead, several or the whole length. The loops can be worked vertically or horizontally or even diagonally for different effects.

STACKS

Stacks are made in the same way as a short fringe where you take the needle through a pivot bead and back through one or more beads to create a short stack of beads. Experiment with beads and bugles.

FRILLS

Use three-bead netting to create a frill effect on a plain tube. For a fuller effect add more beads on the second round.

This illustrates the different ways to add loops of beads to tubular peyote stitch.

Stacks of beads can be added to a single bead or if large enough the beads can straddle a pair of beads.

The top frill has two rows of three-bead netting; the second row of the bottom frill has been increased to five beads.

For short loops try adding three size 11 seeds over size 10 triangle beads or size 15 over delica beads. Longer loops look better with a large bead in the middle. Size 11 and size 8 seeds work well together.

Loops can be worked vertically, horizontally or diagonally for interesting effects.

Using the cotton reel shape (below left), work two rows of netting around the middle of the tube. Increase the beads to five in the second round.

Size 6 and 8 seed beads, held in place with a smaller pivot bead, create a bubbly texture on the surface of the tube. Vary the length of the spikes to create a rounder shape.

Add size 11 seeds and size 10 triangle beads to each end of a short tube to make a cotton reel shape.

A short bugle with a seed bead makes a spiky texture.

Embellished beads look quite spectacular when strung together with attractive large beads and metal rings.

CHAPTER 4:

Fringing, Netting & Tassels

Bead Inspirations

The gorgeous fringing and netting samples shown here give you some idea of the variety of styles of fringing and netting. Shown on ribbon for impact you can, of course, add them to soft furnishings and accessories or use them to make tassels too. Vary the designs by changing colourways or the size and style of beads.

Bright Blackberries

Little blackberry-shaped baubles add weight to the end of fringe strands without taking away from the delicacy of the beads. Space the strands slightly so that the strands hang separately or, for a fuller fringe, add strands without a blackberry in between. Alternating the fresh pastel bead colours in each strand brings a liveliness to a simple but pretty design.

Perfect Pearls

Pearls always add a touch of class to any piece of bead work and fringing is no exception. Beautiful heart-shaped beads with a matt finish bring out the wonderful sheen of the unusual drop pearls. Take care when planning the spacing and length of the fringe strands so that the drop beads slot into the gap created above two heart beads without actually touching.

Diamond Delight

In this unusual design pairs of fringe strands have been joined together at the base to create a gorgeous interwoven net. It looks complicated but is actually rather easy. Simply make a fringe strand with a large bead at the base, come up through a few beads and then add the beads for the second side of the 'v'. Attach to the ribbon and then back track to begin the next 'v'.

Neat Netting

Vertical netting (see page 84) is a super technique for making fringing because it is so easy to create fringe strands as you go along. You can use the continuous thread method or attach individual threads spaced along the edge. Here contrast beads bring out the colours in the ribbon. A more subtle effect is achieved by using the bold pale yellow beads for every second row of the shared beads.

*D*on't you find that it's almost impossible to resist running your fingers along bead netting or through a beaded fringe or tassel? It's a very dramatic way to embellish as the beads glide back and forward so seductively. These three styles of beading are grouped together as they are worked in a similar way with a needle and thread. You can mix and match, using netting to decorate a tassel or fringing to finish a net border. Beginning with a range of fringe styles, this chapter guides you through the basic techniques for making horizontal, vertical and circular netting and then finishes with a selection of tassels, from an embellished thread tassel, to beaded tassel tops and tassel top forms.

Basic Tool Kit

Apart from the usual materials, make sure you have a plentiful supply of tassel heads and decorative beads.

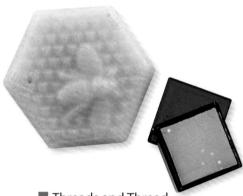

■ Beading Needles

Choose the correct needle for your thread to make threading much easier – beading needles have rectangular holes and are ideal for multifilament threads whereas round twisted threads are more suited to betweens sewing needles, which have a small round eye. As a guide the size of the bead should be a larger number than the needle size, for example thread size 11 beads with a size 10 needle. You may need to use the finer needle to go through beads several times. Use longer needles for fringing and shorter needles for netting.

■ Threads and Thread Conditioner

Twisted threads have a better drape than multifilament threads and are more suitable for fringing and tassels as you want the beads to swing and sway. On larger pieces of netting you need a strong thread that doesn't stretch such as the multifilament Super-lon™. A strong quilting thread gives good results but as it is made from cotton, it can be weakened by mildew over time.

Thread conditioners are discussed in more detail on page 36.

■ Tassel Forms

Tassel heads can be formed over any solid shape that has a hole through the centre. Use glass and other decorative beads that have a large hole or cover wooden beads, pressed cotton balls or wooden tassel tops with smaller beads, yarn or ribbon.

■ Rulers and Pins

Use a ruler or tape measure to mark the spacing of fringing or netting on ribbon or fabric. Fine dressmakers' pins with glass heads are ideal for marking.

Getting Started: Fringing and Netting

Before you can start creating intricate projects you need to learn the basic stitches for adding fringes and netting.

■ ADDING NETTING OR FRINGE TO BEADWORK

You can add fringing or netting to a piece of bead work by passing the thread through the beads or looping through the thread between the beads. Use the diagrams shown on the next page as a guide but bear in mind that you can add fringe or net to each sample and use the loop technique or through bead technique for any of the bead stitches. Remember that some bead holes run horizontally and others vertically so choose the right diagram for guidance. Exactly how you add the beads will depend on the spacing of the fringe or netting.

HORIZONTAL HOLES

In **peyote stitch**, bring the needle through several beads and out of one of the beads that is dropped down lower than the others. Pick up the beads for the fringe and take the needle back through the strand. Pass the needle through the next drop down bead ready to add the next strand.

In **right angle weave**, the thread path is circular through groups of four beads so follow that path for best results when adding a net or fringe. Bring the needle out of one of the bottom beads, add a fringe strand and take the needle back through the next bead. Take the needle through beads as shown.

Square stitch is a compact stitch where the thread is passed through each bead several times in a circular pattern. Add beads or fringing by looping over the multiple threads between the beads. Bring the needle up through a bead, loop over the thread and back through the same bead to lock it in position.

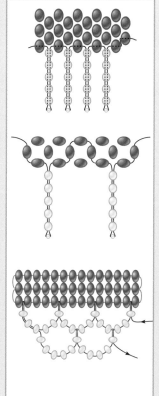

VERTICAL HOLES

With **brick stitch** bring the needle out through a bead on the edge and pick up the beads for the fringe strand. Take the needle back through the fringe strand and through the same bead. Take the needle along between the rows of brick stitch out at the next bead where you want a fringe strand.

Herringbone stitch is worked with pairs of beads so the fringe or netting strand is added between the second bead of one pair and the first bead of the next pair. The bead strand will then hang at the bottom of the 'v' shape formed by the beads. Take the needle through the next pair ready to start again.

You can add fringing or netting through the beads of **ladder stitch** or loop through the threads underneath. When adding a fringe or net to the threads, the beads hang between the beads of the ladder stitch. Bring the needle up through a bead, loop over the thread and back through the same bead to lock it in position.

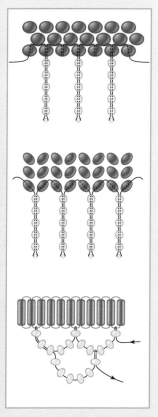

ADDING FRINGES OR NETTING TO FABRIC

Adding fringing or bead netting to soft furnishings and items of clothing will transform them into stunningly beautiful beaded accessories. Consider the weight of the bead fringing or netting before beginning and make sure that the colours of the beads tone in with the fabric. Add beads to a ribbon or tape to be incorporated in a design or use a ready-made item such as a scarf or shawl.

ATTACHING A SINGLE THREAD

Attach a thread to the edge. On a narrow hem scarf begin about 2.5cm (1in) along the edge and take a 1cm (½in) stitch through the hem only. Work two tiny backstitches in the hem on the reverse side and then feed the needle through the hem to the side edge.

MEASURING AND MARKING

Lay the fabric or ribbon flat on the work surface. Measure the width of the item or mark the length of beading required. Work out the spacing remembering that you will get one more strand than the measurement – i.e. on a 10cm (4in) length with 1cm (½in) gaps you will have 11 strands.

Insert the first pin the required distance from the side edge. Work along the bottom edge of the fabric, inserting pins as necessary.

ATTACHING MULTIPLE THREADS

Cut a double length of thread and thread the cut ends into a needle. Make a small stitch through the hem and pass the needle through the loop on the end of the thread. Pull through to secure. Add a double thread at each mark.

Fringing

A fringe is a decorative border of strands that are held closely together at one end and loosely at the other. You can attach a fringe to ribbons, fabric, ready-made items or beaded fabric made using bead stitches or loom work.

■ MAKING A FRINGE

Design fringe strands by picking up beads on an unthreaded beading needle and arrange on a beading mat to create the effect you require. You can use smaller beads at the top of the fringe and large beads for weight at the bottom.

1 To make the fringe, bring the thread out at the edge of the fabric or beadwork. Pick up the beads for the fringe strand from top to bottom and let them drop down to the fabric or beadwork.

2 Pick up a pivot bead and take the needle back through the other fringe beads on the strand only. Take a short stitch through the edge of the fabric or bead fabric (see page 79) ready to begin the next strand.

TIP TAKING A TINY BACKSTITCH AT THE TOP OF EACH FRINGE STRAND SECURES EACH STRAND INDIVIDUALLY.

■ DECORATIVE FRINGING

Fringes styles can vary from simple, plain strands of seed beads to ornate creations with unusual decorative beads. Consider adding a bead charm, a small loop of beads or even a bead blackberry.

When the fringing is densely packed rather than spaced out add larger embellishments to every other strand so that the fringe strands still hang straight.

ADDING A LOOP OR BLACKBERRY

Fringing tends to swing and hang better if there is a slightly heavier bead as the pivot bead at the end of each strand. If you don't want to add a bead, however, a bead loop or blackberry can add interest to a fringe without the need for an ornament.

1 To make the loop pick up several pivot beads and then take the needle back through the fringe beads on the strand. The size of the loop will depend on the number of pivot beads added.

2 To create the blackberry, bring the thread back down to the loop at the end of the fringe strand. Pick up a bead and pass the needle through the loop. Pick up a second bead and pass the needle through the loop. Keep adding beads one at a time to make the berry shape. Take the needle back through the fringe strand.

MAKING A BRANCHED FRINGE

Add branches to the main fringe strand to create interesting coral-like effects. You can add as many or as few branches as you like and alter the lengths for different effects.

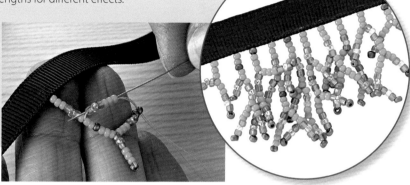

1 Pick up the beads for the fringe strand, including the pivot bead, and then take the needle back through only a few of the beads on the fringe strand.

2 Pick up a few beads to make a short fringe branch including a pivot bead. Take the needle back through the branch beads. If you want to make a second branch, take the needle through a few more beads on the strand. Make a second branch and then take the needle back through the remaining beads on the strand.

Using a variety of beads adds interest and sparkle to branched fringing.

Bead Something Now
Coral Bracelet

Have you got a box where you keep all the leftovers from your bead projects until you have time to sort them all out? This is the perfect project to use some of them up. Use the branched fringe technique given above to add beads of all shapes and sizes to a single line of large seed beads and create this gorgeous bracelet in just a few hours. The fullness of the bracelet is achieved by working back and forwards along the base row of beads, adding a new row of branched fringing to create the crinkly coral effect. You can finish the bracelet with a loop and blackberry fastening (see page 80) or attach a pretty toggle fastening, as pictured. Full instructions are given on page 162.

Netting

Netting is a series of loops linked together to create a mesh. The loops can be worked horizontally or vertically, depending on the effect required.

◼ USING NETTING ◼

The net patterns are simple but there are innumerable variations using different sizes, shapes and colours of beads. Most often netting is added to the edge of fabric items or beadwork as an alternative to a fringe but it can also be used to make stunning pieces of jewellery. Netting can be worked flat or in a circle to make a bag shape or cover a round object (it can also be worked as a tubular rope, see page 61). Refer to Getting Started on page 78–79 to find out how to measure and mark a fabric edge or how to add netting onto beading.

Bead Terms for Netting

Shared beads are the beads that link the rows of netting and have two threads passing through them.
Bridge beads sit between the shared beads and generally have one thread passing through them.

HORIZONTAL NETTING

This method of netting is worked from one side to another. When worked flat, this style of netting naturally forms a 'v' shape as each row gets shorter by half a loop at each end. To keep straight sides a new string of beads has to be added at each end; the rows of netting link into the side strands to create a straight-sided piece (see below).

1 Begin with a long thread at the edge of the work. Pick up a shared bead, the required number of bridge beads (in this case seven), a shared bead, seven bridge beads and a shared bead.

2 Take the needle through the fabric at the next mark and back through the last shared bead. Beginning with the bridge beads, pick up the same sequence of beads to make the next loop and continue to the end of the fabric.

3 To make a shaped net fringe: take the needle back through the beads in the last loop to the other side of the shared bead at the bottom of the loop. Work back across, adding bead loops as before. This time, however, instead of passing through your fabric, you will stitch through the bead at the bottom of each loop.

To make a fringe with straight edges bring a new thread and needle through each end shared bead. Pick up sufficient bridge beads and a shared bead to link into the next row of netting. Add more beads to the end threads as required when you work more rows of netting.

INCREASING AND DECREASING

Horizontal netting is easily increased or decreased as you simply add more or fewer beads in one or more loops.

Add extra shared or bridge beads to increase the length of a bead loop. Increase gradually by adding extra beads on one loop or quickly by adding extra beads on several loops. When looping through beads add an odd number of beads each time and add an even number for looping through threads.

Reduce the number of beads in one or more loops to decrease. The amount of decrease depends on the number of beads removed in each row. When looping through beads remove an odd number of beads each time and remove an even number for looping through threads.

WORKING HORIZONTAL NETTING

Horizontal netting can be worked by looping through shared beads or by looping over the threads between the beads.

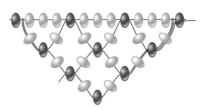

The most common way to work netting – pass the needle through a bead without catching the previous thread and pick up an odd number of beads. The centre bead is a shared bead and can be a different colour or shape.

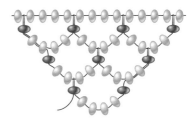

Loop the working thread over the thread between the beads on the previous row. You need an even number of beads in each loop and the shared beads sit in the opposite direction to the bridge beads.

Bead Something Now
Netted Scarf

An elegant shawl or scarf is ideal for keeping the chill off your shoulders when wearing an evening gown. This delightful embroidered scarf has a panel of horizontal netting (see page 82) to add extra colour and sparkle and of course the weight of the netting helps to keep the scarf in position. If you prefer a fringe along the bottom of the netting use either the single or multiple thread versions of the vertical netting technique shown on page 84. Remember that there are a lot of beads in the netting so choose beads to suit the weight of the fabric in the shawl or scarf. Full instructions are on page 162.

VERTICAL NETTING (SINGLE THREAD)

Working vertical netting with a single thread is a similar technique to the horizontal netting technique except that the threads go up and down rather than horizontally. It is the perfect technique for creating delicate bracelets and necklaces using a multi-strand clasp.

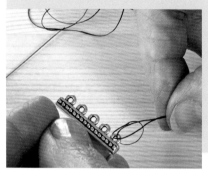

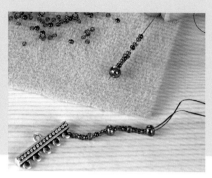

1 Thread the cut ends of a double thread on to the needle. Take the needle through the first hole on your clasp and back through the loop to begin.

2 Pick up the required number of bridge beads (in this case 11) and a shared bead. Repeat to get the length required, making sure there is an even number of shared beads and ending with the bridge beads.

3 Go through the end hole on the other part of the clasp and *take the needle back through the last seed bead.

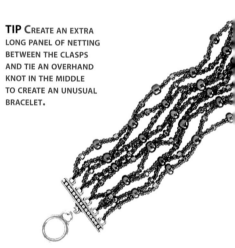

4 Pick up 10 more seed beads and a shared bead, then 11 more seed beads. Miss a shared bead on the first strand and take the needle through the next shared bead. Repeat to the end.

5 Take the thread through the next hole and then repeat from *. Go back and forwards until all the holes are filled. Go back through a few beads, tie a half hitch knot (see page 17), repeat again to make the thread really secure and then trim the end.

TIP Create an extra long panel of netting between the clasps and tie an overhand knot in the middle to create an unusual bracelet.

VERTICAL NETTING (MULTIPLE STRANDS)

With this technique the netting is created on multiple threads attached along the edge of fabric or on to beads in a string or panel. The holes in the beads run vertically over the netting and is ideal if you are going to end the netting with a fringe.

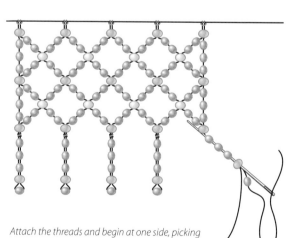

Attach the threads and begin at one side, picking up all the beads in the first strand. For the second strand, pick up beads in sequence, remembering to omit every second shared bead – instead take the needle through the appropriate shared bead on the first strand. Once the netting is complete, add a pivot bead to each pair of threads, go back through some of the beads and secure the thread with two half hitches (see page 17).

Fringing, Netting and Tassels **85**

Tassels

A tassel is essentially a fringe rolled up to create a bundle of dangling strands. Decorate ready-made tassels with beads or make wonderfully ornate tassels using wooden tassel tops.

Either bead the whole tassel or simply bead only the head or the fringe strands. You can attach the tassel to a ribbon or cord by tying a knot on a jump ring inside a bell cone to create a loop, or simply bringing the two cut ends through the top of the bell cone.

SIMPLE TASSELS

Beaded tassels can be as simple or as ornate as you like. The easiest tassels to make are simply lots of fringe strands tied together with an end cap used to cover the thread ends.

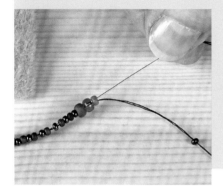

1 Pick up the selection of beads for the fringe strand. Pick up a pivot bead and then take the needle back through the other beads. Cut the thread, leaving a long tail.

2 Make sufficient strands to create the size of tassel you require. Feed the threads through an eye pin and tie with an overhand knot (see page 17). Secure threads with a little clear glue and trim the ends.

TIP TO ADD RIBBON OR CORD INSIDE THE BELL CONE END TIE THREADS TO A JUMP RING INSTEAD.

3 Feed an end cap on to the eye pin so that the threads are completely covered. Trim the end of the wire to 7mm (3/8in) above the end cap and bend to one side. Make a loop with round-nose pliers (see techniques page 117).

COILED RIBBON TASSEL

This pretty tassel uses ready-made fringing or you can create your own length of fringing using the techniques on page 80. See page 87 for the finished tassel.

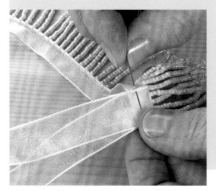

1 Lay the hanging cord or tape across the ribbon. Sew a few stitches to secure near the end of the tape. Begin to roll the fringed tape up, catching the tape each time as you go around.

2 Once the tassel is the correct size, cut off the tape, turn under the raw edge and stitch securely. Wrap the head of the tassel with ribbon or tape and sew in position.

3 Attach strong thread to the top of the tassel head. Pick up sufficient seed beads to reach the bottom. Take the needle through the tassel head and continue adding more beads until the head is covered.

BEADED BEAD TASSEL

Pressed cotton balls are ideal for tassel tops as they are lightweight and can be painted or dyed to match the bead colour. Round wooden beads are a suitable alternative but make sure the hole is large enough to attach the threads from the beaded strands. See page 87 for the finished tassel.

1 Tie a long thread through the hole in the large bead or pressed cotton balls. Pick up sufficient beads to reach round from one hole to the other. Take needle back through the hole.

TIP INSERT A COCKTAIL STICK TO STOP THE BEADS GOING DOWN THROUGH THE HOLE

2 Keep adding rows of beads all the way round. Go back, filling in with shorter bead rows, and then tie the thread ends together.

TIP TRY TO KEEP THE SHORTER BEAD ROWS EVENLY SPACED AROUND THE BALL.

3 Make several bead strands (see page 85). Tie the threads through an eye pin with an overhand knot and apply glue to secure. Trim the ends. Feed the eye pin up through the hole in the beaded bead, making a wrapped loop at the top. Attach a ribbon loop or cord.

BEAD NETTING TASSEL

Alternatively add beads around a bundle of threads to make a pretty tubular beaded tassel top. These instructions are for three-bead netting, but any of the tubular stitches in Chapter 2 (see page 61) would be suitable. See page 87 for the finished tassel.

1 Cut a skein of size 5 pearl cotton in half, or wrap decorative thread around a piece of card to create the size of tassel you require. Cut along one edge and lay the threads on the work surface in a flat bundle.

2 To make a loop for hanging the tassel, fold a length of cord in half and tie with a knot near the end. Position the cord loop so that the knot is just below the mid point of the thread bundle. Wrap a thread around the cord loop and bundle a couple of times and tie tightly to secure. Pick up by the loop and let the thread bundle drop down over the knot.

3 Pick up enough beads to reach around the bundle of threads (for three-bead netting you need a multiple of four) and tie in a circle near the top. Pick up three seed beads, miss three beads and take the thread through the next bead.

5 Work the next round of netting going through the middle bead on each loop. Continue until the netting tube is the length required. Secure the ends.

4 Work all the way round until you reach the first loop again. Take the needle down through the first two beads on the loop ready to begin the next round.

Bead Something Now
Beaded Tassel Box

This gorgeous tassel, made from a variety of space dyed yarns looks equally stunning attached to this gorgeous silk covered box or dangling from the wardrobe key. The tassel is decorated with the bead netting technique shown on page 86. To create the subtle diamond pattern on the netting you do need to add a specific number of beads and this is explained clearly on page 163. The box is made by covering a plain tin gift box with patterned paper to match the tassel and aged with an antique gold inkpad. Full instructions are on page 163 but if you are short of time you can simply attach the tassel to a ready made box.

Bead Tassels

There are lots of different ways to make tassel tops and one of the most attractive is a beaded bead. Using a pressed cotton ball or large bead with a big enough hole to take the fringe strands, you can work different beading stitches, such as peyote stitch (see page 48) or three-bead netting (see page 52) over the surface or simply cover the bead with rows of small beads.

Ready-made fringing makes a quick and easy tassel. Look for exquisite bead fringing in soft furnishing departments.

Using different beads for the tassel strands adds interest and texture. Sew extra strands around the base of the bead for a fuller effect.

Match the bead colours to the threads for a co-ordinated look. You could make a longer piece of netting for a more elegant tassel or add some beaded strands over the threads.

Taking It Further

Now you can start to discover different uses for fringing, netting and tassels. Learn how to create asymmetric fringing with intricate loops and designs, decorate tassel tops with unusual materials and circular or tubular netting to cover 3-D objects and make projects such as doilies, beads and baubles. Think carefully about the bead order, laying the beads out on a bead mat to plan the design.

FRINGING

Fringes don't have to be straight along the bottom. Think about creating a diagonal line, either asymmetric or symmetrical with a chevron or zigzag pattern. Create curves by rounding off the diagonal shape in the middle of the fringe or by draping loops of fringing from one side to the other. Mix loops with fringing for really ornate designs or create more random effects with strands of different lengths. See below for tips on creating diagonal lines, loops and interesting fringes.

Create diagonal lines by adding extra beads in each strand at the top of each strand only. This way the bold pattern created by the fringe beads is unaffected.

Loops are simply fringe strands attached at both ends. Make the loops different lengths and drape over straight fringe strands for an ornate effect.

Many fringes rely on their symmetry for impact. Keep the bead order for a balanced effect but use random strand lengths to create a really interesting and unusual design.

TASSELS

Tassel top forms are shaped pieces of wood that can be decorated with thread or beads to make a tassel. You can decorate the wood shape with beads by sticking the beads in place, attaching them with wire or working a bead stitch such as peyote stitch (see page 48) over the surface. The tassel fringes are attached around the preformed neck on the wood shape and the tassel hung by attaching ribbon or cord through the hole that runs down the centre.

Use contemporary materials such as brightly coloured raffia and marabou feather trim to make a really funky tassel or try pearls and bugles for classic style.

DECORATING READY-MADE TASSELS

One of the easiest ways to make an ornate beaded tassel is to use a ready-made tassel bought from a soft furnishing store and then decorate it with beads. You can add beads to the fringe strands, embroider beads around the neck or work one of the many bead stitches onto the tassel top (see page 88).

1 Attach a thread into the top of the tassel fringe. Pick up the beads for the first strand as well as the pivot bead, miss the pivot bead and then take the needle back through the other beads. Make a small stitch at the top and add the next strand. Continue all the way round.

2 To decorate the tassel top or neck pick up beads and stitch into the tassel so that the beads are secured in a random or set pattern.

3 Pick up enough beads to fit around the neck of the tassel and go back through the beads to form a ring. Tie the ends, pass through a few more beads and trim. Repeat until filled.

NETTING

Netting can be worked in the round to cover 3-D objects. Tubular netting can be used to embellish tassels (see page 61) or to create a rope or cord, shown on page 73, but you can also work circular netting to make doilies, flower shapes or cover round objects like beads and baubles.

By changing the number of beads in each loop circular netting can be worked as a flat piece or shaped to cover a bead or bauble.

1 Pick up 10 beads in alternating colours and tie in a circle. Pass needle through beads, coming out after a dark (shared) bead. Pick up a light (bridge) bead, a shared bead and a bridge bead. Take needle through next shared bead.

2 Repeat all the way round. Take the needle through one half of the first loop again, ready to begin the next round of loops. Pick up two bridge beads, a shared bead and two bridge beads. Pass the needle through the shared bead in the next loop. Repeat all the way round. Continue adding more beads in each loop to keep the beading flat.

3 When working circular netting over a round bead or bauble add sufficient beads in each round to allow the netting to drape over the shape. Decrease beads as you pass the mid point.

CHAPTER 5:
Threading and Stringing

Bead Inspirations

These three simple necklace ideas use a variety of stringing materials and beads to create quite diverse designs. To make the Frosty Flowers design refer to the instructions for the tigertail necklace on page 101. The other designs are based on the simple knotting techniques on page 99. The ideas are simple enough for a beginner but could be used as a base for multi-strand necklaces.

*N*ecklaces and bracelets are probably the most popular items of jewellery to make as everyone can wear them – even men! Although essentially just a string of beads, there are so many different styles that you will never run out of ideas; from simple leather thongs to exquisite tigertail necklaces and fabulous knotted designs using gorgeous ribbons and cords. Beginning with a guide to designing your own necklace, this chapter covers all the techniques you need to string beads on any type of thread or cord, including planning the design and learning basic stringing, making a simple fastening, using slider beads, and much more. You can dip into specific techniques to refresh your memory or, if you are a beginner, work through the chapter, practising different techniques and trying your hand at the gorgeous 'Bead Something Now' projects as you go along.

Organza Ovals

Experimenting with a selection of stringing materials can make quite a difference to the finished look of a necklace. These gorgeous semi-precious stones were originally strung on a thick wax cotton cord but soft organza ribbon adds a delicacy and softness to the design. Including some juicy glass beads makes the whole necklace look almost good enough to eat.

Frosty Flowers

Delicate frosted glass beads have such a wonderful translucent quality, especially the pretty leaves and flowers, that you need to keep everything as simple as possible. Strung onto a coated wire, such as tigertail, the beads hang in a soft but firm curve that lets the leaves fan out. To finish the design, look for a tubular crimp clasp (see page 97), which is one of the neatest ways to fasten a tigertail necklace.

Precious Pink

Large semiprecious stones in deep pink make an absolutely fabulous necklace but as the stones are heavy, keep it short with a screw fastening (see page 97) to secure. Adding small round pink-dyed jade beads pulls the design together and adds freshness to the necklace. Use a double length of space-dyed rayon cord so that the knots don't slip through the large holes in the beads.

Basic Tool Kit

Apart from pliers, needles and thread, all you will need for this chapter are findings and fastenings.

■ Beading Needles

Twisted wire needles and big eye needles are the most useful needles for bead stringing as they have large eyes (see page 12). The loop on twisted wire needles collapse when you go through a bead. For larger beads, tapestry needles are useful or you can stiffen the end of the thread with nail varnish to create a built-in 'needle'.

■ Findings

These are the metal bits used to finish jewellery, neatening raw ends and making it easy to attach fastenings. The type you choose will depend on the materials chosen to make the jewellery. Use the table below as a guide. Head pins and eye pins are featured on page 109.

■ Pliers

The basic set of jewellery pliers: round-nose, flat-nose and wire cutters are used to attach findings and fastenings. If you use crimps regularly, crimping pliers make a much neater finish. Size 2 crimps are ideal for medium thickness thread or tigertail.

■ Fastenings

Fastenings range from the basic lobster claw and trigger clasps to the most ornate magnetic, screw, toggle and clasp fastenings. They can have one or more rings depending on the number of strands. Choose a style that is secure enough for the weight of the beads and will suit the design. For example, bracelet and necklaces both suit toggle fastenings. Plated metal, sterling silver or gold-filled are popular, although alternative metals and antique finishes are also available.

toggle
ornate hook
screw fastenings
metallic fastenings
trigger clasp
lobster claw
multi-strand fastenings
crimp fastenings

Reference	Findings	Uses
1	Thong ends	Secure to the end of leather thong or cord using flat nose pliers so that a fastening can be attached (see page 97).
2	Spring ends	Thread ribbons and cords into the springs and squeeze the end spring with pliers to secure. Attach a fastening (see page 97).
3	Knot cover	Also known as calottes or clamshells, these findings hide the knot or crimp at the end of bead thread or tigertail and make it easy to attach a fastening (see page 98).
4	End cones	Used to hide knots and raw ends of ribbon and multiple threads at the end of necklaces and other jewellery (see page 98).
5	Round & tubular crimps	Secure these findings with crimp (see page 97) or flat nose pliers. Generally used on thread that can't be knotted, such as tigertail (see page 95) to attach fastenings and space beads along the length (see page 100).
6	Jump rings	These round or oval rings, which have a slit for opening and closing, are used to link components and attach fastenings (see page 97).
7	Split rings	Split rings do not have a slit opening and so are more secure than jump rings. Use split ring pliers to attach fastenings to prevent broken finger nails.
8	Spacer bars	Used to hold strings of beads at an equal spacing. Use end bars with the same number of rings or holes (see page 102).
9	End bars	Use end bars with rings for attaching multiple strands of beads on necklaces and bracelets. Solid bars have teeth for grip and can be secured to ribbon or beadwork with pliers.

■ Threads

There are new innovations in threads becoming available all the time. Look out for nylon cords that have the same handling properties of silk or a beading wire that drapes better than tigertail and can be knotted. Traditional threading materials such as waxed cotton, rattail, satin cord and leather thong now come in a wide range of contemporary colours. See the guide on page 93 for choosing thread for each technique.

Getting Started

There is more to completing jewellery than just adding fastenings – you have to know which string to use, how to size up thread thicknesses and lengths, consider bead weights and think about the overall design.

■ CHOOSING THREAD

Anyone planning to make a necklace or bracelet asks the question: 'What string do I use?'. There are dozens of traditional threads and cords for bead stringing as well as new materials appearing all the time. Don't be daunted by the variety – just feel encouraged to try out the different materials and experiment to find out which threads you prefer. When choosing threads think about the design of the jewellery: whether the threads will be hidden or be an integral part of the design, if you are planning a chunky style or something more delicate, and whether you have particular beads in mind?

Whichever you choose, consider the weight of the beads and use the strongest thread available.

Nymo™ B

SuperLon™ D

Silamide size A

Nylon thread size 4

Silk size 5 /0.68mm

Silk size 10 /0.9mm

Wax cotton 0.8mm

Wax cotton 1mm

Rattail

Leather thong

THICKNESS OF THREAD
Not only is there a vast array of threading materials, but most come in a variety of thicknesses as well, so how do you match threads with beads? When stringing beads the aim is to match the size of the bead hole to the stringing material because loose beads rubbing against thread creates friction and it's more likely to snap. Using a double strand of thinner thread is more secure than one thicker thread. Thread sizes vary, depending on the make, with either a letter or number indicating the size.

■ DESIGNING A NECKLACE

String an interesting selection of beads together and you've got a simple necklace; however a little thought about the style and arrangement will create a better design. First of all, consider for whom the necklace is to be made, as this will affect your choice of style, colour and length.

SINGLE STRAND NECKLACES
The simplest necklace has beads of the same type and size strung together. The most popular design has graduated beads starting with the smallest at the back, working round to the largest in the middle at the front. These two necklace styles are considered formal as the design is symmetrical and both sides are of equal weight. Informal necklaces are more of a challenge to create, as the two sides are different. This style of necklace often features a larger bead as a focal point on one side and, although the design is asymmetrical, it appears balanced. Mosaic necklaces are also usually asymmetrical but are more eclectic and use a variety of beads with mixed shapes and colours. Although it sounds simple, this style of necklace is often the most difficult to get absolutely balanced.

Formal Style
Pearls and semi-precious stones look absolutely stunning when strung in a formal style, especially if the beads are carefully graduated.

Informal Balance
An informally balanced necklace can be anything but informal. Designed well, this style is one of the classiest necklaces to wear.

Mosaic Composition
Although it looks like it's made from 'bead soup' a mosaic necklace should be planned just as carefully as the other styles.

PLANNING THE DESIGN

When making a necklace, first decide if you want to have a focal point, such as a large bead or a cluster of beads and, if so, where to have it. This is usually in the centre, either strung on the bead string or hanging below as a pendant. A focal point at one side is known as a station. Flat pieces work well in this position and can be extremely flattering close to the collarbone.

Lengths of Necklace

These are standard lengths of necklace but take into account the height of the person and their body shape and adjust if necessary. Necklaces shorter than 61cm (24in) require a fastening unless strung on elastic.

Choker: 36–41cm (14–16in) depending on neck measurement
Pendant: 46cm (18in)
Matinee: 51–61cm (20–24in)
Opera: 71–81cm (28–32in)
Rope: 101–114cm (40–45in)
Lariat: over 114cm (45in)

Necklace design is a little like colour theory with primary, secondary and tertiary beads instead of colours. The primary beads are the main focus of the necklace and are usually the most expensive, secondary beads frame and enhance the primary beads and tertiary beads, which are less expensive, fill the gaps in between! You can lay beads out on a beading mat or work surface but it is much easier to use a bead board as you can arrange the beads in stages to build up the design, knowing exactly how long it is going to be. Play about with sizes and colours of beads for a while to get everything absolutely right before you string a bead!

Using a Bead Board

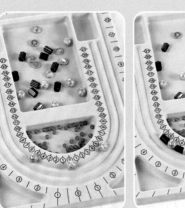

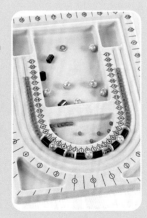

1 Decide on the length of your necklace and arrange the primary or focus beads on the bead board. This arrangement is for a symmetrical necklace.

2 Place the secondary beads either side of the focus beads. Choose beads that frame and enhance the primary beads so that they are still the main focus.

3 Add tertiary beads to fill the strands. You can use slightly larger beads on the lower half of the necklace then similar smaller beads to fill up to the fastening.

BASIC STRINGING

There are many ways to string beads and lots of different materials so how do you choose what to use? The first consideration is the style you are looking for – perhaps a fun piece, or a more substantial design in an ethnic, classic or contemporary style. This can give an indication of the stringing material such as elastic for a fun bracelet, wax cotton for an ethnic style, silk thread for a classic design or organza ribbon and tigertail for a contemporary look. Take into account the beads you have chosen too; their weight and the size of the holes determines the strength and thickness of the threading material as you don't want the jewellery to stretch, break or fray.

CONTINUOUS LOOP
Bracelets and basic necklaces made using elastic thread can simply be knotted to join the ends.

Thread the beads onto elastic thread so that there is a bead with a large hole at one end. Tie the ends together using a reef knot (see page 17), pull tight. Trim the ends and the knot will be hidden inside the hole of the large bead.

TIP IF SOME BEADS HAVE A LARGE HOLE, THREAD A SMALL BEAD ON AT THE SAME TIME THAT WILL SIT INSIDE THE LARGER BEAD TO STABILISE IT.

• Bead String/Cord
Bead string necklaces over 60cm (24in) in length don't need a fastening. Simply tie the ends using a reef knot (see page 17) or overlap the ends for a neater finish.

1 Before you begin, make sure you can pass a double length of thread through the bead holes. String the beads, allowing about 10cm (4in) at each end. Pass one end of the string through five or six beads

2 Using the tail thread, work a half hitch knot (see page 17) over the main thread. Pass the end through another two beads and knot again. Secure each knot with a drop of glue. Repeat with the other tail working in the opposite direction. Pass the ends through a few more beads and trim the ends neatly.

TIGERTAIL AND COVERED WIRES
For threads that don't knot, such as tigertail, thread crimps between the beads and then secure the crimps with crimp or flat-nose pliers.

TIP CRIMP PLIERS COME IN SEVERAL SIZES – USE THE CORRECT SIZE FOR YOUR CRIMPS.

RIBBONS
All sorts of ribbons are ideal for stringing. You can use narrower satin ribbons in the same way as thong and waxed cotton or go for a wider soft organza ribbon to contrast with the hard shiny surface of the beads. Torn fabric strips add a ragged gypsy look to a string of beads or try funky fibres, usually sold for cardmaking and scrapbooking to create an eclectic design. Mesh ribbon, which is a tubular wire mesh, makes an excellent bead string. Thread the mesh ribbon through beads with larger holes or drop the beads inside and knot either side to secure. When you are ready, take a look back through the chapter to find techniques to add fastenings that suit your particular design.

Delicate organza ribbon complements the shiny surface of the large semi-precious stones on this simple necklace.

MAKE A SIMPLE FASTENING

With thicker cords and thongs you can make simple slide fastenings to allow you to take the jewellery on and off. Cut the cord or thong long enough to go over your head, hand or foot, depending on what type of jewellery you are making and allow about 20cm (8in) extra for the knots and slide fastening. Thread beads on to the length of cord and position them in the middle.

USING SLIDING KNOTS

1 Arrange the cords so that they are parallel and the ends are at opposite sides. Pass the left end under the other cord and then work an overhand knot.

2 Repeat with the right hand end, tying the knot so that the end is facing in the opposite direction to the first knot. Pull the knots apart to shorten the necklace and away from each other to lengthen. Adjust the knots along the length until you get a good fit.

USING A SLIDER BEAD

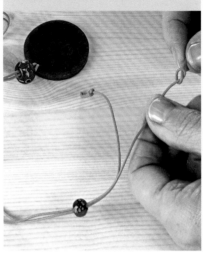

Thread a large bead over both ends. This bead should be a fairly tight fit. Knot the ends to prevent the sliding bead coming off.

TIP To prevent rattail fraying, paint the ends with Fray Check liquid or clear nail varnish.

A slider bead works as a fastening, as well as adding to the decoration of the necklace.

Bead Something Now
Wax Cotton Bracelet

Wax cotton is fabulous material for stringing beads to make informal necklaces and bracelets. It is available in a wide range of contemporary colours that you can co-ordinate with beads to make really stylish pieces of jewellery that are ideal for wearing with casual clothes. The beads in this delightful bracelet are spaced using simple overhand knots (see page 17) and there are clever sliding knots (see above) so that you can adjust the diameter to take it on and off. Choose pretty colours for a girl or try natural beads and neutral colours to make something for a young lad. Full instructions are given on page 164.

ADDING FASTENINGS

Some fasteners come with a built-in crimp that simply attaches to the end of the thread but usually you need to cover the thread ends first and then attach the fastening. It can be tricky trying to work out the best way to neaten the ends of bead strings but if you look at the following examples, you can choose the method that best suits the material and design.

USING A CRIMP

This method is ideal for tigertail wire that can't be knotted and can also be used for beading thread.

1 Pick up a crimp bead, a jump ring or necklace fastening and take the needle back through the crimp bead. Secure the crimp with pliers. Add the beads over the tail of the wire, as well as the long length.

2 At the other end pick up a crimp and the jump ring or fastening. Feed the wire back through the crimp and several beads. Secure the crimp with pliers and trim the wire end.

USING GIMP

Gimp, or French bullion, is a tight spiral of fine wire that is traditionally used when stringing pearls to protect silk thread from fraying. The gimp covers the short section of thread that goes through the fastening.

 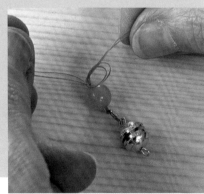

1 Cut a 1cm (½in) length of gimp and pass the needle and thread through the middle. Feed on the fastener then bend the gimp gently and tie the threads together with a reef knot (see page 17). Pick up the beads on one of the threads.

2 Pass the tail through the first bead and work a half hitch knot (see page 17) over the main thread. Repeat with the second and third beads and trim the end. Reverse the process at the other end once the remaining beads are strung.

TIP FOR EXTRA SECURITY YOU CAN APPLY A LITTLE BEAD GLUE TO EACH KNOT BETWEEN THE BEADS.

Crimp Ends

Thicker threads and cords can be simply finished using one of the many crimp ends available. These are available in a range of metallic colours.

Spring Crimps Use flat-nose pliers to squeeze the last ring of the spring into the thong so that it is held securely.

Leather Crimps
Use flat-nose pliers to flatten one side against the thong. Repeat with the other side so that it is held firmly.

Crimp Fastener Look out for fasteners with an inbuilt crimp. You simply insert the thread and squeeze the crimp ring or the end of the fastening to secure.

Gimp is available in a range of metallic colours as well as gold and silver.

You can buy purpose-made tube fastenings for nylon-coated wire. Simply feed the wire or wires into each end of the fastening and squeeze with flat-nose pliers.

USING A KNOT COVER

This little finding, sometimes known as a calotte, is a neat way to finish the thread ends securely. There are two styles, one has a hole in the side of the cover and the other, known as a clamshell, has the hole in the hinge and is much more secure.

Calottes are available in a range of styles and metallic finishes.

1 Feed the thread through the hole in the hinge and tie an overhand (see page 17) or figure of eight knot (see page 17) so that the knot is inside the clamshell.

TIP IF YOU ARE USING A DOUBLE THREAD YOU CAN TIE A REEF (SQUARE) KNOT INSTEAD (SEE PAGE 17). IF THE THREAD YOU ARE USING DOESN'T KNOT EASILY, USE ONE OR TWO CRIMP BEADS INSTEAD TO SECURE THE THREAD.

2 Apply a drop of bead glue onto the knot, as shown, and trim the ends. Squeeze the sides of the clamshell together to hide the knot and thread ends. Then attach the fastener of your choice.

3 If the calotte has a hole on one side simply tie a figure of eight knot at the end of the bead string, trim the end and apply a drop of glue. Tuck the knot inside the calotte so that the thread is in the groove on the bottom of the calotte and then close with flat-nose pliers.

END CONES

Knot covers and end cones serve a similar purpose as they are both designed to cover knots. End cones tend to be more decorative, coming in all shapes and sizes to suit every style of bead or necklace imaginable. Choose an end cone that will fit closely around the bead strands you have chosen as a cone that is too small or too large just looks wrong.

Using End Cones with Tigertail
Make a loop on the end of each necklace strand using crimps. Attach the loops to an eyepin. Slide the cone end over the eyepin and finish as above.

1 Design the strands of the necklace so that the accent beads don't line up, leaving at least 15cm (6in) of beading cord, ribbon or wire at each end. In this example beads have been added to both ribbon and wire strands. Tie the wire and ribbon together at one end with an overhand knot (see page 17).

2 Cut a length of 0.6mm (24swg) craft wire and wind one end around the ribbon and wire overhand knot (see page 17). Trim the end of the wire close to the knot, leaving the other tail to make a wrapped loop.

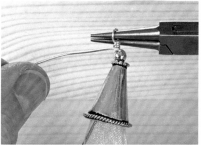

3 Apply glue to the knotted ribbon and wire and slide the cone end over the wire. Make a wrapped loop, trim the end of the wire and attach the fastening.

TIP IF THE END CONE HAS A LARGE HOLE AT THE TOP, PICK UP A SMALL ROUND METAL BEAD BEFORE MAKING THE LOOP.

Bead On

Once you have mastered the basics, you can move on to more advanced bead threading and stringing techniques.

■ SPACING BEADS

Necklaces aren't always simply strung on a string. It is sometimes necessary, and often a style choice, to space beads along a thread or wire and there are many ways to do this. The method you choose to space out your necklace or jewellery depends on the style of the necklace and the material that you are using to make it with.

KNOTTING

Bead strings are usually knotted to prevent the beads from rubbing together and also to stop all the beads falling off if the thread snaps. There are several methods of knotting: the one needle method is more skilful and traditionally used for pearl necklaces; a quicker technique with a slightly untidier knot, known as the double thread method, is ideal for larger beads. The third technique adds knots over a second thread and is ideal for adding knots to a tigertail necklace. You need plenty of thread to string the beads for any of these techniques as each knot uses at least 3mm (⅛in) with fine threads and more for thicker threads.

• One Needle Method

This is the traditional method used for stringing pearls. Add fasteners using a knot cover (see page 98) or with gimp (see page 97).

1 Attach a fastener or calotte/knot cover to the end of the thread (see page 98). Tie an overhand knot on the thread by looping the tail over and under the main thread (see page 17). Pick up the first bead and tie another loose overhand knot.

2 Insert a large needle or fine tweezers into the loop of the knot. Begin to pull the knot tight, guiding the knot along the main thread until it sits next to the bead. Remove the needle as the knot tightens.

3 Continue adding beads one at time, tying a new knot after each. To add a calotte continue to the end of the strand. If the bead string is to be finished with gimp (see page 97), tie the last three beads without knots. Attach the fastener with gimp, leaving a little slack on the main thread. Pass the thread back through the first bead and work a half hitch (see page 17) over the main thread. Add a knot between the remaining beads and secure the end.

• Double Thread Method

This is easier to work but the knots aren't quite as neat. It is ideal for necklaces with chunky beads.

1 Attach a fastener so that there is a double thread and tie a reef knot (see page 17). Thread a needle on each end or work with a big eye needle that is easy to thread quickly each time you tie a knot.

2 Pick up a bead by passing both threads through the hole in the same direction. Tie a reef knot (see page 17) on the other side of the bead. Repeat to the end of the necklace

• Spacing Beads on Tigertail

Nylon-coated wires can't be knotted but, if you like the way beads hang on tigertail, you can still get the knotted look using this simple technique. The beads need to have a hole that is large enough to take both thread and wire.

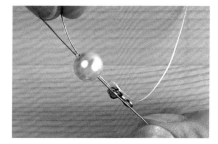

1 Secure a beading thread and tigertail into a knot cover using crimps (see page 97) and pick up the first bead on the tigertail. Using a needle, pass the thread through the first bead.

2 Tie an overhand knot (see page 17) using the beading thread, over the tigertail and use a needle to guide the knot down to sit next to the bead. Repeat to the end and attach a knot cover.

SPACING BEAD WITH CRIMPS

When spacing beads with long gaps in between, use crimps. Generally used for tigertail or other coated wires, crimps of different sizes can be used to space beads on ribbon, fine thong or thread. You can mark spacing on the thread or wire before you begin or simply hold the work against a ruler or measuring tape.

TIP ALWAYS CHECK THAT THE CRIMPS ARE QUITE SECURE BEFORE MOVING ON TO THE NEXT.

1 Attach a fastening using a crimp loop (see page 97). Pick up a crimp bead and then the bead, followed by another crimp. Secure the first crimp with pliers.

2 Move the bead up against the first crimp and then hold the wire so that the second crimp falls against the bead. Secure the second crimp, as shown.

■ MULTI-STRAND STRINGING ■

Necklaces with more than one strand need a little forward planning to work out the best method of construction. Multi-strand necklaces can either have all the strands the same length or be graduated with loops hanging one under the other.

To make the classic Parisian loop, string two strands of beads with a 2.5–8cm (1–3in) difference in length and attach both strings to a clasp. This style is often used for stringing pearls.

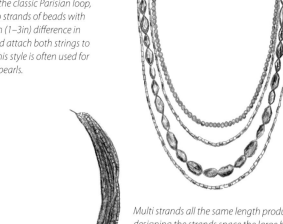

Create a much bolder necklace with several strands. Make each bead strand slightly longer so that they hang gracefully one under the other or increase the differential for a contemporary design.

Multi strands all the same length produce a much fuller effect. When designing the strands space the large beads out so they are not lying together and reduce the size of beads towards the clasp.

The multi-strands can all begin at the back of the necklace or you can begin with a single strand necklace and then change to two or more strands for a more interesting effect, as with the Bead Something Now: multistrand necklace (see page 103).

Bead Something Now

Tigertail Necklace

Tigertail is often used for what people call an illusion necklace where the beads are more prominent than the threads – the beads then appear to be floating in air. You can simply make a necklace with a single strand of beads, spacing the beads with crimps and attaching a crimp tube fastening (see page 97). When using tigertail you do have more impact if there are several strands. The technique is exactly the same as making a single strand, you simply add a different type of bead to each strand and then attach a larger tube crimp fastening. If you need more information about arranging beads in multistrand necklaces look at the detailed instructions on page 100. Full details for making this necklace are on page 164.

SINGLE TO MULTI-STRAND
The easiest way to make a necklace that goes from a single to multi-strands is to use several fine bead strings. It works best with two or three separate strings.

1 String beads onto different bead strings to create the multi-strand section of the necklace. Thread the ends at each side through a large accent bead and then through the remaining beads on the necklace. Attach knot covers and a necklace fastening.

2 Alternatively you can use end cones to finish the multi-strands and then attach a single strand of beads or length of chain to finish the necklace. See page 98 for how to use end cones with a range of threads.

USING MULTI-STRAND CLASPS
You can use the techniques learnt for single strand necklaces to add two or more strings. Either choose a decorative end bar with integral loops and attach a fastening or use a special multi-strand fastening, often used to string pearls.

1 Attach a bead thread to each loop on the multi-strand fastening using crimps or by knotting between the beads (see page 99).

2 Add the beads you need on the strands, graduating the length as required and then attach each strand into the multi-strand fastening at the other end, making sure none are twisted.

ADDING A SPACER BAR
When making multi-strand bracelets and more formal necklaces, separate the bead strands with spacer bars. These thin metal strips have holes along the length to correspond with the number of loops on the clasp or end bar. Plan where the bars will lie on the jewellery before beginning.

1 Thread the required number of beads on each strand. Feed the threads through the holes on the bar and then continue stringing, adding further bars as required.

TIP WHEN MAKING A NECKLACE INCREASE THE BEADS BETWEEN THE SPACER BARS IN EACH ROW SO THAT THE BEADS HANG IN A SOFT CURVE TO FIT ROUND YOUR NECK.

Different styles of bar end clasps and bar ends are available to match the spacer bars. Choose one with the same number of rings as there are threads.

Bead Something Now
Multistrand Necklace

One of the reasons for making a necklace in a single colour is that it's fun collecting the beads and you can really go to town mixing shapes and sizes. This stunning jet-black necklace is made from a selection of beads, some semi-precious, some glass and even a few plastic collected over the last year. The necklace uses the single to multi-strand technique on page 102 and has three strands all the same length. It's important to design all three strands at the same time so that the larger beads don't lie together. The beads get much smaller at the end of each strand; add long bugles or cylinder beads to reduce bulk. Secure the strands using a calotte (see page 98). Full instructions for making the necklace are given on page 165.

Taking It Further: Macramé

Often when stringing beads the colour of the thread doesn't matter too much as it is hidden. However, with thicker stringing materials, the cord, thong and ribbon are as much a part of the jewellery design as the beads. Macramé is a versatile knotting technique that can be used to create a wide range of stunning knotted necklaces and bracelets.

■ MACRAMÉ

There are three simple macramé knots used for jewellery that can be used in different combinations to create knotted necklaces and bracelets; half knot, square knots and half hitch knots. You can work overhand knots to create simple pieces, or use basic macramé knots to make stunning contemporary jewellery, such as the Macramé Necklace shown on page 105. You can add beads to the threads before you begin knotting so that they are incorporated in the design.

HALF KNOT
This is essentially half a reef (square) knot; repeated in the same direction so that the threads naturally twist into a spiral.

1 Arrange the cords in a row with the two shorter cords in the middle. *Pass the right-hand cord under the two centre cords and over the left-hand cord.

2 Take the left-hand cord across the two centre cords and pass it through the loop on the right. Pull the threads taut. Repeat from * until the spiral is the length required.

SQUARE KNOTS
This flat knot is worked using a reef (square) knot over the centre threads.

1 Arrange the cords in a row with the two shorter cords in the middle. *Work a half knot, passing the right-hand thread under the centre threads and over the left-hand cord. Take left-hand cord across two centre cords and pass it through loop on the right.

2 Reverse the knot, passing the left-hand cord under the centre threads and over the right cord then take the left cord and pass it through the loop on the right. Repeat from *.

HALF HITCH
A series of double half hitches is usually worked over one of the side threads to form a thick rib effect. The knots can be tied so that the resulting rib is horizontal or diagonal.

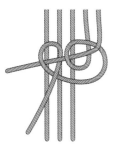

Arrange one of the outer cords across the other cords horizontally. Bring the new outer vertical cord over the horizontal cord and back under it again to the right-hand side. Take the same cord over the horizontal cord and this time bring it out to the right-hand side through the loop. Repeat the two knots using each of the vertical cords in turn, to create a thick rib.

TIP THE CENTRE THREADS (USUALLY TWO) ARE THE LENGTH OF THE JEWELLERY PLUS 15CM (6IN) AT EACH END FOR FINISHING. THE OUTER KNOTTING THREADS ARE MUCH LONGER; ALLOW ABOUT THREE TIMES THE FINISHED LENGTH SO THAT YOU DON'T HAVE TO JOIN ON EXTRA THREAD.

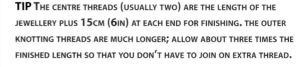

Working Macramé

Fix the piece you are working on to a hard surface. Use tape or 'T' pins to secure the work to a corkboard or macramé mat. When working macramé, especially when arranging cords at a particular angle or to create a loop or curve, use pins to hold the cords in place ready to tie the knot. The pins help to keep the work straight and flat as you progress.

MULTI-STRAND MACRAMÉ
Create different designs and patterns by splitting thread strands.

ADDING BEADS
Create interesting effects by adding beads to either the core or outer threads. The beads you choose need to have a hole large enough for the thread or cord.

When adding beads to the core threads, the outer threads go around the bead holding it in position. When working half knots the macramé naturally twists and you get best results adding further beads once you have worked enough knots to bring the outer threads are back round to the sides. With square knots you can add beads either side of the complete knot or after one half knot so that the bead is in the middle of the knot.

You can create all sorts of different effects adding beads to the outer threads and as you are only threading beads on to a single strand the beads can be smaller. Add beads as you go so that you can tie knots with a plain thread. Single beads on the outer threads create a picot effect. To create an interesting texture for a bracelet, swap the core and outer threads between knots.

If there is more than one knot across in the design you can split the threads in subsequent rows to create different patterns. Alternating square knot uses two cords from one knot and two cords from the adjacent knot to make a knot in the middle. Vary the design by working several knots before going back to the original arrangement.

Bead Something Now
Macramé Necklace

If you thought that macramé was only for making ethnic style of jewellery, try making this stunning necklace with fine paper string or wax cotton for any elegant occasion. Choose a large focus bead and smaller beads with holes that are large enough to take four strands of thread. The necklace is worked using a half knot (see page 104), which automatically twists as you knot. Find out how to add gold spacer beads as you go along by looking at the samples above. Finish the cord ends with leather crimps and attach a pretty fastening. Ring the changes with black and silver beads for that little black dress or brighten it up with your favourite party colours. Full instructions are on page 165.

CHAPTER 6:
Wire Work and Jewellery Techniques

*W*ire is a super medium to use with beads as it allows you to control the shape of the finished product and to make things that are much more three-dimensional than with other beading styles. The basic twisting technique is so easy, and needs no special tools, that you can make quite exciting pieces like a wedding tiara within minutes of getting started! Jewellery is an extremely popular way to work with wire and you will find all the basic techniques in this chapter, including how to use wire products such as eye pins, headpins and chain. The more adventurous can try their hand at making gorgeous flowers for decoration or accessories using the French beading techniques on page 122.

Bead Inspirations

Wire is one of the most inspiring materials to use with beads. It can be used in lots of different ways and, as it also comes in all sorts of colours, finishes and thicknesses, there is an endless variety of textures and shapes that can be created.

Wire Works

Wire is much stronger once it has been twisted and even quite fine wire will support the weight of fairly large beads. This technique, shown on page 111, is often used to make tiaras but you can wrap the wire around soft materials like suede thong to create a necklace or embellish a candlestick. The wrapped suede will hold an intricate shape.

Chain Mail

Chain is one of the standards for jewellery making but it is also a versatile material in its own right. You can thread ribbon through the links, as shown on page 120, or push the chain along so that it bunches up to create a scrunched wire effect. Space bead charms along the length or cut shorter lengths and string between large beads.

Flower Power

Coated wire is less likely to kink than plain wire as the plastic or thread coating helps to soften any curves. In the same way, threading seed beads onto wire has the same effect. To create a thick cord twist two strands of plastic coated wire together and then wrap the finer thread coated wire around the twists. Embellish the flowers with tiny wire springs.

Prince Charming

Rather than simply hanging charms from a length of chain decorate the chain itself first. You can thread cord or ribbon through the chain, as shown on page 120, or join short lengths together with bead links as shown here. Use a selection of different beads to make the charms. The techniques for making bead links and headpin charms are on page 116.

Basic Tool Kit

As well as basic jewellery tools needed for this chapter, such as pliers and other basic tools, you will also need basic wire working equipment, such as a jig.

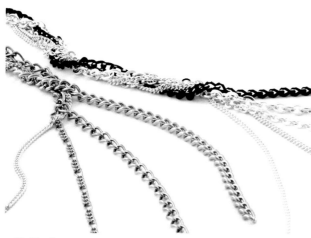

■ Chain

You can make your own chain using wire or buy ready-made chains in a range of styles, colours and finishes. Precious metal chains are generally more expensive, not only because of the increased price of the metal, but because the links are individually soldered. Most costume jewellery chain has links that can be opened and so are not as strong. When choosing chain, consider the weight and how the bulk or delicacy of the chain relates to the size of the beads or charms.

■ Pliers

A set of jewellery tools consists of three basic pliers that can be used to make most wire work and jewellery items. Round-nose pliers are used to make jump rings or loops with wire. The tapered jaws make rings of different sizes. Flat-nose pliers are the general wire working tool. Choose snipe- (chain) nose pliers that have tapered jaws for fine work and avoid serrated jaws as they can damage the wire. Use wire (side) cutters rather than scissors to cut wire. The blades are shaped so that you can cut a tapered or flat end depending on the way the pliers are held. Look for specialist tools rather than DIY tools which are much larger. I prefer tools that are sprung so that the blades open after use but some beaders prefer unsprung tools.

■ Bead Mat (illustrated on page 15)

A bead mat is an essential piece of equipment for beading. The pile surface prevents beads rolling away and lets you pick up beads on to the wire easily. Other materials with a pile surface, such as velvet or nubuck suede, are ideal too. Felt is not so good as the longer fibres catch on the wire as you work.

■ Wire Jig

These boards either have loose pegs or are made with the pegs fixed. There are various shapes of board available with different arrangements of pegs, for example, the square or rectangular boards have straight rows and the round boards have concentric rings. Metal wire jigs are better quality than plastic and easier to use with thicker wires.

Wire

Most jewellery wire is either plated or enamelled over a base metal such as copper although you can buy solid precious metal wires to make special pieces of jewellery. Memory wire is a hard wire that holds its circular shape. It is available in ring, bracelet and necklace size and should be cut with heavyweight cutters only. Coated wires are becoming more popular. These wires, covered in plastic or wrapped with thread, add a contemporary look to jewellery making and other crafts. All wires are available in a range of thicknesses. Look at the table below for more information about which wire gauge to buy.

• Types of Wire

Jewellery wire is generally either a metallic shade, such as gold or silver that has a plated finish, or a colour, which is generally enamelled with a copper core. Copper is a fairly soft metal so craft wire is easy to bend and shape. Anodised aluminium wires are very soft wires, usually available in thicknesses over 1mm (19swg) that can be shaped by hand. The anodising process creates very bright vibrant colours.

Wire Gauges

Craft wire is measured in either millimetres (mm) or by the standard wire gauge (swg). The most popular craft wires range from 1mm (19swg) down to 0.375mm (28 swg), which means that thinner wires have a larger swg number. A good all-round wire to start with is 0.6mm (24swg), which holds its shape fairly well. If you want to make jewellery or wire work components that won't pull out of shape you can buy harder wire from specialist wire suppliers or use long headpins or eye pins that are generally less pliable than craft wire.

mm	swg	mm	swg	mm	swg
4	8	0.63	23	0.15	38
3.25	10	0.56	24	0.132	39
3	11	0.5	25	0.125	40
2.65	12	0.45	26	0.112	41
2.36	13	0.4	27	0.1	42
2	14	0.375	28	0.09	43
1.8	15	0.315	30	0.08	44
1.6	16	0.28	31	0.071	45
1.4	17	0.265	32	0.06	46
1.25	18	0.25	33	0.05	47
1	19	0.236	34	0.04	48
0.9	20	0.212	35	0.025	50
0.8	21	0.2	36		
0.71	22	0.17	37		

Jewellery Findings

These are the metal bits used to finish a piece of jewellery. Those detailed here are the main findings used in wire work and jewellery techniques, however, other useful findings are listed on page 92.

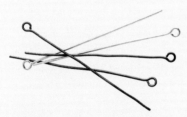

Eye Pins These are used to make bead links or dangles. Look for extra long eye pins to make decorative coiled ends for earrings or pendants.

Headpins Look for those with decorative ends that are ideal for making dangles for a charm bracelet or earrings.

Jump Rings Available as circles or ovals; they come in a range of sizes. The rings can be opened then closed again to link components in wire work.

Split Rings These look like jump rings but have two coils of wire one on top of the other, so are more secure. Split ring pliers make it easy to open the rings.

Earring wires These come in a variety of styles suitable for pieced ears, or you can buy screw fitments. They are available in a range of metals and finishes.

Fastenings

Choose fastenings to suit the style or the materials used to make the jewellery. Fastenings can have single or multiple holes to accommodate one or more strands. Multistrand fastenings are also ideal for attaching to knitted or crocheted wire (see page 139). You can slot wire straight into crimp fastenings for a secure and neat way to finish jewellery (see page 97).

toggle *multistrand*

crimp fastening *toggle*

multistrand *toggle* *crimp fastening*

Getting Started

Once you have a basic set of jewellery tools, you can use all the techniques explained in this chapter on different thicknesses and colours of wire, so you can adapt the skills to make your own unique pieces.

■ WORKING WITH WIRE

Wire-based jewellery or wirework projects are one of the most satisfying crafts to learn as the techniques are easy but produce stunning results in a minimal amount of time.

STRAIGHTENING WIRE
Wire is generally sold in coils and reels and as a result is curved when unwound. This curve can be useful when making coils but often it is better to begin with straight wire.

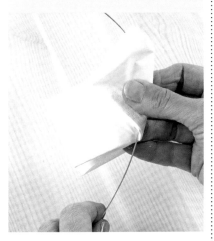

1 To take a gentle curve out of craft wire, fold a piece of tissue and pull the wire through between your finger and thumb then exert pressure to straighten out the curve.

2 To straighten wire that has been stored badly with lots of kinks along the length either secure one end in a vice or use two pairs of flat-nose pliers and pull as hard as you can in opposite directions. This stretches the wire slightly and removes any kinks.

CUTTING WIRE
You can use strong craft scissors to cut finer wires but it is better to invest in a pair of good quality wire cutters. Wire cutters have a flat side and an angled side that allow you to cut the end straight or tapered.

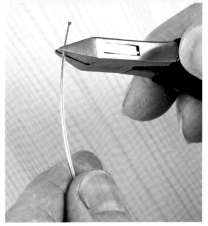

1 Cut with the flat side of the wire cutters towards the work to get a straight cut on the end of the wire. Make sure the flat side of the pliers is perpendicular to the wire so that the cut is straight and not at an angle.

2 When cutting a wire that crosses over another wire, use the very tips of the blades to get as close as possible to the crossover point. Hold the flat side of the wire cutters next to the work.

MEMORY WIRE
This extremely hard wire is available in coils of various diameters to make rings, bracelets or necklaces. The wire always springs back into its circular shape.

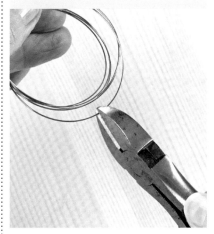

1 Cut the wire using special memory wire cutters or heavyweight wire cutters as fine jewellery wire cutters or scissors will be damaged by such a hard wire.

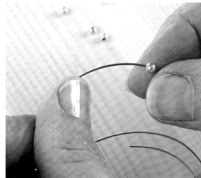

2 The end of the wire can be bent over using flat-nose pliers to finish or you can glue on special memory wire ends, which are small balls with a hole drilled in one side to cover the sharp ends.

BENDING WIRE

Wire doesn't bend on its own. You need to be quite firm to get the wire to bend where you want. Choose flat- or snipe (chain) nose pliers to bend wire at an angle. Avoid pliers with a serrated surface that will damage the wire.

 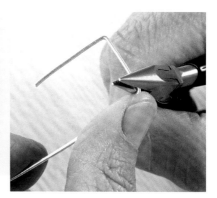

1 Hold the wire firmly with the flat-nose pliers so that the edge of the jaw is exactly where you want the wire to bend. Rotate the pliers to create a particular angle.

2 To create a right angle, hold the tail of the wire and push up against the jaws of the pliers with your thumb.

TWISTING WIRE

Twist wire to create texture and add body to the wire so that it supports the weight of a bead or holds its shape better. Twisted wire is easy to curve or coil as it is less likely to kink than single wire. It also looks more delicate than using a thicker craft wire and, as a result, is a popular technique for making tiaras and wedding accessories.

1 Use a bead to give you leverage for twisting the wire. Hold the bead between your finger and thumb and roll it round and round until the wire is evenly twisted along its length.

2 Rather than making a single twist, create short branches by only twisting for a short length and then adding a bead to one tail and twisting to make the branch. Add other branches as required.

3 If you are using thicker wire and find it easier to twist the wire rather than the bead, splay the wires out at right angles so that you can exert a more even pressure to make a neater twist.

MAKING TWISTED WIRE

Lengths of twisted wire can be used to make jump rings (see page 118) or used to give a textured appearance to jewellery and wire work. A cord maker or hand drill is ideal for twisting lengths of wire.

TIP MAKE A SUPPLY OF TWISTED WIRE, READY TO USE IN A VARIETY OF PROJECTS.

1 Fold a long length of wire in half and loop the folded end over the hook. Secure the cut ends in a vice (or get a friend to hold the ends with pliers) and turn the handle until it is twisted evenly along the length, as shown.

2 Take care when releasing the wire as it can spring. You can use an electric drill if it has a slow speed setting. Simply fit a cup hook in the Chubb instead of a drill bit.

Tiara

Tiaras have always been associated with royalty and wearing one, whether it is for a ball or on your wedding day, will always make you feel like a princess. This particular tiara is extremely easy to make, as you only need to use the twisting techniques shown on page 111 to complete the design then simple wire wrapping is used to attach the beads along the tiara band to finish – full instructions are on page 166. I used genuine Swarovski crystals, as you can't beat the quality and sparkle, then teamed these with imitation pearls as I liked their round shape, but if you choose freshwater pearls then the tiara will be completely unique. Use a ready-made tiara band or twist two lengths of 0.8mm (21swg) wire together to make your own.

WIRE JIG

Wire jigs are a great way to make lots of different wire work designs, ensuring that the pieces are all a uniform size and shape. There are a variety of styles of wire jig and each has a different arrangement of pegs or holes for pegs. Add earring wires to a wire jig motif to make quick and easy earrings, use the motifs as a component of a necklace or link lots of pieces together to make a bracelet. You can make components like bar ends for multistrand jewellery or even hooks for fastening using the larger pegs.

USING A WIRE JIG
As with all tools, you get what you pay for and more expensive metal jigs are definitely easier to use with thicker wires. To try out the technique, a basic plastic jig is ideal. Straighten the wire before you begin using the techniques on page 11.

1 Set out the pegs on the board to create the motif pattern you require. This arrangement of four pegs makes a figure of eight filigree motif.

2 Hold the wire diagonally across between the pegs and take the wire around the centre top peg. Holding the wire tight, pull it taut and take it around the right hand peg.

3 Sweep the wire out to the left hand side peg and then down and around the bottom peg to create the figure of eight. Tap the wire motif down with the eraser tip of a pencil.

4 Lift the motif off the pegs, trying to disturb it as little as possible. Trim the tails of wire close to where the wire overlaps. You can flatten the motif with flat-nose pliers or tap it with a hammer on a steel block.

ADDING BEADS

Beads can be incorporated into the wire jig design with some forward planning. You can either work one side then take the wire motif off the jig to add the bead or arrange the pegs to incorporate the bead.

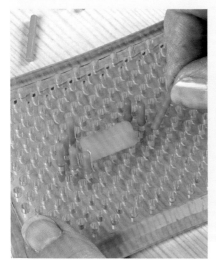

1 Arrange the pegs for one side of the wire jig design. Lay the bead on the board and arrange the pegs for the second side.

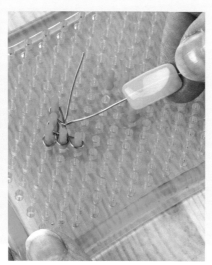

2 Cut a length of straightened wire and create the wire design on one side. Pick up a bead on the wire and push it into position on the board.

3 Wrap the wire around the pegs on the other side in the opposite direction. Lift the motif off the pegs and trim the wire ends. Flatten the wire with pliers or a hammer and block.

Making Simple Wire Jig Jewellery

Sometimes, when you get a new tool like a wire jig, it is fun trying the technique but not so easy to visualise how to use the pieces you have made in actual jewellery. The examples below show how effective wire jig jewellery can be.

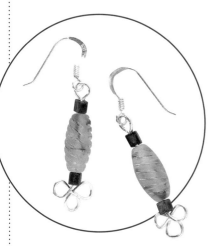

Arrange the pegs so that you can make a decorative end, add beads and then make a hanging ring for quick and easy earrings.

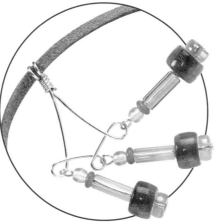

A wrapped loop is a secure way to finish pendant motifs. Add bead dangles to the loops and then hang from a ribbon or thong.

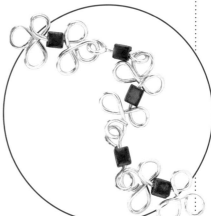

Join wire jig motifs with bead links to make a bracelet or necklace. Full instructions for making the bead links are on page 116.

◼ COILING WIRE

Coils of wire add a decorative touch to jewellery making. Use round-nose pliers to begin and flat-nose pliers with smooth jaws to bend the wire in a loose or tight coil.

LOOSE COIL

 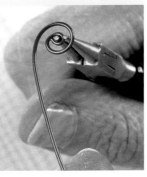

1 To begin use round-nose pliers to make a small loop at the end of the wire. Hold the wire at the very end of the pliers and bend the wire round until it touches the tail again.

2 To make the coil hold the wire a few centimetres (an inch) from the pliers and bend the wire gently round, moving the pliers in the loop until it is the size required.

TIGHT COIL

1 To begin, make a small 'u' shape on the end of the wire rather than a loop, using round-nose pliers.

2 Hold the 'u' sideways in flat-nose pliers and bend the straight wire round. Move the tiny coil around a few millimetres (tenths of an inch). Bend the wire round against the loop. Keep rotating the coil and bending the wire around until the size required.

◼ CAGED BEAD

Wrapping wire around beads is an elegant way to assimilate the beads into wire work jewellery. You can wrap the wire in a random fashion or make attractive little coiled cages to enclose the bead.

1 Cut a 20cm (8in) length of 1mm (19swg) wire. Make a small 'u' shape on one end with round-nose pliers and begin to make a tight coil.

2 Coil the other end of the wire and wind both coils into the centre so that they are the same size and form an 's' shape.

3 Push the centre of each coil with round-nose pliers to form two domes. Bend the domes towards each other to form an oval cage.

4 Use pliers to open the cage slightly and slide in a bead. Adjust the coils with pliers. You can bend the wire with pliers to tighten the cage against the bead. To make a bead link, insert an eye pin through the hole and make a loop at the other end (see page 116).

Use your imagination to make all sorts of interesting jewellery with wrapped, caged or spiral beads.

Bead Something Now
Keyring Charm

It's hard to lose a set of keys when they are attached to a large keyring but that doesn't mean it has to be dull and boring. This exquisite accessory has colourful spiral beads, shown below, set into these unusual square-shaped beads. The turquoise beads are semi-precious and have a hole drilled through two sides so that the spiral beads can be secured in the middle. Link the large beads with short lengths of spring and attach to a large spring hook. You can then attach the keys and hook safely to a belt loop or inside your handbag. Full instructions are given on page 167.

■ SPIRAL BEADS

Use the spring technique to make delightful wire beads. You can make short or long beads depending on the length of the spring. Try different thicknesses and colours of wire to make delicate or chunky beads.

1 Wrap 0.6mm (24swg) wire around a thin knitting needle (size 0000) or 1.2mm (18swg) wire to make a 4–5cm (1½–2in) spring. Remove the spring and trim the ends.

2 Leaving a short tail for leverage, wrap 0.7mm (22swg) wire around the knitting needle four or five times. Trim the long tail to about 20cm (8in) and slide the long spring down to the knitting needle.

3 Holding the short tail for leverage begin to wrap the spring around the knitting needle. You will need to push the spring down as you wrap, catching the last coil with your nail to stop it sliding up the wire.

4 Once the spring is wrapped around the knitting needle, wrap the core wire around four or five times and then slide the spiral bead off. Trim the ends of the wire neatly.

■ WRAPPED BEADS

Open out a spiral bead and position it around a large bead to make an attractive wrapped bead.

1 Make a spiral bead as above. Loosen the spiral by holding each end and turning the ends in opposite directions.

2 Slip a suitable bead into the loose coil and adjust to fit. Feed an eye pin through the holes in the spiral and bead. Trim the end to 7mm (⅜in) and make a loop with round-nose pliers (see simple loop, page 117).

■ MAKING A SPRING

Wrap wire around a mandrel (knitting needle or similar object) to make a tight spring.

1 Hold the tail of the wire in the palm of your hand and carefully wrap the other end around the mandrel so that the wires fit tightly together.

2 Slide the spring off the mandrel and trim the ends neatly using the flat side of the wire cutters.

■ EYE PINS

An eye pin is a piece of straight wire with a loop at one end. They are generally used to connect beads or jewellery components, such as simple earrings or bead charms.

Ready-made eye pins are made from quite a hard wire that holds its shape well. Make your own eye pins as the first stage of a bead link.

MAKING AN EYE PIN

1 Cut the wire straight at the end. Hold the wire about 6mm (¼in) from the end of the round-nose pliers so that the tip of the wire is level with the jaws.

2 Bend the wire around the pliers with your thumb until it touches the tip of the wire.

TIP THE DISTANCE YOU HOLD THE WIRE FROM THE TOP OF THE PLIERS DETERMINES THE SIZE OF THE LOOP.

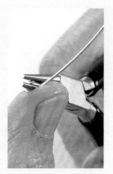

3 Reposition the round-nose pliers, as shown. Bend the loop back until it is central above the straight wire.

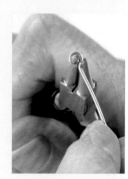

MAKING AN EYE PIN DANGLE

Eye pins are often used to make simple earrings or bead charms for jewellery. Simply bend the wire over to secure the beads or make a more decorative end by coiling.

1 Pick up the beads you require on the eye pin. Trim the end about 6mm (¼in) from the beads and fold the wire over using snipe-(chain) nose pliers.

2 For a more decorative end, bend the end of the eye pin to make a loose or tight coil (see page 114).

MAKING A BEAD LINK

Bead links have a loop at each end of the wire with one or more beads in the middle. They can be joined together to make earrings, bracelets and necklaces. This method for making the second loop is ideal when you have made the eye pin with craft wire. When using a ready-made eye pin, which has harder wire, use the simple headpin loop technique instead (see opposite).

1 Make an eye pin loop on the end of the wire. Pick up the beads you require. Hold the wire in the jaws of the round-nose pliers. Wind the wire around the pliers to make a loop.

2 Cut the wire where it crosses, using the very tip of the wire cutters. Hold the ring with round- or chain- (snipe-) nose pliers and bend back to straighten.

Attaching the Earring Wire

Open the loop on the earring wire using flat-nose pliers. Push the open end of the loop away from you; attach the bead link and then close with the reverse action.

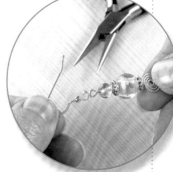

Joining a Link to a Bead Dangle

To join a link to a bead dangle use a pair of pliers to open one of the loops by pushing the cut end back, attach the other section and then close by reversing the action. Attach an earring wire in the same way.

HEADPINS

Headpins, which look like large dressmaker's pins, are used to make bead charms that can be dangled from bracelets and necklaces or attached to an eye pin bead link to make earrings.

SIMPLE LOOP

This is an easier way to make a loop on headpins and eye pins as they are made with a harder wire than normal jewellery wire. If the bead slides over the headpin, add smaller bead, such as a seed bead, first.

1 Trim the wire to 7mm–1cm (⅜–½in) above the top bead. The distance will depend on the thickness of the wire and the size of the loop required. Make a right angle bend close to the bead using snipe- (chain) nose pliers.

2 Hold the tip of the wire with round-nose pliers and rotate the pliers to bend the wire part way around the tip. Reposition the pliers and continue rotating the pliers until the tip touches the wire. Check the position of the loop and adjust until it is central.

WRAPPED LOOP

The wrapped loop is stronger and more secure than a plain loop. It is ideal for beads with slightly larger holes or for more precious beads or charms that you don't want to lose. Use longer headpins to allow for the wrapping. If you find it difficult to wrap the wire by hand, use flat-nose pliers for more purchase.

1 You will need at least 3cm (1¼in) of wire above the last bead. Using snipe (chain) nose pliers, hold the wire above the bead leaving a small gap and bend at a right angle.

2 Hold the wire close to the bend with round-nose pliers and wrap the tail all the way round to form a loop.

3 Hold the loop firmly in flat-nose pliers and wind the wire tail around the stem covering the gap between the loop and the bead. Trim the tail.

TIP IF THE HEADPIN PULLS THROUGH THE BOTTOM BEAD, ADD A SMALL BEAD FIRST AS A STOPPER AND THEN THE LARGER BEAD.

Bead Something Now

Earrings

Struggling to find the perfect earrings for your big night out? It can be frustrating looking for the ideal colour of accessory to go with a special outfit but it is much easier to buy just the right colour of bead, as there are so many to choose from and then you can make your own. These gorgeous earrings are made using the eye pin bead link technique on page 116 and finished with a headpin bead dangle with a plain loop, shown above. The headpins have a decorative end, which inspired the choice of cylinder beads. If you can't find similar headpins, add two tiny metal doughnut-shaped beads to a plain gold headpin before you begin. Full instructions are on page 167.

◼ JUMP RINGS

Jump rings are round- or oval-shaped pieces of wire with a gap for opening and closing. They are generally used to attach findings or join elements together but can be used in their own right to make stunning chain maille jewellery.

MAKING JUMP RINGS

1 Choose a rod of the required diameter – knitting needles or large nails are ideal. Hold the end of the wire at one end and wrap tightly around the rod.

2 Slide the closely wound spring off the rod. Pull the spring open slightly by hand or with two pairs of pliers. Use wire cutters to trim one end of the wire straight.

3 Line up the pliers with the first cut so that the flat side of the pliers is away from the cut end. Turn the pliers round and trim the new end each time with the flat edge of the wire cutters before cutting the next jump ring.

OPENING AND CLOSING

1 Hold the jump ring with two pairs of pliers, ideally two flat-nose or use the round-nose with a pair of flat-nose pliers. To open the ring, bring one pair of pliers towards you.

2 Attach another ring, chain or jewellery finding. Reverse the action to close.

3 To tension the jump rings so that they stay closed, push the ends slightly so that they overlap on one side and then the other. Pull back and the ends will then spring together.

TWISTED WIRE JUMP RINGS

Add texture and interest by making jump rings out of twisted wire. Use two different colours of wire for a two-tone effect or try two different gauges of wire for a more unusual look.

1 Fold a length of 0.5mm (25swg) wire in half and twist using a hand drill as described on page 111. Coil the wire around a rod in the same way as for plain jump rings and cut into individual rings.

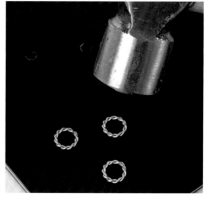

2 After tensioning, twisted wire jump rings should be hammered lightly with a hammer on a hard surface to fuse the wires together.

◼ CHAIN MAILLE

Linking jump rings together to make chain or jewellery is known as chain maille. This ancient technique is still used to make chain mail garments today. There are several distinct styles – European designs have the main rings overlapping in one direction, Japanese have rings set at right angles to each other and Persian has intricately linked pairs of rings. There are simple patterns such as two-in-two chain and flower chain but you can experiment and create some of your own.

TWO IN TWO CHAIN

Jump rings can be linked to make a length of chain. Have a supply of open and closed rings ready to make this chain. You can simply link single jump rings together or link together in pairs or even threes to make a more ornate chain.

1 Open two jump rings and loop one through four jump rings. Close the ring with two pairs of pliers. Attach a second ring through the four rings in the same way.

2 Hold so that you have a chain of pairs of jump rings (three to start). Pick up two closed rings on an open ring and loop through the top pair on the chain. Close the ring just added and add another through the same four rings.

FLOWER CHAIN

Interlink three jump rings together to make little 'flower' shapes and then join all the flowers together to make a pretty chain with jump rings.

1 Join two rings together. Open a third ring and loop it through where the first two overlap. Close the ring.

2 Group the rings into a flower shape. If the flower shape isn't compact, like the sample on the right, you need to flip the loose ring so that they all nestle close together, like the sample on the left.

3 Make several flowers. Loop an open jump ring through two flower shapes and close. Pick up further flowers one at time with a jump ring, loop through the end flower in the chain and close.

JAPANESE CHAIN MAILLE

Linking jump rings at 90°, so that some are horizontal and others vertical, then arranging in a geometric pattern is known as Japanese chain maille. The technique is generally used to make a chain mail fabric that can be used for brooches or small pouches. The small rings need to fit snugly over the larger rings so make your own large jump rings using a thicker wire. 12mm (18swg) wire works well with 0.5 or 0.6mm jump rings.

Join two large jump rings with a pair of smaller jump rings. Open the rings out so that they are flat and add a third large ring to one side using another two small rings.

Make two two-ring rows. Lay the sections out either side of the longer row. Link the rows together with pairs of jump rings. Each time you add a pair of rings lay the piece down to see where to add the next pair.

Chain Maille Variations

Alternate pairs of twisted wire rings with pairs of plain rings to create an attractive texture . Use brightly coloured wire to give the chain a contemporary look or add beads to some jump rings as you go along .

Vary the look of the flower chain by making coloured jump rings to link the 'flowers' together, and use two or three for more impact. You can add beads to the linking jump rings or make simple bead links (see page 116) to give the chain a completely different look.

Use different shades of wire for the small jump rings to add a touch of colour. Work out a colour plan so that the same colours of rings don't sit together.

Bead Something Now
Chain Maille Bracelet

These exquisite beads have a crushed ice finish with a pretty silvery effect that makes the beads and chain maille really come together in this simple bracelet. The little chain maille flowers are shown above and the bead links technique for attaching the beads shown on page 116. If you can find a plain silver toggle fastening made from a similar thickness of wire as that used for the chain maille it blends in to the design rather than detracting from it. Full instructions for making the bracelet are on page 168.

Bead On

Having learnt the basic techniques, now try working with chain, making your own jewellery fastenings and how to give wire an antique appearance.

■ WORKING WITH CHAIN

Chain for jewellery making is available in a variety of styles, sizes and materials. More expensive chain has soldered links but the majority of jewellery chain has open links.

CUTTING CHAIN

Measure the length of chain required and then cut through the next link on one side. If the chain is thick or made from hard wire cut through both sides so that the link falls away.

TIP USE THE TIP OF YOUR WIRE CUTTERS TO SNIP INTO THE LINKS.

JOINING CHAIN TO FASTENINGS
Attach chain to fastenings or other jewellery findings using small jump rings.

1 Open the jump ring with two pairs of pliers, loop through the last link of the chain, add the fastening and then close the jump ring.

2 Bead links and dangles hang better on a charm bracelet if they are attached to one side of the chain. Lay the chain down on the work surface or a beading mat so that it is flat and untwisted. Attach jump rings or charms to one side on alternate links.

■ THREADING CHAIN

Threading ribbon, cord or elastic through the links alters the appearance of the chain and adds variety to jewellery designs.

ADDING RIBBON
A wide sheer ribbon will bunch out through the links, giving a very soft appearance. Experiment with different widths and types of ribbon to find the effect you are looking for. Depending on the style of chain you can miss links or weave through every one.

1 Loop the ribbon through a large eye needle and weave it back and forwards through the links, leaving a long tail at each end.

2 Thread the ribbon through a large tube crimp, then a jump ring and back through the crimp. Thread it through the last link in the chain and back through the crimp again. Pull the ribbon with both ends until you manoeuvre the chain, crimp and jump rings close together. Repeat at both ends of the chain, squeeze the crimps to flatten and then trim the ribbon tails.

ADDING ELASTIC

If you thread elastic through the links of chain it will scrunch up to make a very textured metal bracelet. The links can be embellished in the same way as a charm bracelet.

1 Loop a double length of elastic thread through a large eye needle and weave it back and forwards through the links.

2 Decide on the size of the bracelet. Tie the elastic threads together with a couple of reef knots or secure the ends by passing both ends through a couple of crimps from opposite ends (see page 97) and flatten with pliers.

◼ MAKING JEWELLERY FASTENINGS ◼

Using basic wire working techniques it is easy to make a simple hook and eye fastening for necklaces and bracelets.

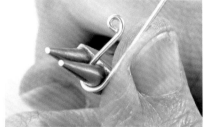

1 Form a tiny loop at the end of a 5cm (2in) piece of 1.2mm (18swg) wire using the very tip of round-nose pliers.

2 Hold the wire at the base of the jaws about 12mm (½in) away from the loop and wrap the wire around the jaws until the loop touches the wire again.

3 Grasp the wire near the base of the round-nose pliers. Bend the wire round to make a loop at right angles to the hook. Reposition the pliers and bend the loop back to straighten. Hold the loop with flat-nose pliers and bend back to add a soft curve to the hook.

4 To make the other part of the fastening make an eye pin with a 4cm (1½in) length of 1.2mm (18swg) wire. Make a larger loop with the other tail of the eye pin and straighten to make a figure of eight.

5 Hold each loop of the figure of eight in flat-nose pliers and twist around until the loops are perpendicular to each other.

TIP FOR A PROFESSIONAL FINISH FLATTEN THE RINGS AND HOOK TIP WITH A HAMMER AND BLOCK.

Antiquing Wire Work

Jewellery and wirework components can be artificially aged to give it an antique look in minutes. The technique works on silver, copper or brass wire. You can antique jewellery with most beads attached, although bone, ivory and polymer clay are not suitable.

1 Working in a well-ventilated area, drop a chunk of liver of sulphur into a small bowl of hot (not boiling) water and stir until completely dissolved. Use pliers to lower the jewellery into the solution until it is submerged. Leave for a few minutes and then lift out. Rinse the jewellery out in a bowl of lukewarm water. Pat dry with kitchen towels and leave for several hours or overnight to allow to dry.

2 Protect the work surface with kitchen towel. Polish the jewellery with grade 0000 steel wool, polishing in one direction only for best results. Use a stiff wire brush to clean out bits of steel wool trapped in any crevices. Polish the jewellery with a soft cloth. A chemically treated cloth like a Sunshine cloth™ will speed up the process.

Taking It Further: Beaded Flowers

Now that you have got the hang of wire work, there are many projects you can learn to complete. French beaded flowers look quite exotic but are actually quite easy to make.

FRENCH BEADED FLOWERS

There are only a few simple techniques to learn which can easily be adapted to make a variety of flowers. As well as loops and petal or leaf shapes you can also use the wire twisting techniques used for the bridal tiara on page 113 to make interesting flower centres.

Before beginning to make any of the components of a French beaded flower you will need to pick up beads onto the wire (see page 139). You can do this by transferring pre-strung beads directly on to the wire, by scooping loose beads from a dish or bead mat, or by using a bead spinner.

THE BASIC FRAME

This classic French beading technique is used to make a variety of leaf or petal shapes. Alter the number of beads on the centre wire to change the length and add more rows to make the shape wider.

1 For a basic shape, work directly off the reel of wire, picking up the required number of beads. The quantity depends on the style of flower but 45cm (18in) of beads is sufficient for most medium pieces. If you need more later, estimate the quantity of wire required, cut the end and add more beads.

2 Make a small loop on the end of the wire to prevent the beads falling off. Drop 15 beads down to the loop (this quantity will change depending on the length of the leaf or petal). Leave a tail of 8cm (3in), wrap the wire around four fingers and twist about five or six times to make a large loop. The beads on the short tail will form the centre row of the leaf. The long tail is the working wire.

3 Bring the working wire with 16 beads up beside the centre row. Hold the working wire at 90° and wind it around the centre wire once. Bring another 16 beads down the working wire and repeat the winding sequence at the bottom of the petal. Keep working from top to bottom adding one–two beads extra each time until you begin to create the petal shape. The more rows you add the wider the leaf or petal shape will become.

4 To make a more pointed shape at the top of the petal or leaf, change the angle at the top to 45° to make a slightly pointed end. Once the leaf petal is the size required wind wire around at the bottom end and trim. Cut the wire at the top and bend over.

MAKING STAMENS

Stamens are the spiky bits in the centre of a flower. You can make the stamens any length you want and add larger beads at the end if required.

Pick up seven beads on a fine wire (0.315mm, 30swg). Miss the last bead added then take the wire back through the remaining beads. Repeat the process to make a continuous row of stamens.

MAKING LOOPS

Loops are used to make flower centres or simple petal or leaf shapes. All three techniques are based on a basic loop shown in step 1, below.

• Plain Loops

These can be worked singly or in a continuous row and are ideal for making flower centres, small leaves and calyxes.

1 Bring the required number of beads down the wire. Form the beaded wire into a loop and twist the wires together at the base.

2 To make continuous loops work down the wire making more loops side by side. Twist the wires on each loop in the same direction to prevent the beads falling off.

Bead Corsage

Part of the delight of French beading is endeavouring to make flowers using their true colours and striving to recreate the intricate details to make each one look as realistic as possible. These flowers do look stunning in a vase or as a decoration in the home but for accessories it is fun to alter the colours to suit an outfit or individual. This stunning bloom is reminiscent of an echinacea flower. Use the techniques shown on these pages to assemble this exquisite accessory. Full instructions and details of the beads used are on page 168.

• Crossover Loops

This is a plain loop with a second loop perpendicular to the first, forming a cluster.

1 Make a plain loop and twist the wires together once or twice. Bring the working wire with the same number of beads as the first loop up to the top and over the other side.

2 Wrap the wire around underneath the loops to complete the shape. You can work these singly or in a continuous row to make a flower component.

• Wraparound Loops

This is a plain loop with one or more loops circling around the outside and secured at the bottom.

1 Make a plain loop of beads and twist the wires together once or twice. Bring the working wire full of beads up around the first loop so that the second loop is slightly larger.

2 Wrap the wires around at the base to secure. Add more loops to make a round petal shape suitable for peonies or similar flowers. Wraparound loops can be worked singly or in a continuous row.

ASSEMBLING A FLOWER

Once you have made all the separate components they can be combined to make the finished flower. Each flower is slightly different but you can use these general instructions as a guide.

1 Twist the wires of the flower centre by hand or with flat-nose pliers. Attach a finer wire to the top of the stem and use to attach the petals one at a time, wrapping the wire around the twisted stem each time to secure.

2 If the flower has a calyx, position around the stem and wrap the finer wire around to secure. Trim the wire stems so that the stem is thicker at the top and tapers towards the end.

3 To finish the flower, wrap the stem with floral tape.

CHAPTER 7:
Bead Embroidery

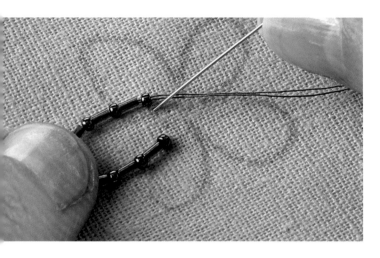

Bead Inspirations

Buttons are fun to make and you can really go to town and try out lots of different embroidery techniques. If you are worried about using a bead embroidered button through a buttonhole try a loop fastening or use studs as a closure instead. Experiment with different styles to create lots of button designs, such as beaded chain stitch, beaded buttonhole stitch and a mixture of tent stitch and cross stitch buttons.

*B*ead embroidery is one of the most tactile ways to work with beads and, because fabric is used in so many household and fashion items, there is literally no limit to what you can embellish. In this chapter the basic techniques for attaching beads to fabric, such as single stitch, lazy stitch, couching and backstitch are all covered in detail but many bead embroidery stitches are simply traditional embroidery stitches with beads added. It is exciting and inspiring to see how the stitches are transformed with the addition of beads. Only a few basic embroidery stitches are covered but you can experiment with adding beads to all your favourite stitches, and if you want to take things a little further try the traditional technique of tambour embroidery, shown on page 135.

Love Heart When beading a fabric completely you can create different textures using a variety of stitches. Backstitch is ideal for the heart as you can add several beads at a time on straighter lines and one or two for curves and filling gaps. The background is filled with the more random texture of single stitch, accentuated by pretty triangle beads.

Snake Charmer With lazy stitch you can literally take the beads for a walk to create wonderful snakelike patterns. Work the first stitch in the middle of the shape using quite large beads and then work the stitches so that they fan out in one direction and then after a few stitches, reduce the size of the centre beads and fan the opposite way.

Sizzling Sequins Overlapping sequins look absolutely fabulous. You can simply stitch them in place using the technique on page 134 or learn how to use a tambour needle to add the sequins. Begin in the centre of the marked circle and add each sequin so that it covers the thread on the one before. Spiral round to fill the area completely.

Blooming Lovely Couching is ideal for these pretty little flowers as it is easy to make nicely rounded petals of the same size. Make two loops with 11 beads to create a figure of eight then add only nine beads on the next two petals and pass the needle through two of the centre beads. Use a single stitch stack (page 128) for the flower centres.

Tubular Bells Almost impossible to pass through a buttonhole this is a fabulous design for a purely decorative button or a small brooch. Use bugles and seed beads to create a range of heights and textures, adding different coloured 'pivot' beads at the top of each stack. Work the tallest stacks in the middle and finish with single beads at the edge.

Basic Tool Kit

**For this chapter you will need embroidery equipment
as well as ordinary beading tools.**

■ Scissors

Small scissors with a fine sharp point are ideal for
embroidery as you can cut ends of threads close to
the fabric. For cutting the actual fabric use a pair of
dressmaker's shears. Keep separate scissors just for
fabric as paper quickly blunts the blades.

■ Needles

Bead embroidery needles are shorter than
regular beading needles so that it is easier to
stitch through the fabric. A size 10 is suitable
for most work or choose a size 13 for sewing
tiny beads. Sharps needles, often used for
quilting, make a good substitute. Use a tapestry
needle for evenweave fabric.

■ Thread

Ordinary polyester sewing thread is quite suitable
for embroidering beads if the item is not in regular
use. For items, such as bags or clothing that will be
handled or washed use a stronger thread such as
Nymo™ or quilting thread. Stranded cotton and other
embroidery threads can be used when incorporating
beads in embroidery stitches, but you may need
a larger needle and beads with bigger holes to
accommodate the thicker thread.

■ Fabric Markers

Water soluble or vanishing markers
are both suitable for marking designs on fabric
for bead embroidery. The vanishing marker disappears
over several hours and is ideal when you are working
on a small area or on fabric that can't be wetted. The
water-soluble marker is more permanent as it won't
disappear until sprayed lightly with water.

■ Transfer Paper

This coated paper is useful for
transferring designs from a
template onto smooth fabric.
It is available in a range of colours
– choose a colour that is similar to
the fabric so that it will be almost
invisible under the stitches.

■ Embroidery Hoop

When stitching small areas of bead embroidery use an
embroidery hoop to stretch the fabric. There are plastic hoops
with a metal spring or the traditional wooden hoops in a range
of sizes. If you bind the inner hoop with narrow fabric tape, the
fabric is less likely to slip through in use. Tambour hoops are
larger and have a stand or support so that you can work with
both hands at one time.

Getting Started

Most fabrics, from the sheerest georgette or organza to heavy denim and furnishing fabric, are suitable for bead embroidery. When working embroidery stitches there is always a tendency for the fabric to pucker and this is especially problematic with bead embroidery as it is difficult to press the fabric to smooth out any creases. Fabrics can be stabilised by stretching in an embroidery hoop or by attaching a backing fabric.

Embroidery Hoops

Bind the inner hoop of the embroidery hoop with fabric tape before use to prevent the fabric slipping in use. It is advisable to use a backing fabric, even with a hoop, so that you can secure the threads on the reverse.

Backing Fabrics

Heavier fabrics, such as denim or felt, do not need a backing fabric as they are less likely to pucker and you can secure threads into the reverse side of the fabric without it showing on the right side. When using an embroidery hoop with finer fabrics a lightweight lawn is usually sufficient. If you are not using a hoop either stitch backing fabric to the main fabric before you begin or use an iron on interfacing. For a slightly padded effect, fine quilting wadding can also be layered between the fabric and the backing before embroidery.

■ TRANSFERRING DESIGNS ■

When working a set pattern or motif you will get better results if the design is transferred to the fabric before you begin. A traditional method is 'prick and pounce', where a series of holes are pricked along the lines of the motif and then a small muslin bag of talcum powder is tapped over the template to transfer tiny dots of powder onto the surface of the fabric. You then draw along the dotted lines with an embroidery marker.

• Direct Transfer

This is the easiest method of transferring a design. The fabric doesn't even need to be translucent; for dark or dense fabrics tape the template and the fabric to a light box or window before you begin.

Tape the template and the fabric onto a worksurface. Draw along the lines with an embroidery marker.

• Transfer Paper

You can use a pencil or a dressmaker's wheel to draw along the lines when using transfer paper but remember to protect your work surface, as you will need to exert quite a lot of pressure. A pencil will only work with fairly smooth fabrics.

Lay the paper coated side down on the fabric and position the template on top. Draw along the lines with a pencil or dressmaker's wheel.

■ BEGINNING AND FINISHING THREADS ■

It is important to secure threads carefully when working bead embroidery to prevent the beads falling off. When beginning, avoid a knot as it can unravel or pull through the fabric; work with a double thread even if the thread is apparently quite strong.

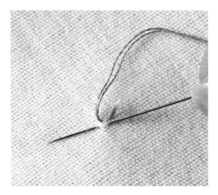

1 Take a tiny stitch on the reverse side of the backing fabric and then work a second tiny stitch on top to secure the thread. This is an ideal way to secure the thread at the end too.

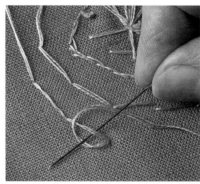

2 A quick method for finishing threads is the half hitch (see page 17). Make a loop of thread, take the needle under a previous stitch, through the loop and pull through. Repeat a couple of times for extra security.

◼ WORKING ON EVENWEAVE FABRIC

Counted thread bead embroidery is worked in either tent stitch (used in needlepoint) or cross stitch. Tent stitch is a single diagonal stitch; cross stitch has two diagonal stitches and both are worked on evenweave fabric such as canvas, aida, hardanger fabric or evenweave linen. You can incorporate the beads as part of a cross stitch or needlepoint design or create the entire design with beads. For the most popular evenweave fabrics that are 28 count or 14 count aida, use size 11 seed beads.

TENT STITCH

This stitch can be worked over a single block of aida or over pairs of threads on evenweave linen. Changing the stitch direction to the opposite diagonal will vary the angle of the bead.

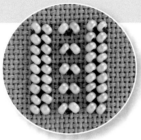

Change the angle of the bead by working a stitch from top right to bottom left instead.

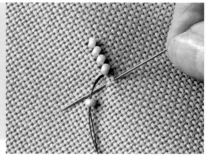

1 Secure the thread on the reverse side. Bring the thread out at one corner of a block and pick up a size 11 seed bead. Then take the needle back through the hole diagonally opposite.

2 To continue adding beads, bring the needle out at the hole to the left of where the needle went in last. Pick up a bead and take the needle through the hole diagonally opposite again.

CROSS STITCH

When working cross stitch you can complete each stitch as you go or work a row of beaded tent stitches and then go back along the row to finish the cross stitches.

If you take the needle through the beads from top left rather than from bottom right, as shown, the beads will lie horizontally.

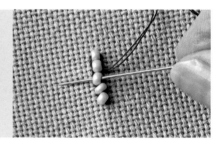

1 Work a tent stitch from top left to bottom right with a bead added. Bring the needle out directly above where the thread last emerged. Take the needle through the bead again from right to left.

2 Pull the thread through and then pass the needle back through the hole diagonally opposite from where it emerged. Continue working cross stitches one below the other.

Stacking Single Beads

Add larger beads or lots of small beads one above the other to create a range of different textures. Bugle beads also work well adding extra height to a design. Vary the sizes of the beads in each stack to create a range of shapes and textures. Make a row of stacked beads along the edge of a piece of fabric to create a fringe. Use bugle beads to quickly add height and interest to a piece of bead embroidery.

1 Bring the thread out where you want to add a large bead. Pick up the large bead and a small seed bead. Take the needle back through the larger bead only and through to the reverse side.

2 To create a stack, pick up several small beads and a small pivot bead, which can be the same or a contrast to the other beads. Miss the pivot bead and take the needle back through the other beads and through to the reverse side of the fabric.

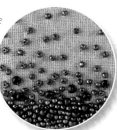

Work the stitches close together so that the fabric is almost completely covered in beads or fill an area with a smattering of beads.

Stitch in a straight line adding beads to disguise a seam or outline a motif or shape.

Using embroidery thread, make the stitches longer so that thread is showing at each end.

■ SINGLE STITCH ■

Attach individual beads using single stitch. If the beads are spaced far apart, go through each bead a second time to prevent the beads pulling out.

1 Secure the thread on the reverse side (see page 127) and bring out to the right side. Pick up a bead, drop it down to the fabric and hold the thread at the angle you wish to stitch.

2 Insert the needle close to the end of the bead so that the needle is perpendicular to the fabric and take it through to the reverse.

Bead Something Now

Little Bag

A loosely woven tweed fabric makes a pretty background for this gorgeous selection of glass beads. Stitch the beads onto the fabric individually, using single stitch, before the bag is made up. Pick beads that tone into the fabric colours and then select a few stronger shades such as the rich plum size 6 seed beads, which will give the beading a lift. As the bag is so small you can stitch the side seams by hand or use a sewing machine with a zipper foot attached so that you can stitch close to the beads. The instructions for making the bag are on page 169 or, if you are short of time, you could add beads to a ready-made bag.

▪ LAZY STITCH ▪

This traditional stitch is often found in Native American bead embroidery. The stitch is similar to satin stitch and often has a similar distinctive appearance with closely packed rows side by side. There are two methods of working the stitch, straight and diagonal and you will probably swap from one to the other when working a design or motif. Depending on the size of the beads, usually between four and eight are added on each stitch. Avoid adding too many beads at a time.

• Straight
Use this technique to make tightly packed short rows of beads or for making a change of direction.

 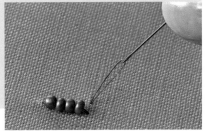

1 Secure the thread on the reverse side (see page 127) and bring the needle out to the right side. Pick up four beads and hold the thread taut so that the beads are lying where you want them to be. Holding the needle perpendicular to the fabric, take it back through at the end of the last bead.

2 Bring the needle up a bead's width from where it went down through the fabric. Pick up four more beads and holding the thread taut, pass the needle back through at the end. The beads should be lying flat with each row neatly side by side.

• Diagonal
Working the stitches diagonally makes the beads less likely to fall to one side and is ideal for rows of beads that are spaced slightly apart.

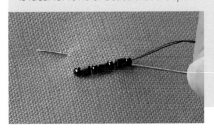 

1 Pick up four beads as described in step 1 above. Take the needle diagonally back towards the other end of the bead row. Bring the needle out about 6mm (¼in) from where the thread last emerged.

2 Pick up another four beads; hold the thread taut, pass the needle back through at the end and pick up beads for the next row.

BACKSTITCH
This simple stitch is a secure way to add a few beads at a time or a quick way to create curved lines. The needle goes back through the last couple of beads each time.

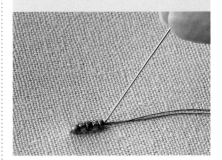

1 Secure the thread on the reverse side (see page 127) and bring it out to the right side. Pick up five beads and drop them down to the fabric. Hold the thread taut so that the beads are lying where you want them to be.

2 Take the needle down through the fabric at the end of the beads and back up between the third and fourth beads, as shown.

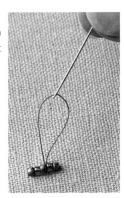

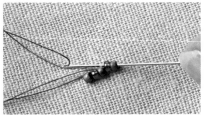

3 Pass the needle through the last two beads. Pick up the next five beads ready to work the next backstitch.

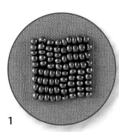    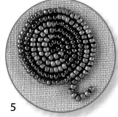

1   **2**   **3**   **4**   **5**

Work blocks of straight stitches in alternating directions to create a basket weave effect (1). When making a flower shape or fan use straight lazy stitches when the ends are close together and diagonal lazy stitches when they are further apart (2). Alter the length of lazy stitches by adding fewer or more beads in each stitch. Don't add too many or the beads will not lie flat (3).

When working backstitch bead embroidery pick up fewer beads if you are working a tight curve and more beads for a straighter line (4). If you are filling an area with backstitch it is important to space the lines out slightly so that the beads don't bunch up as you add more rows (5).

COUCHING

Although is seems an odd word couching describes the stitch exactly as it is derived from the French verb 'se coucher', which means to lie down. Strings of beads are laid across the fabric and small stitches hold the line of beads in place. You can work short lengths of couching with a single thread or use two threads for longer lines.

• Single Thread

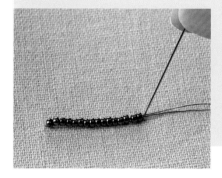

1 Secure two strands of thread on the reverse side (see page 127) and bring them out to the right side. Pick up enough beads to complete the line you want to create. Hold the thread taut and take the needle back through the fabric at the end of the beads.

2 Bring the needle back through the fabric between the second and third beads from the end. Take the needle back through on the other side of the bead thread. Work back along the row of beads, taking a small stitch over the bead thread every two or three beads.

To create a curved line with a single thread use your thumb to hold the beads in the shape you want and then stitch over the beading thread one or two beads from the end to secure before working back along the line.

TIP WORK STITCHES BETWEEN EVERY TWO OR THREE BEADS IF THE LINE IS CURVED SO THAT THE SHAPE IS SMOOTH.

• Double Thread

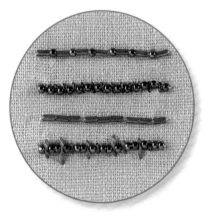

1 Bring a thread up where you want to begin and pick up enough beads to complete the line. Secure the thread beyond the end of the line by wrapping it around the needle or a pin.

TIP WHEN COUCHING ON A CURVED LINE SECURE THE THREAD AND HOLD THE BEADS IN POSITION WITH YOUR THUMB.

2 Bring a second thread up between the fourth and fifth beads and take it back through on the other side of the bead thread. Work back along the row of beads taking a small stitch over the bead thread every four or five beads. Once the beads are couched, take the bead thread to the reverse side and sew in the thread ends.

For double thread couching use one thread to hold the beads and a second thread to stitch them down. The second thread can be thicker so that it is visible between the beads and you can create a decorative effect by stitching between every bead.

Bead On

This section covers more complex stitching techniques and embroidery methods, such as chain stitch, buttonhole stitch, fly stitch and tambour embroidery.

■ EMBROIDERY STITCHES ■

Embroidery stitches take on a whole new look when beads are added. You can completely fill the stitch with beads or just add beads to a particular part of the stitch. With beaded embroidery stitches use an attractive thread such as stranded cotton, fine perlé cotton or silk thread as it is generally more visible than with ordinary bead embroidery.

CHAIN STITCH

Use chain stitch to make a double row of beads. You can either work ordinary chain stitch where the threads emerge and go back through the same point or space the threads to create a straighter effect.

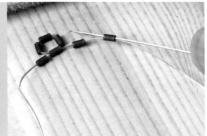

Use a variety of bead sizes to create a richly textured line of beads. Vary the tones of the beads within one colourway to avoid making it too 'bitty'.

1 Bring the needle up through the fabric and pick up four beads. Hold the beaded thread in a small loop then go back down through the fabric where the thread emerged.

2 Bring the needle back up in the middle of the loop and pull the thread through to form the first chain stitch. To make an individual chain (lazy daisy stitch) simply catch the loop down with a tiny stitch.

3 To create a line of chain stitches, pick up another four beads and form the second chain stitch loop. Take the needle back down where the thread emerged. Repeat as required.

4 To work the wider stitch, bring the needle up through the fabric, add the beads and form a loop. Take the needle back through the fabric about 3–6mm (⅛–¼in) from where it emerged. Make the second loop with the same spacing between the threads.

BUTTONHOLE STITCH

Buttonhole or blanket stitch is ideal for edging. You can sew two pieces of fabric together as you go, adding the beads so that they sit along the edge of the fabric or on the other leg of the stitch to make a pretty border.

Vary the length of the stitch to create a zigzag or wavy line, adding more beads to cover the extra length of thread.

1 Bring the thread up through the fabric and pick up two beads. Work a vertical stitch about 3–6mm (⅛–¼in) further across. Pass the thread under the needle so that the beads are between the needle and where the thread first emerged from.

2 Pull the needle through to create the 'L' shaped stitch. Pick up two more beads and take a vertical stitch again. You can also leave the beads on the vertical leg of the stitch.

TIP You can also work buttonhole stitch on the edge of fabric or along a fold.

FLY STITCH

Use fly stitch to create little loops of beads or add beads on the tail as well to create a 'y' shaped stitch.

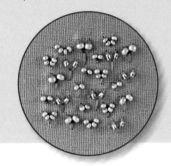

Vary the stitch by adding beads to the tail only or add beads to both the 'v' and the tail. Work single stitches side by side to create a border.

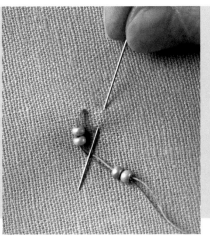

1 Bring the needle up through the fabric and pick up four beads. Next, hold the beaded thread in a small loop then go back down through the fabric about 3–6mm (⅛–¼in) from where it emerged.

2 Bring the needle back up in the middle of the loop and pull the thread taut to create a 'v' shape. You can either work a tiny stitch over the bead thread to hold it down or a longer stitch to create a tail.

Bead Something Now
Patchwork Pincushion

The delightful little pincushion was inspired by Victorian Crazy patchwork, which was embroidered and often embellished with beads. The bright pastel colours and pretty matt beads bring the technique up to date. The contemporary design has small rectangles sewn together in rows and then the rows stitched together to make a square. The patchwork doesn't need to be precise but if you are unsure you can of course simply add the bead embroidery to a single piece of fabric. Choose some of the bead embroidery stitches shown on pages 132-133 to decorate the cushion or incorporate beads in your own favourite stitches. Full details of how to make the cushion are given on page 169.

■ ATTACHING SEQUINS

There are several ways to attach sequins to fabric. You can sew the sequins individually or overlapping in a row. These techniques are also suitable for attaching washer style beads. Sequins can also be attached using a tambour needle (see Taking It Further, page 135).

• Secure the thread on the reverse side. Position the sequin where you want it and bring the needle up through the middle of the sequin. Take the needle back down at the side. A second stitch secures the sequin and a third in a 'y' shape will make is secure enough to launder.

• Secure the thread on the reverse side. Position the sequin where you want it and bring the needle up through the middle of the sequin. Pick up a seed bead and take the needle back down through the hole in the sequin only. You can make a tiny backstitch on the reverse side for added security before attaching the next sequin.

Sequins can be sewn in straight or curved lines. It looks a little magical as the stitch that secures the last sequin is hidden by the next sequin sewn on top.

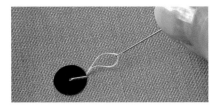

1 To attach sequins in a row, position the first sequin and take a stitch from the centre hole and over the right hand edge. Bring the needle and thread back through to the right side.

2 Position the next sequin so that it covers the last stitch. Bring the thread up through the hole in the second sequin and over the right hand edge. Repeat until the line is as long as required.

Bead Something Now
Picture Frame

A fabric frame embellished with beads is a really attractive way to display a cherished photograph and if you make it yourself you can co-ordinate the colours with your décor. Use a plain fabric and trace or transfer a design onto the fabric or try embroidering over a pattern. You can simply couch beads (see page 131) along the edges of any design and then embellish areas with sequins and contrast beads to get fabulous effects. This gorgeous fabric has lots of interesting details incorporating a large leaf print, which becomes an asymmetrical abstract design when the centre area is cut away. Full instructions are on page 170.

Taking It Further: Tambour Embroidery

If you are enjoying bead embroidery, why not try your hand at tambour work? This technique, named after the frame or tambour used to stretch the fabric, uses a hooked needle to attach beads or sequins to fabric. Using a tambour needle takes a little bit of practice but the finished result has a much better finish than couching, especially on curved lines. This high quality technique is still used for haute couture, and evening bags that are densely covered in overlapping sequins have generally been attached using a tambour needle.

HOW IT WORKS

The needle pulls loops of thread through loosely woven fabric to create a chain stitch on one side and the beads or sequins are added in the straight stitches on the other side. The large frames traditionally used for tambour work are similar to an embroidery hoop but have a clamp or stand attached so that you can work with both hands. To prevent the fabric slipping as you work, wrap a narrow fabric tape around the inner ring to provide grip. A tambour needle is similar to a very fine crochet hook but with a sharp point like a needle that is fitted into a small handle. Net or loosely woven fabrics such as muslin or fine linen work well as it is easy to draw embroidery thread through the open weave.

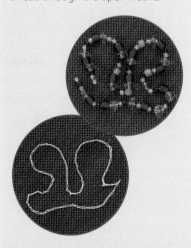

To create a pattern draw a light pencil line on the fabric before beginning. One or more beads can be added at a time although you get a smoother curve if there is a stitch for every bead. The reverse of the bead embroidery shows the chain stitch. Make sure you pull the tail through the last loop so that it doesn't unravel. For extra security, iron interfacing on the chain stitch side.

WORKING CHAIN STITCH

Tambour needles come in a variety of sizes but all are quite fine. You will find it easier to learn the technique using a tightly twisted sewing thread rather than stranded cotton as the hook is less likely to split the thread.

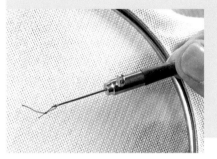

1 Make a small slip knot on the end of the thread. Hold the tambour needle with your right hand above the stretched fabric. Hold the thread in your left hand below the fabric (reverse if you are left-handed). Push the tambour needle through the fabric, catch the slip knot loop with the hook and pull it back through the fabric.

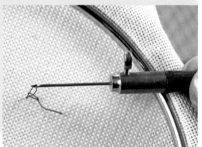

2 Move the tambour needle forward slightly, still inside the loop and then push back through the fabric. Catch the thread again and pull the tambour needle through to make the second loop. Continue working the stitches to create a long line of chain stitch.

ADDING BEADS AND SEQUINS

If you turn the chain stitched fabric over you will see a row of straight stitches on the other side. You can work the tambour stitch so that the chain stitch is on the reverse of the fabric adding beads or sequins on the straight stitch side. Begin by pulling a slip knot through from the right side.

1 Pick up beads on the thread and drop one close to where the thread emerges. Catch the thread with the tambour hook on the other side of the bead and pull through the fabric and through the previous loop on the reverse side. Continue adding beads one at a time.

2 When adding sequins, position each sequin so that hole is directly over where the thread emerges and bring the tambour hook through the fabric at the edge of the sequin to catch the thread and pull through the other side. Each subsequent sequin hides the previous thread.

CHAPTER 8:
Knitting and Crochet

Knitting and crochet are traditional textile skills that can be transformed with the addition of beads. You can use fancy stitches and intricate shaping, but in general, the basic stitches are all that is required. It is helpful to know how to cast on, knit, purl and cast off for the knitting section, and with crochet the basic chain, double (US single) and treble (US double) crochet stitches are all that is required. This chapter focuses on how to add beads to these traditional textiles with clear step-by-step instructions for both yarn and wire. Knitting and crochet are perhaps the most versatile techniques for working with beads because of the variety of stitches, materials and beads that can be used. Look out for the 'Bead Something Now' projects as you work through the chapter, which use techniques shown on the same page. Full instructions for the projects are on pages 171–172.

Bead Inspirations

These gorgeous embellishments illustrate the wide range of textures and shapes that can be created when knitting and crocheting with beads. You can wear the motifs as brooches, if you attach a brooch back, or they can be used to embellish bags, shoes and other items. Knit or crochet a cord or strap and attach one of the motifs to make a unique piece of jewellery.

Beaded Bow

Bows are easy to knit, as there is no shaping required. Knit a long rectangle using two colours of 0.315mm (30swg) wire together and wrap a beaded band around the middle. Swarovski crystals add a luxury touch to this fun embellishment.

Knitted Rose

Pick up 100 seed beads on no. 5 cotton perlé then cast on 100 stitches and knit 2.5cm (1in) in stocking stitch. Cast off adding a bead on each stitch. Gather the bottom edge and roll up to make the rose. Knit leaves with beads down the centre and sew in position.

Beady Rectangle

Moss stitch has a wonderful crinkly texture that holds its shape well. The texture is enhanced when worked using metallic stranded cotton. Pick up about 50 assorted beads and add in the centre of the rectangle to make a stylish brooch.

Crinkly Crochet

Crochet a long rectangle and fold in three to make a dense crinkly mesh. Sew the layers together with running stitch. Work a wheel with large crystals and attach, adding a large round bead in the middle for a finishing touch.

Daisy Design

Cast on using the half hitch technique and then cast off immediately to make long tendrils. Leave one stitch on the needle each time until you have 28 stitches and then finish like the rosette on page 145. Sew semi-precious chips in the middle to finish.

Crochet Flower

Pick up a selection of seed beads on no. 8 variegated cotton perlé and crochet a spiral circle with beads. Crochet a plain round of treble (US double) crochet and then use filet crochet techniques from page 151 to add a decorative border.

Basic Tool Kit

In this chapter all you really need is knitting needles and crochet hooks, as well as yarn, thread or wire and, of course, lots of gorgeous beads!

■ Big Eye and Twisted Wire Needles

These needles have two points with a long eye nearly as long as the needle that can accommodate almost any yarn. They are available in two lengths 5.5cm and 11.5cm (2¼in and 4.5in). Twisted wire needles are available in a range of thicknesses. The large eye is easy to thread but collapses as you pull the needle through beads.

TIP MAKE YOUR OWN TWISTED WIRE NEEDLE USING A FINE WIRE SUCH AS **0.315** OR **4MM (10**SWG). CUT A **15**CM **(6**IN) LENGTH AND BEND IN HALF OVER A KNITTING NEEDLE. HOLD THE WIRE ENDS AND TWIRL THE NEEDLE UNTIL THE WIRE IS TWISTED TO THE END. TRIM THE ENDS NEATLY.

■ Yarns and Threads

When knitting and crocheting it is easier to add beads to smoother yarns and threads and, because the beads are generally fairly small, embroidery threads such as cotton perlé and crochet cottons are ideal. Crocheting ropes is easier with slightly stiffer threads such as fine nylon cord.

■ Wire

Wire for knitting and crochet needs to be soft and pliable so that it can be manipulated without breaking. You can use general craft wire or look for crochet wire that is ideal for both knitting and crochet. Wire up to 0.6mm (23swg) or 0.7mm (22swg) is reasonably easy to use but the most common thickness is 0.3mm (30swg). Doubling up thinner wire is easier to work than the equivalent thicker wire and gives interesting effects if you use more than one colour.

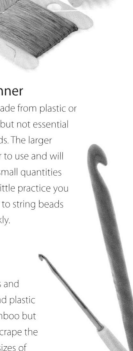

■ Bead Spinner

Bead spinners, made from plastic or wood are useful, but not essential for stringing beads. The larger models are easier to use and will work with quite small quantities of beads. With a little practice you will soon be able to string beads surprisingly quickly.

■ Knitting Needles and Crochet Hooks

These essential pieces of equipment come in a range of materials and sizes. Basic knitting needles are generally metal in smaller sizes and plastic in the larger sizes and both are suitable. For yarn you can use bamboo but use older needles and hooks for wirework as the metal tends to scrape the surface. You can experiment to achieve closer work with smaller sizes of needles and hooks and lacier effects with larger sizes.

Getting Started

Before you begin knitting or crocheting you have to choose beads and yarn, thread or wire. You can add beads to just about any type of stringing material so long as the holes in the beads are big enough. In general the greater the anticipated wear on your garment, the stronger the yarn you'll need as the beads double the amount of friction on the yarn.

STRINGING BEADS

Sometimes it is easier to string beads onto a finer thread and then transfer them to the thicker yarn. Picking beads up direct from a bead mat lets you select the order or distribution of accent beads along the length but it can be time consuming. A bead spinner is an excellent tool for picking up strings of beads quickly but the order of beads is completely random. Generally it is better to put all the beads you require on the yarn at one time but if the yarn is quite fragile you should transfer only four–five in at a time and then join in a new batch of beads at a later stage.

• Bead Strings

Beads that have been pre-strung are ideal for knitting and crochet. It is easy to transfer the beads onto your yarn. Separate one string from the hank and secure the beads at one end with a large knot or a bead stop spring (see page 37).

Lay the yarn over the bead string thread and tie the string in an overhand knot (see page 17). Carefully ease the first few beads over the knot. The beads should now transfer quite easily over the flattened knot.

• Bead Spinner

It takes a little practice to become proficient but you will soon be able to string beads surprisingly quickly. There are special curved needles for stringing, as shown here.

Attach your yarn or thread to the curved needle. Pour beads into the bead spinner. Turn the handle slowly to get the beads spinning (they don't have to be going too fast). Lower the needle into the beads so that it is fairly horizontal and the beads should whiz up the needle. Alternatively you can use a twisted wire needle bent into a curved shape at the end.

ATTACHING FINDINGS

Fastenings can either be attached directly to the wire or to a jump ring. Very fine wire can slip through the gap in jump rings even though they look tightly closed so where possible use a split or solid ring instead. When attaching the finding make sure any sharp ends are tucked away or woven back through the knitting or crochet to avoid them irritating the skin.

WORKING A SLIP KNOT

Both knitting and crochet often begin with a slip knot.

1 Make a loop with a long tail and then take the yarn across the back of the loop.

2 Pull the yarn through the loop and pull tight to make the knot.

BEGINNING A NEW THREAD

It is likely at some point that you will need to join on a new thread either because you have come to the end of the yarn or have run out of beads.

Stop knitting or crocheting at the side when there is still a reasonable tail. Pick up sufficient beads on the new yarn and then begin knitting for a few rows leaving a long tail. Pull the two ends so that the stitches are the correct size and tie a loose reef knot (see page 17). At the end of the project untie the reef knot and use the tails to sew a seam or stitch them in along the seam.

Knitting

Knitting with beads is easy as there are no fancy stitches to learn. So long as you know how to cast on and off and can knit you will be able to make all sorts of wonderful beaded items.

◼ BEAD KNITTING

There are several techniques: bead knitting, beaded knitting and adding beads with a crochet hook. With bead knitting the beads sit in front of the stitches and hide the yarn altogether, making it possible to create patterns or images with the beads. In beaded knitting the beads sit between the stitches and are an integral part of the fabric. You can also add beads without pre-stringing

them using a fine crochet hook. It is easier to learn to knit beads using a fairly smooth yarn so that you can see exactly where the beads lie in relation to the stitches. Cotton yarns such as crochet cottons or no 5 perlé cotton embroidery thread are ideal. When you are learning each technique knit the first two rows and knit the outside two stitches of any sample without beads.

BEAD KNITTING – HORIZONTAL BEADS

This quick and easy technique adds beads to the back of the knitting as you work, although this will be the right side of the knitting. The beads are added on every second row of garter stitch and lie more or less horizontally. Knit the sample with cotton perlé no 5 on size 12 needles.

Although beads are only added every second row, the beads cover the knitting well with no large gaps between the rows.

1 Pick up sufficient beads on the yarn. Cast on 14 stitches and knit two rows. Bring about 2.5cm (1in) of beads up near the right-hand needle and tension the yarn around your little finger. *Knit two stitches and bring a bead up to the right needle at the back of the knitting.

2 Knit the next stitch, making sure you don't pull the bead through the loop of yarn. Add beads on every stitch to the last stitch. Knit the last stitch.

TIP Keep the yarn fairly taut so that the bead is held firmly in position.

3 On the next row the beads will show on the front of the knitting. Knit the row without beads and then repeat from *. At the end of the piece of knitting knit two rows without beads and cast off.

ADDING BEADS ON EVERY ROW

This technique is often used to make small bags where progressively more beads are slipped between the stitches to increase the beading and shape the bag. Rows are worked in pairs as the beads lie back to back so that the back looks similar to the front. You can work several pairs with the same number of beads so that the increase is more gradual.

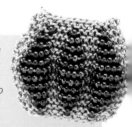

Use size 0000 knitting needles with size 8 perle cotton and size 10 or 11 seed beads to make delicate shell-like bead work.

1 Pick up beads on the yarn. Cast on 12 stitches to make the sample and knit one row. Knit three stitches. *Bring a bead up to the right-hand needle and knit the next three stitches. Repeat from * to the end of the row.

2 On the next row repeat adding a single bead every three stitches.

3 On the next two rows knit three stitches and bring two beads up to the right-hand needle. Then increase the beads by one every two rows.

BEAD KNITTING – CHEVRON BEADS

This slightly more advanced technique, worked in stocking stitch, creates a densely packed covering of beads that is ideal for pictorial work. The beads are added every row and sit diagonally, changing direction each row. Knit the sample with cotton perlé no 5 on size 12 needles.

1 Pick up sufficient beads on the yarn. Cast on 14 stitches and knit one row then purl the next row. *At the beginning of the next row knit two stitches. Put the right-hand needle into the back of the next stitch. Bring a bead up close to the right-hand needle.

2 Take the yarn around the needle in the usual way and then, holding the bead in place with your left index finger, lift the loop over the right-hand needle and push the bead through as you go.

3 Continue adding a bead on every stitch until you reach the last two stitches. Knit these two stitches without beads.

4 On the next row purl the first two stitches. Put the right-hand needle into the front of the next stitch. Bring a bead up close to the right-hand needle. Take the yarn around the needle in the usual way so that the bead nestles between the needles at the front.

5 Pull the stitches to make the loops slightly larger and then push the bead through the loop with your left thumb as you complete the stitch. Add beads on every stitch to the last two stitches. Purl the last two stitches.

6 As you knit the next row you will be inserting the needle in stitches that already have a bead on them. Repeat from * until the knitting is the length required. Knit two rows and cast off.

In this technique the stitches are twisted as the beads are knitted into the stitch and so are held very securely.

Which to Choose?

Horizontal and chevron bead knitting are similar techniques, both ideal for knitting a bead fabric. There are subtle differences between them as detailed below.

Bead Knitting – Horizontal Beads
The beads sit in a regular horizontal position. It is knitted in garter stitch (all knit rows) and has quite a textural appearance, as the stitches are visible like little seeds between the beads. This technique is particularly good when you are using an attractive yarn for a knitted garment, bag or other item.

Bead Knitting – Chevron Beads
The beads sit in a chevron pattern giving it an interesting beaded texture. It is knitted in stocking stitch with alternate knit and purl rows but when the beads are large enough in relation to the thread, there is almost no thread visible at all. This technique is particularly good for pictorial or intricate patterned beading.

■ BEADED KNITTING

Beaded knitting has more emphasis on the knitting with beads lying between the stitches rather than densely packed on one side.

SLIPPING A STITCH
This technique adds beads to the front of the knitting as you work. You add beads every second row and there is at least one stitch between the beads, as you need to knit a stitch to secure the bead. Knit the sample with cotton perlé no 5 on size 12 needles.

1 Pick up beads on the yarn. Cast on 13 stitches and knit two rows. Knit the first two stitches of the next row. *Bring the yarn to the front between the needles. Slip the next stitch purl-wise onto the right-hand needle.

2 Slide a bead up to the slipped stitch. Take the yarn between the needles and back to the rear of the knitting.

3 Knit the next stitch to secure the bead. Add beads on each stitch to the last two stitches. Knit these stitches without beads. Knit or purl the next row. Repeat from * until the knitting is the length required. Knit two rows and cast off.

Garter stitch (all knit rows) has a rough texture that can be enhanced with a knobbly yarn.

Stocking stitch (alternative knit and purl rows) has a neat regulated appearance that works well with a smooth or silky yarn.

USING A CROCHET HOOK
If you don't want to pre-string beads because it is too time consuming or the yarn is too fancy or fragile you can add beads as you go using a fine crochet hook. Choose a hook that will fit through the hole in the bead. Beads added with a crochet hook sit vertically rather than horizontally.

1 Knit to where you want to place the bead. Pick up a bead on the crochet hook. Catch the next stitch with the hook and pull it off the needle and through the bead.

2 Slip the stitch back onto the left-hand needle and knit the stitch. The bead will be held very securely. Add a bead on every stitch, or as often as required. Knit a row and then add beads on the next row as before.

When all the rows are knitted, the beads sit between the ridges of the garter stitch.

Crochet is ideal for adding the occasional bead to a piece of knitting. In stocking stitch the beads add texture.

It is also the ideal technique for adding beads if both sides are on view as the beads show on both sides.

Bead Something Now
Beaded Scarf

Using a fine yarn to add beads into knitting gives you the opportunity to knit with almost any yarn you like and makes it easy to knit stunning items like this gorgeous silk scarf. The beads are strung on to fine cotton perlé in a similar shade to the main yarn so that it is almost invisible when knitted. You can simply add beads to the border at each end but knitting in size 8 seed beads on the main body of the scarf adds extra texture and sparkle. Full details of how to make the scarf are on page 171.

ADDING BEADS TO FANCY YARN

If the beads you want to work with have too small holes or the yarn is too thick, knobbly or fragile, you can string beads onto a fine yarn and then knit the two strands together as one, or string the bead yarn behind the knitting and only include it when you want to add a bead.

String the beads onto a thin yarn or thread. Hold the two yarns together and work as one thread. Cast on and knit until you are ready to add a bead. Bring the bead up the finer yarn to the needle ready to add the bead with your chosen technique.

TIP IF YOU KNIT WITH THICKER YARN AND ONLY BRING THE THREAD INTO THE STITCH WHEN ADDING A BEAD, MAKE SURE THE FINER THREAD ISN'T TOO TIGHT ACROSS THE BACK OF THE KNITTING.

KNITTING WITH WIRE

Wire is super material to knit as it is ideal for making three-dimensional projects and creates wonderfully textured knitted fabric. Garter stitch, where every row is knitted, is the most popular for knitting with wire as it has a gorgeous rough texture. Stocking stitch, where a knit row is followed by a purl row, has a smoother texture on one side.

CASTING ON

When casting on with wire it is better to cast on fairly loosely so that the bottom edge is not too tight. As wire doesn't unravel in the same way as yarn you can cast on with half hitches to make an attractive looped edge. You can also casting on with wire in the regular way with your thumb or using two needles.

1 Hold the tail of the wire in your left hand. Pass your right thumb under the wire to make a loop.

2 Tuck the needle into the loop and pull taut. Pass your right thumb under the wire again to make the next loop and pull the wire taut.

3 Cast on as many 'stitches' as you need, spacing the stitches with a gap the same width as the knitting needles.

ADDING BEADS ON THE EDGE

It is easy to add beads as you cast on so that the knitting has a beaded edge. Pick up the beads required for the body of the work first and then the number of beads required for casting on.

1 Using the half hitch method you can simply drop a bead down to the needle before forming the next half hitch. You can add a bead on every stitch, either every two stitches or randomly along the edge.

2 You can also add beads easily using the thumb method of casting on, dropping a bead down to the needle before casting on the next stitch. If the beads are larger than the width of the needle it is better to use a larger needle just for casting on.

ADDING BEADS TO THE MESH

Beads are generally strung onto the wire before you begin and then knitted in as you go using one of the techniques on pages 140–141. It is worth making a small sample in each technique as the knitted wire meshes look similar but feel completely different. My preference is for beaded knitting as the slipped stitches produce an attractive mesh that is stable and easier to make jewellery or other items with.

• Bead Knitting Wire

Cast on using the half hitch method and knit a row. Using the instructions for bead knitting – horizontal beads on page 140, add beads between the stitches on the reverse side on every other row. Wire doesn't have any 'give' so don't make the stitches too tight. Keep the loop carrying the bead between stitches fairly taut so that the bead stays in position.

• Beaded Knitting

Cast on and knit a row. Following the instructions for beaded knitting on page 140, knit to where you want to add a bead and bring the wire forward. Slip the next stitch onto the right needle purlwise, bring a bead up to the needle and then pass the wire back to the reverse side. Knit a stitch.

Bead Something Now

Wire Knitting Corsage

This beautiful wire and bead embellishment would look equally stunning pinned to your lapel as a large brooch or corsage, attached to a bag or you could even make two to transform a pair of plain shoes for a special occasion. Knitting blue and silver wire together makes the design much livelier but you could of course use any two colours of wire and choose beads to match. Details of how to make the corsage are on page 171,

CASTING OFF

Wire knitting doesn't unravel in the same way as knitting and so it is not always necessary to cast off in the traditional way although you do need to secure the last row in some way otherwise the knitting will unravel when handled.

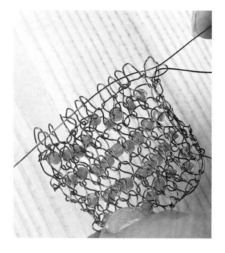

Make the stitches loose so that they can be lifted one over the other easily. If you struggle to cast off with wire in knit stitch, try casting off with a purl row instead. You can simply remove the needle and then pass the tail through the last row of stitches. With thicker wire flatten the stitches to secure the wire. For a decorative edge, add beads as you cast off. Bring the bead up to the needle and knit or purl the next stitch. Lift the first stitch over the second. For bead knitting where beads are added on the back of the knitting, knit to cast off. For beaded knitting where beads are added to the front, cast off with purl stitch.

SHAPING WIRE KNITTING

You can shape wire knitting by increasing and decreasing stitches in the same way as knitting with yarn but, because it is very malleable but still holds any shape, there are alternative techniques.

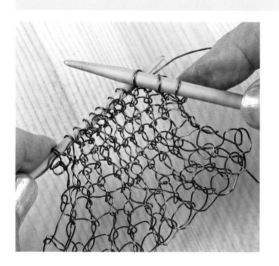

Rather than working out where to increase or decrease you can simply push or pull the mesh once the knitting is complete to make the shape you want. Alternatively shape the knitting by changing the size of your knitting needles. Moving to a larger size creates an increase in the size of the stitch and using smaller needles decreases the size of the stitch.

FOLDING THE MESH

You can change the delicate properties of wire mesh by folding it to make it denser and more stable.

Knitted mesh is generally folded horizontally between rows. Fold alternate rows in opposite directions. Secure the layers of knitting mesh by oversewing or working running stitch using a similar or contrast wire.

MAKING A ROSETTE

Circles can be made by increasing and then decreasing to make a flat shape but it is more attractive when knitting with wire to keep the cast on edge on the outside of the circle. Half hitch casting on is particularly good as the stitches form an attractive looped edge. You can add beads as you cast on and in any row (see Wire Knitting Corsage opposite)·

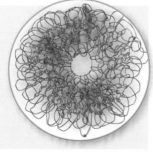

1 Using the half hitch technique, cast on 50 stitches on size 3 knitting needles. Then change to size 10 needles and work stocking stitch (alternate knit and purl rows) for the next three rows. On the next row purl two together and repeat to the end (25 stitches). On the next row, knit one and then *knit two together. Repeat from * to the end.

2 Slip the stitches off the needle and thread the tail through the loops. Pull up to form the rosette shape. Sew the side seam with the tail of the wire and stretch the outside edge to make a fuller rosette.

Crochet

Crochet is a great technique for working with beads. It is quick to learn, versatile and you can take your work anywhere since there is only one stitch to worry about unravelling!

Bead crochet can be worked as a chain, a panel, a circle, as a rope or in a tube to create a huge variety of jewellery and other items. There are a range of stitches from chain to sextuple treble that increase in height by a loop at a time. You can add beads to any of the stitches but for most projects you will use chain stitch, slip stitch, double (US single) and treble (US double) crochet stitches.

CHAIN STITCH

Chain stitch can be used to make beaded strands and, when worked with wire, makes simple and attractive jewellery (see page 149). It is also used to make a foundation or base chain for a piece of crochet. This is the equivalent of casting on in knitting.

1 Pick up beads on the yarn. Make a slip knot and insert the hook. Hold the crochet hook in position with a few beads between your left index finger and the hook.

2 Bring a bead up to the side of the hook. Take the yarn over the hook (YOH) on the other side of the bead. It is easier to manoeuvre the hook rather than the yarn.

3 Pull the yarn through to form another loop. Continue adding beads in the same way. You can add beads every loop or work one or more plain loops between the beaded loops.

SLIP STITCH

This is used to make a chain stitch circle, work a row without adding height and for making tubular ropes.

1 Crochet a chain. Insert the hook into the last chain of the base chain. YOH and pull the yarn through both loops in the one movement.

2 To work a slip stitch insert the hook in the next chain, YOH, draw the yarn through the chain and the loop on the hook in the one movement. Add two chains at the end of the row for turning slip stitch then insert the hook into the second chain from the hook.

Turning Chains

Turning chains are used in flat pieces of crochet to bring the hook up to the height needed to make a stitch. At the end of the base row of chain stitches you need to work one or more stitches ready to turn – one for slip stitch, two for double (US single), three for treble (US double) crochet and so on. These extra chains keep the piece the same width as you work.

DOUBLE CROCHET (US SINGLE CROCHET)

Double (US single) crochet makes a flat fabric that is densely covered in beads on one side with bare crochet fabric on the other. Beads are added every second row. It is the stitch most often used to make flat beaded crochet for jewellery and other items.

1 Crochet a chain, adding two chains for turning. *Bring a bead up to the back of the hook. Insert the hook into the second chain from the hook. YOH, draw the yarn through the chain only to leave two loops on the hook.

2 YOH, draw the yarn through both loops on the hook. Continue to the end. Crochet two chains and turn the work.

3 Insert the hook into the second chain from the hook. Work double (US single) crochet without beads to the end, inserting the hook through both loops in the previous row each time. Work two chains and turn the work. Repeat from *.

TREBLE CROCHET (US DOUBLE CROCHET)

Treble (US double) crochet makes a flat fabric with deeper rows of crochet and so the beads are spaced further apart. Larger beads sit on the surface of the crochet on one side and so are added every two rows. Smaller beads and washer style beads sit attractively between the stitches and are added every row. The fabric looks the same back and front.

1 Crochet a chain, adding three chains for turning. *Bring a bead up to the back of the hook. YOH, insert the hook into the fourth chain from the hook. YOH, draw the yarn through the chain only to leave three loops on the hook. YOH, draw the yarn through the first two loops on the hook.

2 YOH, draw the yarn through the last two loops on the hook. Work treble crochet (US double crochet) with a bead in each chain to the end of the row. Crochet three chains and turn the work. Repeat from * adding beads on every row.

CROCHETING IN THE ROUND

There are lots of different circular motifs that can be worked by crocheting in the round. You can either spiral round and round or create a step-up at the end of each round ready to start the next one. To keep the work flat you need to increase (adding more stitches). If you don't increase enough the work will be bowl shaped rather than flat.

This spiral sample (left) uses flat disc beads added every second stitch. You can add a bead every stitch on every round if the beads are small.

If you prefer work in concentric circles (right) it is necessary to step up at the beginning of each round. The height of step up will depend on the stitch you are working, two for double (US single) crochet and three for treble (US double) crochet.

• Make a Spiral

1 Crochet four chains and use a slip stitch to join into a circle. *Work a double (US single) crochet into each chain.

2 In the next round drop a bead down to the hook and work a double (US single) crochet into the first chain, work another double (US single) crochet into the same chain. Repeat these two stitches to the end of the round.

3 Mark the last stitch with a short piece of thread or wire. Repeat from * until the circle is the size required, changing from a plain round to a beaded round and vice versa each time you reach the marker again.

• Create a Step-Up

1 Crochet four chains and use a slip stitch to join into a circle. * To step up crochet two chain and then work a double (US single) crochet into each chain in the circle. Use a slip stitch to join the last stitch to the first.

2 To step up to the next round, crochet two chain. Work two double (US single) crochet stitches into each stitch in the previous round. Then work a slip stitch to join the last and first stitches.

3 On the next round, step up and then work two stitches into each chain, adding a bead on every second stitch. Continue alternating rounds without beads (one stitch into each chain) and rounds with beads (two stitches into each chain).

Bead On

This section covers more complex knitting and crochet techniques and methods, such as single stitch tube crochet, crochet ropes, crocheting with wire, crocheting wire fabric and beaded wire crochet.

◼ SINGLE STITCH TUBE CROCHET

Tubular crochet is a little tricky to learn but it is well worth the effort. The rope is crocheted in rounds of six beads and depending on how the beads are added you can create beautiful spiral patterns with different colours or try a range of different bead sizes for a stunning textured effect. To make the technique as easy as possible to learn, use a stiff thread such as a bonded nylon bead string and work with a contrast colour of beads. Some people advocate repeating six different colours in each round which creates a spiral pattern but I have found that threading the beads in alternating colours, in sets of six beads, means that you know exactly when you have finished a round. To practice, string about 15cm (6in) of beads to make a short length.

The rounds of seed beads stack neatly together to make a densely beaded rope.

1 Using a size 4 bonded nylon bead string, string size 6 beads in groups of six alternating between dark and light beads. Make a slip knot (see page 96) and insert the hook.

TIP PRACTICE WORKING SLIP STITCH ON A FLAT PIECE OF CROCHET SO THAT YOU BECOME COMFORTABLE PULLING THE HOOK THROUGH BOTH LOOPS IN ONE SMOOTH MOVEMENT.

2 Work six chain, inserting a bead on each stitch. Form the beaded chain into a circle with beads on the outside. Insert hook into first beaded chain. Drop a bead down to back of hook so it's on outside of bead ring. YOH and pull thread through both loops on hook in one movement. Take thread through one loop at a time until it's easier to manipulate thread. Work all the way round the base circle, adding a bead in each chain.

3 On the next and subsequent rounds you need to *insert the hook into the thread loop on the left hand side of the next bead in the previous row. This rotates the bead so that the thread is running vertically through the centre and ensures that the beads stay on the outside of the circle.

4 Once the hook is in position to the left of the bead, bring a bead up to the back side of the hook. YOH and pull the thread through both loops in one smooth movement.

5 Repeat from * to complete the next round. If you look from the top into the tube you should see the six dark beads sitting out in a ring with the threads in the middle.

6 Continue adding rounds of beads. After a few rows the pattern becomes more obvious and you can see the way the beads sit on top of one another in a neat brick pattern.

Mobile Phone Pouch & Charm

As many mobile phones have cameras included it is a good idea to protect the lens when you are carrying the phone in your bag or purse. This delightful little crochet pouch is made to measure – the phone fits snugly inside so there is no need for a flap and as a result it is easy to slide the phone in or out. You could also make a pouch for your MP3 player as well. Make a crochet rope bead charm to attach to the phone or on to the pouch instead. Full details of how to make it are on page 172.

CROCHET ROPES

Beaded ropes are easy to make with crochet. You can simply crochet chains or create loops on a chain to make gorgeous textural jewellery but the most spectacular ropes use a tubular technique that creates a firm rope completely covered in beads.

CROCHET STRAP

You can simply crochet a single chain adding beads with every stitch but treble (US double) crochet makes a super strap with beads visible on both sides.

1 String beads onto the yarn. Work chain the length of strap required. Crochet three turning chain. Bring a bead down to the hook, YOH, work a treble (US double) crochet into the third chain from the hook. Work along the chain working a treble with bead on each stitch.

2 Crochet one chain and turn the work. Work slip stitch crochet down the other side to finish the strap.

CHAIN LOOP CROCHET

This gorgeous rope has loops of beads suspended from a centre core of crochet. It is easy to work and by stringing different beads you can create a wide range of designs.

1 String the beads onto the thread in the order required. This sample has size 6 seed beads in two alternating colours. Make a slip knot on the end of the thread. Bring the first six beads down to the hook, YOH and pull the thread through the loop on the hook.

2 Bring the second set of beads down to the hook, YOH and pull the thread through. Make sure you pull the thread taut after each stitch so that the rope is fairly tight.

3 Continue bringing down six beads at a time and working a single chain to join each loop. When the rope is the length required cut the yarn with a tail and pull through the last loop. Attach a fastening at each end using the tails.

▉ CROCHET WITH WIRE

Crocheting with wire is easy as you only use basic stitches but it is extremely satisfying because the finished results are so stunning.

You can create fine beaded chain, wire fabric of all shapes and sizes and pretty circular forms that make gorgeous earrings.

BEAD CHAIN

This is the easiest technique as it only uses chain stitch but it is versatile as you can add any sort of bead and either incorporate the beads every stitch or spaced down the chain. Several chains together make a stunning necklace.

1 Pick up beads on 0.315mm (30swg) wire. Make a slip knot and insert the hook. The hook should be large compared to the thickness of the wire, try size 2.5mm. Crochet three chains and bring a bead down to the hook.

2 YOH on the other side of the bead and pull the wire through the loop on the hook. *Crochet three chains and then add a bead on the next chain. Repeat from * until the chain is the length required.

WHEELS

Crochet wheels are ideal for making earrings, brooches or an embellishment. This simple wheel has only one round but you can work a second round to make a larger embellishment.

1 Pick up beads on 0.315mm (30swg) wire. Make a slip knot and insert the size 2.5mm hook. Crochet four chain and join the ends in a circle with a slip knot (see page 96).

2 Crochet three chain to create the step up ready for working a round of treble (US double) crochet. Bring a bead down to the hook, YOH and pass the hook through the crocheted wire circle. YOH again and bring the wire through two loops.

3 YOH again and bring the wire through the remaining two loops. Treble (US double) crochet through the crocheted wire circle between 15 and 20 times depending on the size of beads. Use a slip stitch (see page 142) to join the last stitch to the first stitch.

▉ CROCHETING WIRE FABRIC

When adding beads to crocheted wire the same rules apply as for crocheting with yarn. With double (US single) crochet, the beads are added on every second row whereas with treble (US double) crochet they are generally visible from both sides.

1 Pick up beads on the wire. Work chain the length required adding two chains for turning. On the first row it is easier to crochet into the single wire loop on each chain. Take the hook into the second chain from the hook, YOH and pull through the first loop.

2 YOH and pull through both loops on the hook. Work double (US single) crochet in each chain. At the end of the row work two chains and then turn the work.

3 On the next row, work double (US single) crochet without beads. This time take the hook under two wires at the top of each stitch in the previous row.

Taking It Further

The techniques covered so far in this chapter are fairly basic, but if you would like to develop your skills a little further, why not try French knitting or filet crochet? French knitting is a tubular knitting technique that makes versatile wire or thread mesh; filet crochet is used to make mesh or more ornate shaping in flat or tubular crochet.

FRENCH KNITTING

French knitting is a great way to create long tubes of knitting that can be embellished with beads. You can work on a simple cotton reel with four or six nails hammered in around the top or use a French knitting nancy. Crank style tools also allow you to create long tubes quickly. Add beads inside or thread small beads onto the wire before knitting to create simple jewellery. Plain wire can also be flattened and twisted to create interesting textures that can be embellished with beads.

1 Using the wire straight off the reel, pass it over the guide and down through the centre of the knitting tool. Make a loop on the end and attach a weight. To cast on turn the handle so that the wire goes into the first hook, misses the second, goes into the third and misses the last hook.

2 Add more weights to the wire loop and hold so that the weights hand down freely. Continue turning the handle, making sure the wire goes into each hook. The previous loop must always go below the latch on the hook as you create a new stitch otherwise the knitting will cast off.

3 You can add beads inside the tube as you knit. Make sure the beads will fit easily through the centre hole and then simply push down into the knitted tube. You can space them evenly by sight or by turning the handle a set number of times.

FILET CROCHET

In filet crochet you create a mesh where some areas are solid and others are open. Working with basic stitches you can create a wide range of effects by grouping stitches together and creating gaps.

1 Create gaps in a row of treble (US double) crochet to make basic filet crochet. Work a group of three treble into the base chain and then work a single chain. Miss a stitch on the base chain and work the next treble into the next stitch along. Increase the gap size by crocheting two or three chain and missing the same number of stitches on the base chain.

2 The groups don't always need to be square. Make triangle shaped blocks and gaps by working three stitches into one hole. Miss a hole and work three stitches into the next hole and so on.

3 Use the different heights of crochet stitches to make a picot edge. Either work into one hole or make longer holes with chain as shown. Work a double crochet (US single), treble crochet and double treble through the chain loop, then treble again and finish with a double. To work double treble, put the YOH twice before working the first stitch and work like treble until back to one stitch on the hook.

Bead Something Now

The projects on the following pages are interspersed among the techniques in the main chapters of the book. Each project relates to a particular set of skills so, if something catches your eye, it is a good idea to look back at the appropriate page to refresh your memory or learn the appropriate techniques so that you can make the project with ease.

CHAPTER 1:

Bead Loom Weaving

Bugle Bracelet (page 25)

This simple bead loom bracelet is made from two different types of beads that fit together beautifully in alternate rows because they are both the same width. The bugles and hex beads give the bracelet a lovely texture, reminiscent of a bamboo mat. Use two different shades of bugle to create the mottled appearance.

YOU WILL NEED:

- Purple iris matt, lilac satin and white satin bugles, 3mm, 5g of each
- Silver-lined clear, hex beads, 3mm, 5g
- Nymo™ or Super-lon™ thread
- Size 10 beading needle
- 24mm bar ends and fastening
- Bead loom
- Flat-nose pliers
- Glue
- Scissors

1 Set up the bead loom with eight 45cm (18in) individual warp threads so that the threads are about 3mm (⅛in) apart. Tie the weft thread to a side thread about 15cm (6in) from one end (see page 22).

2 Mix the different short bugles on the beading mat and pick up seven in a random order. Position the bugles under the warp threads and take the needle back through the beads so that it passes over the warp threads.

3 Weave six rows of bugle beads and then pick up seven hex beads and weave as before. Continue adding rows of bugle beads and hex beads to create a random pattern. Work the bead band about 15cm (6in) long or to suit your wrist measurement.

4 Weave thread across both ends of the bracelet (see page 23) and then take off the loom. Tie the thread ends together in pairs and trim.

5 Open a bar clasp and apply a little bead glue inside. Position the end row of beads inside the teeth and tuck in any stray threads. Apply a little more glue and then carefully close the bar clasp with flat-nose pliers. Repeat at the other end. *The quantity of beads shown is for a 75mm diameter candle.*

Beaded Candle Border (page 28)

This delightful bead panel looks equally attractive wrapped round a candle or draped around your wrist as a cuff-style bracelet. The loop edging is worked while the bead work is on the loom and you don't need a pattern as you simply change the number of beads you pick up by one on each row to create the zig zag pattern.

YOU WILL NEED:

- Ice blue triangle beads, size 10, 20g
- Deep blue triangle beads, size 10, 5g
- Silver-lined clear, triangle beads, size 10, 10g
- Organza ribbon, 1m (39in)
- Five painted metal flower beads
- Scissors
- Thread needle
- Pins
- Glue

1 Set up the bead loom with 20, 60cm (24in) individual warp threads. Tie the weft thread to a side thread about 15cm (6in) from one end (see page 21).

2 Pick up 19 ice blue triangle beads. Position the beads under the warp threads and take the needle back through the beads so that it passes over the warp threads. Work a bead panel long enough to fit around your candle, allowing a 1cm (½in) gap between the ends.

3 Use the current thread or add a new length so that the thread merges from the last bead. Pick up six silver-lined (s-l) triangle beads and a deep blue triangle bead. Take the needle back through the last five beads on the next row, towards the edge, so that the beads sit on the surface of the work. Pick up five s-l beads and a deep blue bead and take the needle back through the last four beads on the next row.

4 Continue picking up four s-l beads and a deep blue bead and go through the last three beads. Then pick up three s-l beads and a deep blue bead and go through the last two beads on the next row.

5 Continue adding looped edging by picking up three s-l beads next row and increase by one bead each row until you are back at six s-l beads. Continue along the edge with the zig zag loop edging. Work a matching design along the opposite edge so that the peaks of the triangles are on the same row on both sides.

6 Weave thread across both ends of the bead band (see page 23) and take off the loom. Tie the thread ends in pairs and trim. Spread a thin layer of beading glue over the woven bands and fold back onto the bead band on the reverse side.

7 Arrange the flower beads along the panel and mark their position with a pin at the edge. Sew the beads on by bringing a double thread up through the bead panel, picking up a flower bead and a small triangle bead. Take the needle through the flower bead again to the reverse side. Sew through a bead several times on the reverse side to secure thread and then attach the other flower beads in the same way.

8 Cut a piece of paper to fit just inside the bead panel. Stick a piece of organza ribbon down the centre and then stick the bead panel on top. Tie around the candle.

Evening Bag (page 31)

One of the delights of designing is marrying different textures together so that each component looks even more stunning than before. This design uses three different textures in the beads, wool and buckle that are all similar shades. I chose the buckle first and then found a ball of yarn to match and finally picked beads to tone in. Use wool that knits on the same size of needles so that the finished size of the bag is still 18 × 10cm (7 × 4in).

YOU WILL NEED:

- Mix of seed beads, size 10, approx 30g
- Triangle beads, size 5, 5g
- One ball of chunky wool with silky ribbon running through
- Size 6.5mm (10½) knitting needles
- Large buckle with a 35mm (1⅜in) slot
- Scissors
- Craft glue dots
- Pins

1 To knit the bag: Cast on 18 stitches and knit 1 row. Increase one stitch at both ends of the next five rows. Knit four rows without increasing.

2 *Decrease one stitch at the beginning of the next two rows then knit one row without decreasing. Repeat from *twice. Decrease at the beginning of every row until you have 16 stitches. Cast off.

3 Knit a second panel the same size. Sew the bag together around the curved sides and sew in any ends. Plait three 50cm (20in) lengths of yarn and tie an overhand knot (see page 17), 10cm (4in) from each end. To plait, tape the yarn on to a work surface 10cm (4in) from one end. Start with one of the outer yarns, it doesn't matter which side. Cross it over the two yarns next to it and into the middle. Do the same with the outer yarn from the other side. Keep going from side to side, crossing the outer yarns into the middle of the other two yarns, until you are 10cm (4in) from the end of the yarn. Sew the ends into the side seams to attach/form the handle.

4 To bead the panel: Set up a loom with 16, 45cm (18in) warp threads. Tie a weft thread to the warp threads, about 15cm (6in) from one end. Mix the size 10 seed beads on the bead mat and pick up 15 beads. Position the beads under the warp threads and then pass the needle back through over the warp threads. Work a panel 7cm (2¾in) long.

5 Add a further 22 warp threads on either side of the bead panel. You can either take the beading off the loom off and restring with the new threads or add the extra threads using the single warp method (see page 21). You need to add sufficient threads to work another 7cm (2¾in) beading, following the instructions from step 6 onwards.

6 Work the next row, increasing a bead at each end (see page 30). Continue until the beading is five beads wide. Work four rows straight and lift the bead panel off the loom (see page 25).

7 Using a half hitch knot (see page 17) each time, sew in the ends along the diagonal sides and around the buckle strap. Join a new thread at the top of one diagonal side coming out of the first bead after the last four straight rows.

8 To work the stacked picot edge (see page 27), *pick up a seed bead, a large triangle bead and a seed bead. Take the needle back through the triangle and first seed. Feed the needle through the next bead at the edge of the bead panel. Repeat from *.

9 Around the buckle strap, add the picot beads by taking the beading needle through all beads from side to side and working a picot at each side alternately. Finally continue the stacked fringe down the other diagonal.

10 Pin the bag panel along the back edge of the bag. Sew each individual warp thread into the bag, using half hitches (see page 17) for security. Trim ends. Feed the beading through the top half of the buckle. To prevent the strap from slipping, attach a few glue dots along the bar of the buckle then tuck the beaded strap through.

YOU WILL NEED:

- Space dyed mixed yarns – ten, 2m (2¼yd) lengths
- Colour-lined lime and chartreuse AB, triangle beads, size 10, 5g of each
- Cube beads, 4mm
- Nymo™ or Super-lon™ thread
- Bead loom
- Scissors

Medallion Belt (page 33)

Interesting packs of mixed yarns are available from embroidery suppliers. Choose bead colours to tone in with the yarns. If you can't find triangle beads, use seed beads instead, so long as two threaded side by side are the same width as the cube beads.

1 Cut ten, 2m (2¼yd) lengths of mixed yarns. Tie an overhand knot (see page 17), about 15cm (6in) from one end of the yarn and hook over the pin on the bead loom. Wind the dowel ready to begin the first bead panel about 30cm (12in) from the end of the yarn.

2 Space the threads every 4mm (scant ¼in) and secure on the other side of the loom. Cut a long length of matching Nymo™ or similar and knot to the fourth warp thread in from the edge.

3 To work the first half of the bead motifs: Pick up six mixed triangle beads and position under the warp threads so that there are two beads between the four centre threads. Take the needle back through the beads over the warp threads.

4 Increase two beads at each end on the next two rows of triangle beads. Work one row then increase at each end of the next row and work a final row. Add nine cube beads on the next row.

5 For the second side of the circle motif, work two rows of triangle beads, then decrease by two beads at each end of the next row and work two rows. Decrease two beads at each end of the next two rows. Sew in the weft thread ends.

6 Lift the 'belt' off the loom and untie the first knot. Retie so that the knot sits about 3cm (1¼in) from the bead motif. Hook this knot over the pin on the loom and set up the loom again. Measure 10cm (4in) from the last bead motif and tie a thread on the fourth warp thread in again. Make a second bead motif.

7 Lift the belt off the loom and tie a knot between the bead motifs. Continue using the new knot to secure the beading. Ten bead motifs will make a 90cm (1yd) length plus loose ends for tying. Tie the threads at each end to match the other knots and trim as required.

CHAPTER 2:

Off Loom Bead Stitches

Little Bags (page 34)

The little bags were made to inspire you to try off-loom bead stitches but as it is not obvious how to make them from the photograph we have included brief instructions for each bag below. Choose your favourite off loom stitches and enjoy making one or more of these delightful designs. You will need Nymo™ or Super-lon™ beading thread to make up each design.

ZIGZAG BAG

YOU WILL NEED:

- Seed beads, size 11, frosted apricot, frosted burnt orange, transparent topaz AB

To create the peyote stitch bag, pick up three burnt orange seed beads and one apricot seed bead six times. Pick up another burnt orange seed bead and go through the third bead from the end. Pick up a topaz seed bead first to work the next row. Alternate between burnt orange and topaz seed beads to the end. On the next row, add a topaz seed bead each time; on the next row alternate between topaz and apricot seed beads, then a row all apricot. Continue the zigzag pattern to create a square approximately 4 x 4cm (1½ x 1½in) Fold the square in half and sew the side seams adding link beads to fill the gaps. Add a picot edge with rainbow beads around the top of the bag and finish with a four-bead cable stitch strap.

POLKA DOT BAG

YOU WILL NEED:

- Matte turquoise, frosted burnt orange and frosted cream seed beads, size 11

Pick up 16 burnt orange seed beads then two turquoise seed beads. Work square stitch into the last two burnt orange beads. Continue along adding two turquoise beads at a time. The next row is frosted cream beads with the odd burnt orange. On the next row, to increase, pick up three frosted cream beads and work into the last two beads of the previous row. Continue to the end of the row; add three beads on the last pair (18 beads). Work one row. Increase at each end of the next row (20 beads). Work three rows. Increase at each end of the next row (22 beads). Work one row. Make a second panel exactly the same for the back of the bag. Join the bottom seams together with square stitch. Sew the side seams by oversewing through the thread loops. Attach a thread to the top of one side and pick up enough beads for a handle. Sew into the opposite side and take the thread back through the handle to reinforce. Sew end in securely.

SHOPPING BAG

YOU WILL NEED:

- Seed beads, size 11, silver-lined and matte turquoise, frosted burnt orange

Use 36, 8mm bugles to make a ladder stitch band to begin the brick stitch shopping basket. Work brick stitch in sand coloured beads for two rounds. On the next seven rounds decrease one bead on opposite sides of the tube to create the basket shape. On the third, fourth and fifth rounds create the plum/teal diamonds. To make the base, work a 6-bead ladder stitch band and then one row of brick stitch all round to make a long oval. Sew into the base oval. Join a thread into the bead fabric and work a row of straw colour brick stitch around the top edge. Weave the thread through ready to add the handle. Pick up sufficient beads and take the needle back through the ladder stitch border. Reinforce by going back through and then add a matching handle on the other side.

SHOULDER BAG

YOU WILL NEED:

- Silver-lined and matte turquoise, frosted burnt orange seed beads, size 11

Pick up a s-l bead, a matte bead, a s-l and a matte bead, tie in a circle and go back through them to come out the opposite side to the tail. Work five units in a line, then work twelve rows. Fold the panel in half and use the tubular technique (see page 61) to join the side and bottom edges. Join in a new thread at the top of one side and work a cable stitch strap alternating between burnt orange and matte turquoise for the side beads. Embellish the top edge by sewing a burnt orange bead across each unit.

NET FLAP BAG

YOU WILL NEED:

- Frosted cream, transparent topaz AB seed beads, size 11

To begin the netting, pick up a topaz and a cream bead. Repeat until there are 20 pairs in all. Go back through the fourth topaz bead from the end. Pick up a cream, a topaz and a cream bead and go through next but one topaz along. Continue to the end. Pick up five beads in order then turn. Work netting for 4cm (1½in). Change to topaz beads and continue for another 12mm (½in). Fold the bag up and sew the side seams by stitching the topaz beads together. Bring the thread out at the top of one side and pick up topaz beads for a strap. Sew into the opposite side and take the thread back through the strap to reinforce. Sew in the ends and secure with half hitches.

BUCKET BAG

YOU WILL NEED:

- Teal metal iris matte seed beads, size 11
- Light blue bugle beads, 2mm

To make the base, pick up six seed beads and tie into a circle. Add one seed bead between each, then add two between each in the next round. In the next round work herringbone stitch into the pairs of beads and add a bead between each stitch. In the next row add two beads between each stitch, then work herringbone all round. Work ordinary herringbone, pulling the stitches tight so that the sides stand straight. Work three rounds with short bugles, three rounds with seed beads and two rounds with short bugles. On the next round decrease by working *two herringbone stitches and then add one bead on the next stack. Repeat from * all the way round; on the next round work across the gap. To finish the top edge, add a single bead on each stack. Take the needle down to the top of the last band of bugles. Pick up beads to create a strap and secure at the opposite side. Go back through to strengthen the strap and sew in the ends.

CLUTCH BAG

YOU WILL NEED:

- Frosted cream seed beads, size 11
- Green matte AB bugles, 3mm (size 1)

Working in two-drop odd-count peyote stitch, pick up 18 cream seed beads. Pick up a bugle and pass it through the third and fourth seed beads from the end. Miss two seed beads and add a bugle, repeat to the end. Tie the thread ends together and pass the needle back through the end bugle. Pick up a bugle between each bugle. Continue working two-drop odd-count peyote stitch – four rows of bugles and two rows of seed beads until there are six zigzag lines of seed beads. Work seven rows of bugles and then decrease at each end of every row until only one bugle remains in the middle. Sew in the thread ends. Fold the bag up and sew bugles across to create the side panels. Sew five cream beads in a circle to make a small flower shape and sew to the flap. Add a loop of cream beads to one side for a carrying handle.

CLASSIC HANDBAG

YOU WILL NEED:

- Matte turquoise seed beads, size 11
- Silver-lined turquoise seed beads, size 10
- Green matte AB bugles, 3mm (size 1)

Sew 41 short bugles together with ladder stitch. Join the ends together to make a tube (see page 40). Work the next row in brick stitch using the bugles again. Change to size 11 matt turquoise seed beads and work two rounds. You will need to miss the occasional thread loop, as only around thirty seed beads will fit on to the bugle band. Work a round with silver-lined turquoise seed beads. On the next round, in matt turquoise, decrease one bead at each side of the flattened tube. Work one round matt turquoise and then the last round with the short bugles again. Pull the thread tight as you work to shape the top edge. Bring the thread out at the top of a bugle ready to add the handle. Pick up beads and then sew back down through a bugle. Go back through the handle to reinforce. Add a similar handle to the other side. To create the base, sew bugles across the bottom of the flattened tube.

Square Stitch Bracelet (page 39)

Although these top quality seed beads have quite large holes it is essential to use a fine beading needle (size 13) as thread passes through each bead several times. If you are choosing your own beads make sure two seed beads side by side are the same width as the cube beads as sizes vary between manufacturers.

YOU WILL NEED:

- Steel gold iris cube, 28, 3mm
- Gold lustre green tea Toho seed beads, 2g, size 11
- Rainbow metal matte Toho seed beads, 5g, size 11
- Pale creamy yellow round glass beads, 3, 12mm
- 5 hole bar clasp, gold-plated
- Super-lon™ beading thread in dark gold
- Bead stop spring
- Beading needle, size 13

1 Pick up seven steel gold iris cube beads on a 3m (3yd) length of beading thread and drop down to the middle. Secure the beads one side with a bead stop spring. Thread a long fine beading needle on the other end.

2 Pick up two gold lustre seed beads and pass the needle through the first cube bead again, then through the seed beads again. Continue working two-drop square stitch with these beads to the end of the row. Pass the needle back through the cube beads and the row just worked.

3 Change to the matte rainbow beads and work four rows of square stitch. On the next three rows decrease by two beads at each end to leave two beads. Bring the thread out between the two beads. Remove the stop spring from the other end and thread with a needle. Work the other side to match.

4 Make a second panel exactly the same then work two panels with only one pointed side. Join the two large panels together by picking up a gold lustre seed bead, a large round bead and another seed bead. Take the thread through the two seed beads at the top of the second panels and then weave through the bead fabric and secure with one or two half hitches (see page 17).

5 Take the thread from the other side and pass through the beads just added and secure in the bead fabric. Join an end panel to each side in the same way. Check the size of the bracelet and add extra rows at each end if required before attaching the bar fastening.

Brick Stitch Rosettes (page 43)

Swarovski crystals add a touch of class to this pretty embellishment but you could use faceted glass beads or even round beads in the same diameter as the crystals to make a less expensive but equally stunning design. Take care spacing the larger beads so that they have plenty of room otherwise the medallion will buckle rather than lie flat.

YOU WILL NEED:

- Wine round crushed glass bead, 2, 10mm
- Raspberry bronze iris seed beads, 5g, size 11
- Rose Swarovski bicone crystals, 28, 4mm and 32, 6mm
- Nymo™ thread – wine or black
- Beading needle

1 Thread the beading needle with a long length of Nymo™ thread. Take the needle through the hole in the large round bead twice and then tie the tail to the main thread with a reef knot so that the knot ends up next to the hole.

2 Ease the threads round so that there is a thread on opposite sides of the round bead. Work brick stitch along the threads with seed beads. Begin by picking up two seed beads and then continue adding one each time. Take the thread through the first and last beads to complete the circle.

3 Add two small crystals to begin the next round of brick stitch, missing some loops so that the crystals are spaced evenly. Add single crystals thereafter and join the last to the first as before.

4 Work another round of brick stitch with the seed beads and then a round of crystals adding 16 large crystals.

5 To work the picot edge pick up three seed beads and take the needle back through the last seed bead added and pull up to create the picot. Continue in brick stitch alternating between adding one seed bead and then two seed beads, taking the needle through the second seed bead only all the way round. Sew in the thread ends. Make a second rosette in the same way and attach to your shoes by sewing or using strong glue.

Herringbone Tealight (page 47)

This pretty dish is made to measure to fit a tealight 38mm (1½in) in diameter and 17mm (¾in) high but you can easily adjust the size to suit your particular tealight or candle. Work the circular base so that it is one round of beads larger than the tealight and then stop increasing to create the sides.

YOU WILL NEED:

- Purple teal lustre, steel blue metallic triangle beads, size 10
- Emerald raspberry gold lustre seed beads, size 11
- Super-lon™ beading thread
- Beading needle
- Scissors

1 Pick up six purple lustre triangles and tie in a circle. Pick up one purple lustre triangle between each of the beads in the circle and then on the next round add two purple lustre triangles between each bead.

2 On the next round work herringbone stitch, with purple lustre beads, adding a metallic triangle between each stitch. On the next round add two metallic triangles between each herringbone stitch (24 beads) Work one round herringbone stitch keeping the colour sequence.

3 On the next round continue the herringbone stitch, adding a purple lustre triangle between each herringbone stitch all the way round. On the next round pick up two purple lustre beads both sides of the herringbone stitches. For the final round on the base circle work herringbone all the way round. You should have 48 beads.

4 On the next round work a purple lustre herringbone, then a metallic herringbone all the way round. For extra embellishment each time you work a purple lustre herringbone, pick up a small raspberry seed bead between the two triangle beads and work the stitch as normal. Continue working herringbone stitch without increasing for 10 rounds.

5 On the next round add a small seed bead between each herringbone stitch. On the next round add two seed beads and then three seed beads in the third round.

6 Work round the top row of herringbone stitch adding four floating beads between each herringbone stitch and a single seed bead at the top of each nickel stack to match the top bead on the rainbow stacks. Sew in the thread end to finish.

Peyote Stitch Rings (page 50)

These pretty rings are made with peyote stitch, but could be worked in brick stitch too. In brick stitch you would work the band lengthways whereas peyote stitch is worked back and forwards across the width making it easier to adjust the size of the ring. The ring can be embellished as you work or once the band is completed.

YOU WILL NEED:

- Nymo™ thread
- Beading needle

FRILLY RING

- Rainbow metal matte seed beeds, 5g, size 11
- Silver-lined rose seed beads, 2g, size 9

PINK RING

- Pale pink and dark pink short bugles, 5g, 2mm
- Multi iris drop beads, 12, 3 × 4mm

SPIKY RING

- Emerald raspberry gold lustre seed beads, 5g, size 11
- Dark pink short bugles, 2g, 2mm

FRILLY RING

1 Pick up six matt rainbow seed beads for the first two rows. To begin the third row, pick up another seed bead and take the needle through the second bead from the end (see page 48). Continue adding beads to work an even-count peyote stitch band long enough for a ring. This will be about 6cm (2⅜in) depending on the size of your finger.

2 Bring the ends together – the beads should lock together neatly although it may be necessary to add or take away a row to get the right bead sequence. Take the thread back and forwards across the gap to 'zip' the beads together then sew in the ends securely.

3 To make the frilly circular peyote stitch, pick up three silver-lined beads and take the needle back through the beads to make a circle. Pick up a s-l bead between each of these three beads. Continue working rounds (see page 51), to make a circle about 15mm (⅝in) in diameter. To create a slightly frilly circle squeeze in beads as you near the finished size. Pick up a matt rainbow bead between each bead in the final round and sew in the ends.

4 Bring a thread out in the middle of the frilly circle at the end of one of the three centre beads. Pick up ten matt rainbow beads and take the needle back through the centre bead from the other end. Add a loop of beads over each centre bead. Add two more loops in the very centre. Sew the embellishment to the ring band and sew in the thread ends securely.

PINK BAND

1 Begin with four dark pink beads and then work the next two rows in pale pink. Repeat these two rows to make the even-count peyote stitch ring band. Join the ends but don't sew in the tail.

2 Take the tail thread through the adjacent bugle on the edge. Pick up a drop bead on the tail thread and take a backstitch through the bugle and then take the needle through a bugle in the next row in from the edge, which is slightly offset. Pick up a second drop bead and work a backstitch through that bugle. Add two more drop beads in the same way.

3 Continue working back and forwards across the ring band to add three more rows of drop beads. Sew in the ends to finish.

SPIKY RING

1 Pick up eight lustre seed beads and work an even count peyote stitch band long enough for a ring and join the ends together as above.

2 Take the thread through beads to come out in the middle of the band. Pick up three short bugles and a rainbow seed. Take the needle back through the bugles only then bring it out one bead across. Add another two fringe strands with three bugles along the centre of the ring band.

3 Work your way around the three long strands creating strands with only two short bugles and a seed bead. Finally add single bugle bead strands on the outside. Sew in the thread ends.

Beaded Bauble (page 54)

This gorgeous design is designed to fit a 5.5cm (2⅛in) bauble but it is often tricky making sure that the beaded netting fits snugly around baubles as your beads may be a slightly different size. If the netting appears to be tight add one or more extra seed beads both sides of each accent bead when you sew the motifs together.

YOU WILL NEED:

- Gold seed beads, size 10 (2mm), 15g
- Gold seed beads, size 8 (2.6mm), 15g
- Textured gold metal beads, 30, 6mm and six 8mm
- 5.5cm gold bauble
- Nymo™ thread
- Beading needle

1 To make a six-pointed netting star to fit over the top of the bauble, pick up a large seed bead and two small seed beads; repeat until there are 12 large seed beads. Tie in a circle and take the needle back through the large seed bead.

2 For the second round, *pick up three small seed beads, a large seed bead and three small seed beads. Miss a large seed bead and pass the needle through the next large seed bead in the circle. Repeat from * all the way round. Sew in the thread ends.

3 Make 12 five-pointed stars in the same way by picking up a large seed bead and two small seed beads and repeating until there are only 10 large seed beads this time. Work the second round of netting as before and sew in the thread ends.

4 Join a new thread on the six-pointed star and bring out at a point. Pick up a 6mm gold bead pass the needle through a large seed bead on the point of a five-pointed star. Take the needle back through the 6mm gold bead and back through the large seed bead.

5 Feed the needle through the beads to the next point on the six-pointed star. Add another five-pointed star in the same way. Repeat to add a star to each of the six points.

6 Join all the five pointed stars together with more 6mm gold beads. Lay the netting mesh as flat as possible and position a five-pointed star between each of the stars in the previous round. Sew the points together as before with 6mm gold beads. Finally join the remaining side points of the last round together with the 6mm beads.

7 To make the fringe, attach a thread and bring it out at one point at the bottom of the bauble. Pick up three small seed beads and a large seed bead twice. Pick up an 8mm gold bead, a large seed bead and a small seed bead. Take the needle back through the large seed bead and the remaining beads.

8 Go through the large seed bead at the top in the opposite direction and then take the needle through the beads to the next point along. Attach a fringe strand to each of the six bottom points to finish the bauble. String with pretty ribbon or cord to hang.

Butterfly Necklace (page 60)

Bead weaving can be a bit of a challenge but when you complete this beautiful beaded butterfly it will all seem worthwhile! As it is such a gorgeous design use genuine Swarovski crystals to add extra quality and sparkle. Follow the diagram below, referring to page 59 for detailed instructions on bead weaving.

YOU WILL NEED:

- Light peach Swarovski bicone crystals, 58, 4mm
- Indicolite Swarovski bicone crystals, 20, 6mm and eight 4mm
- Matt turquoise faceted beads, 6mm, 12
- Turquoise transparent, faceted beads, eight, 6mm
- Matt peach faceted beads, 26, 6mm
- Light sea foam AB seed beads, size 8
- Illusion beading thread, 0.3mm, clear
- Two clamshells, silver-plated
- Silver-plated necklace fastening

1 Beginning where indicated on the diagram*, pick up a peach matt faceted bead and drop down to the middle of a 1.5m (1.5yd) length of beading thread. Add a 4mm peach crystal to each thread end. Pass one thread back through the other crystal. Follow the diagram to create the body of the butterfly.

2 Using the thread coming out at the bottom right of the motif, pick up the beads to make the right side of the bottom wing. Miss the seed bead and pass the thread back through the next three beads. Pick up the remaining beads to complete the bottom wing. Follow the diagram to complete the top wing out to the 6mm matt bead.

3 Add another thread to the left hand bottom bead on the butterfly body and work the second side to match. Tie off and sew in the thread ends.

4 To create the necklace feed a 1m (1yd) thread through the matt turquoise bead at the top of each wing. Pull through until the ends are level. Pick up a 4mm peach crystal on each end and then thread both ends through a facetted matt peach bead. Pick up a 4mm crystal on each end again.

5 Work right angle weave to add the turquoise beads and the 4mm peach crystals. Working with both threads together, pick up the sequence of beads as shown. Make the second side of the necklace to match. Attach a clamshell calotte to each end, trim the threads, and close the calottes. Attach a fastening.

6mm peach matt faceted
4mm light peach crystal
6mm indicolite crystal
4mm indicolite crystal
6mm turquoise matt
6mm turquoise transparent
Size 8 light sea foam AB seed

* Start point

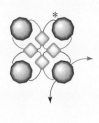

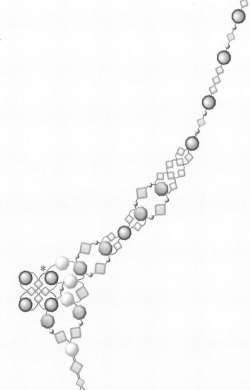

CHAPTER 3:

Ropes and Cords

Spiral Bag (page 66)

A spiral rope makes a really gorgeous handle for this pretty little bag. Choose beads that match one of the colours in the fabric so that the elements of the design work together. This gorgeous fabric is stretchy and has cut-out holes and so has been backed with the same silk as used for the lining. If you choose a lightweight or jersey fabric, stick the two layers together using fusible bonding web and then cut out and work as one fabric.

YOU WILL NEED:

- Fabric 20 x 40cm (8 × 16in)
- Lining 20 x 40cm (16 × 16in)
- Teal matte turquoise beads, size 6, 5g
- Blue-lined triangles, size 11, 5g
- Dark brown seeds, size 11, 2g
- Turquoise washer beads, six
- Brown flat oval beads, 8 × 6mm, three
- Nymo™ thread
- Beading needle
- Sewing thread
- Scissors
- Sewing machine
- Tailor tacks
- Pins

1 To make the spiral bead handle, pick up four dark brown (db) seed beads and this three-bead sequence; a triangle, a size 6 seed bead and a triangle onto Nymo™ thread. Tie in a circle, leaving a long tail, and take the needle back through the four db seed beads again.

2 Pick up one db seed bead and the three-bead sequence. Take the needle through the last three db seed beads on the spiral. Pull the thread up and then take the needle through the last db seed bead.

3 Repeat step 2 to add a second loop of beads. Continue repeating step 2, making sure that the loops lie right next to each other. After four or five repeats the spiral effect will be quite obvious. Join new threads and secure the ends. Continue until the rope is about 20cm (8in) long and leave a tail at both ends.

4 Draw a 17.5cm (7in) square lightly in pencil. Draw a line across 4.5cm (1¾in) from the top edge. Mark a dot 2.5cm (1in) in from each side on the line just added and another dot 1.5cm (⅝in) in from the top corners. Join the dots at each side to create the flap. Draw a line from the bottom corner to the dots on the added line to create the bag shape.

5 Draw the outline of the whole template and trace the flap separately, then cut out both templates. Layer the lining with the fabric and pin the pattern pieces in place. Cut out, leaving a 1.5cm (⅝in) seam allowance all round. Mark the dots on the added line with tailor tacks and then separate the layers. Pin the lining and fabric flaps together with right sides facing. Sew around the flap between the dots and reverse stitch at both ends. Snip into the dots, then trim the seam allowance around the flap. Turn through and ease out the corners.

6 Sew the top edge of the fabric and lining bag sections and press the seam open. Pin the two sections together and sew around the edge reverse stitching at each end. Trim the seams.

7 Pin the two lining bag sections together. You need to fold the flap edges in so that they don't get caught in the sewing machine. Sew the seams, leaving a gap across the bottom of the lining. Trim the seams and turn the bag through the hole in the lining.

8 Sew across the gap in the lining and tuck inside the bag. Press the flap and the bag. Pick up two db seed beads, a washer bead, a large brown bead, a washer bead and a flat oval on one tail of the rope. Sew the thread through at the top of the side seam and then back through the beads just added. Secure the thread in the spiral rope. Repeat to attach the handle to the other side. Attach a thread to the centre of the flap. Pick up a washer bead, a large brown bead, a washer bead, a flat oval and a db seed bead. Miss the seed bead and take the thread back up through the other beads. Secure the thread end in the fabric.

Cellini Spiral Beads Necklace (page 70)

Tubular stitches do not have to be made into long ropes – you can make shorter lengths as beaded beads. Begin with a simple peyote stitch tube for a few rounds and then change to the three different sizes of beads to create a feature spiral in the middle and then go back to the plain peyote stitch to complete the bead.

YOU WILL NEED:

- Gold delicas, matte, 5g
- Gold beads, size 6, 10g
- Red rainbow triangles, size 11, 10g
- Gold ice pearls, 40, 8mm
- Red/orange glass beads, four, 12mm
- Nymo™ or Super-lon™ thread
- Beading needle
- Scissors
- Beading cord
- Big eye or twisted wire needles
- Two calottes
- Necklace fastening

1 Pick up 16 delicas and go through all beads and the first two delica beads again to form a circle. Work three more rows of peyote stitch (see page 69). You'll begin to work the cellini spiral by introducing different beads. You can work around a mandrel (see page 64) if it is more comfortable.

2 On the next round, once you have stepped up, add a delica on the next three stitches. Then add a size 11 triangle bead on the next two stitches. On the next stitch add a size 6 gold bead and then add a size 11 triangle bead on the next two stitches.

3 Step up through the next two delicas ready to begin the next round. Repeat the same sequence of beads each round, remembering that you are adding the same bead as you have just passed through each time.

4 Continue the cellini spiral until there are 20, size 6 gold beads. Add the next two size 11 triangles as normal and step up through the next two delicas. Work five rows of delicas to make a band the same size as at the bottom end. Make another two spiral beads.

5 To make the necklace thread a big eye or twisted wire needle on each end of a 40cm (16in) length of beading cord. Pick up one of the cellini spiral beads. Pick up about nine pebble beads, or similar, to fit inside the spiral. These should fill the space inside the tubular bead and hold it centrally positioned on the thread.

6 Add an 8mm ice gold bead then a size 6 gold bead. Repeat twice more. Pick up a 12mm bead and then reverse the 8mm/size 6 gold beads sequence. Add a second cellini spiral with the pebble beads inside and then the three 8mm bead sequence.

7 To finish the first half of the necklace, add about 11, 8mm beads with small gold beads in between. Thread the second side of the necklace to match. Attach a calotte to each end and then attach a necklace fastening.

Herringbone Earrings (page 72)

These short lengths of herringbone tube flatten when they are folded into a 'U' shape, making it easy to store them away. The earring wires attach quite cleverly through a delica bead, which is more secure than simply sewing several times over the wire loop.

YOU WILL NEED:

- Silver delica beads, 2g
- Nickel matt short bugles, 3mm, 2g
- Gun metal twisted bugles, 7mm, 48
- Nickel matt beads, size 6, two
- Sterling silver earring wires, two
- Nymo™ or Super-lon™ beading thread

1 To work the base band of ladder stitch, pick up four delicas and go back through all four, leaving a long tail. *Pick up two more delicas and go back through the previous two and the two just added. Repeat from * until there are eight pairs of delicas in a row. Join the ends together in a circle by going back through the first two beads and the pair just added.

2 To begin the herringbone stitch, pick up two twisted bugles and go down through the next delica and back up through the next delica along. Add pairs of twisted bugles all the way round. Step up at the end of the round through the next delica and the bugle stacked on top.

3 Continue working herringbone stitch in rounds, stepping up each time. Work two rounds of delicas, two with 3mm bugles, two with delicas, two with 3mm bugles and two with delicas. Add a round of twisted bugles and then complete the second side in reverse order up to the twisted bugles.

4 On the next round add delicas to create a two drop ladder stitch border. Pick up four delicas and pass the needle through the next twisted bugle and back up through the previous twisted bugle and the first two delicas again. Pass the needle back down through the other two delicas and twisted bugle again. Come up through the next bugle along and pick up two delicas. Continue taking through the previous stack and the one just added to the end.

5 To finish the ends, pick up one delica and go down through the next one. Come up through the next and add one until there are four delicas. Flatten the tube and take the needle through all four delicas. Using the long tail, repeat at the other end to add a row of four delicas.

6 Join the two pairs left on either side together by looping the thread through the opposite rows and bring the thread out in the middle of each row. Pick up two 3mm bugles and a size 6 seed bead. Pick up a third 3mm bugle and take the needle back through the other two bugles (these are essentially inside the size 6 seed bead). Attach an earring wire through the top bugle and then sew in the thread ends. Make a second earring to match.

CHAPTER 4:
Fringing, Netting & Tassels

Coral Bracelet (page 81)

This beautiful bracelet in gorgeous blues and silver looks so complicated to make, but is actually quite quick and easy. The pretty branched fringes are added one at a time along a base row and you just keep going back and forward and filling in the gaps until the bracelet has the fullness you require.

YOU WILL NEED:

- Denim blue glass seed bead mix, sizes 15–6, 15g
- Amethyst glass seed bead mix, sizes 15–6, 15g
- Blue glass bead mix, 34g
- Nymo™ or Super-lon™ thread
- Toggle fastening
- Needle

1 Pick up one bead and secure as a stop bead (see page 37). Cut a long length of beading thread. Pick up enough size 8 or 9 seed beads to create the base of your bracelet. To find the length, hold a tape measure loosely around your wrist and take off about 2cm (¾in) for the fastening.

2 Go through the last bead with the needle twice to secure. Thread a second piece of thread and pass through the first four beads, leaving an 8cm (3in) tail. Work a half hitch (see page 17) over the main bracelet thread. *Pick up eight size 10 seed beads, a size 8 seed bead and a size 10 seed bead. Miss the last bead and go through the large bead and the next four size 10 beads.

3 To make the branch, pick up four size 10 beads, a size 8 bead and a size 10 bead. Go back through the large bead, the four small beads on the branch and the four small beads on the 'stem'.

4 Take the needle under the sixth bead on the bracelet base so that the stem straddles the fifth bead. Repeat from * working along the bracelet adding similar branched stems over every other bead, varying the colours occasionally.

5 When you reach the last four beads, begin to work in the opposite direction adding single stems without branches – pick up four–six small seed beads, a large seed and a small seed bead. Miss the last bead and take the needle back through the remaining beads.

6 Take the needle through the next bead so that the stem straddles the bead in between the fringed strands. Repeat to the end.

7 Finally work back along the bracelet base, adding as many extra branched fringes between beads as required to create the effect you like.

8 Release the stop beads and remove the last two seed beads at each end. Thread on the toggle fastening and then pick up the two seed beads again. Sew the fastening securely by going through the beads on the bracelet and through the fastening several times. Secure the thread ends with half hitches (see page 17) and trim neatly.

Netted Scarf (page 83)

One of the easiest ways to embellish a simple scarf is to add a netting fringe. The bead netting adds weight and gives a sheer scarf body. Add interest by threading alternate colours of seed beads and varying the size. Remember to match the size of beads used in the netting to the weight of scarf so that it isn't too heavy.

YOU WILL NEED:

- Scarf, 25cm (10in) wide
- Hematite cube beads, 4mm, 5g
- Pewter seed bead mix, size 15–6, 15g
- Strong fine beading thread
- Needle and pins

1 Measure across the bottom of the scarf approximately every 3.25cm (1¼in) to divide it into eight equal sections and mark with pins (see page 79).

2 Secure two threads on one corner of the scarf, then pick up a cube bead and a large seed on both threads. Remove one thread from the needle. On this thread pick up 15 seeds, a large seed, 15 seeds and a large seed then add a stop bead to secure temporarily. Add a single

thread on the other corner and add the same beads with a stop bead at the end. These two strands of beads are for the straight edges at each end of the netting.

3 On the other thread at the first corner, *pick up five small seeds, a large seed, five small seeds, a large seed and a cube bead. Pick up another large seed then repeat from * to complete the other side of the loop.

4 Take a small stitch through the fabric at the first pin. Take the needle back through the cube and large seed bead. Repeat from * to make loops all the way across the scarf.

5 Take the needle back through the large cube and then through the last beads added, to come out of the large seed bead on the other side of the cube bead in the middle of the last loop. Pick up the seed bead sequence to make the next loop missing out the large seed and cube at the end.

6 Feed the needle through the three beads in the middle of the next loop. Continue to the last loop. Pick up five seeds, a large seed and five seeds and then take the needle through the next large seed on the end string of beads. Work loops across the scarf again, going through the first large seed bead on the end string from bottom to top. Pick up the five seeds, a large seed and five small seeds and take the needle through the middle three beads on the last loop of the first row. Leave this thread to tie in later.

7 Join a new thread on the right-hand side below the second large seed. Bring the thread out above the large seed and work another row of netting all the way across. When you come out of the last large seed on the left hand-side strand, work another row of netting.

8 For the final row of netting, work a half hitch (see page 17) above the last large seed bead on the right-hand side and take the thread back through the last loop to the other side of the middle three beads. Work the last row of netting. Secure the thread end with several half hitches (see page 17).

Beaded Tassel Box (page 87)

This gorgeous tassel with its tiny sparkling beads looks really stunning attached to a pretty tin box covered with Oriental patterned paper and dabbed with antique gold ink to age it. If you are short of time you can simply hang the tassel from a ready-made box or attach to the wardrobe key and it won't go missing so easily.

YOU WILL NEED:

- Pack of space dyed mixed yarns
- Strong fine cord
- Light gold, galvanized green, metallic teal, galvanized aubergine and silver-lined blue zircon, 5g of each
- Needle
- Nymo™ or c-lon™ thread
- Scissors

1 Cut two 15cm (6in) pieces of strong fine cord. Lay one piece horizontally on the work surface. Cut approximately 50, 30cm (12in) lengths of mixed yarns and lay in a bundle on the work surface so that the thread lies across the middle.

2 To attach the hanging cord tie a large knot on one end of the other piece of cord and lay on the tassel bundle so that the knot is just below the horizontal cord. Gather the bundle of yarn around the knot and tie the horizontal cord securely. Wrap around the bundle again and tie once more. Pick up by the hanging cord and let the yarn bundle fall down over the knot to make the tassel.

3 **Base row:** Pick up 32 light gold iris delica beads and go back through to make a circle. Tie in a reef (square) knot (see page 17) to secure. Pull the beads over the top of the tassel. It may be necessary to adjust the size of the tassel to fit as the beads should be a snug fit.

4 **Row 1:** *Pick up three light gold iris beads, miss three beads and go through the next bead. Repeat from * all the way round. Take the needle through the next three beads to come out after the middle bead on the first loop.

5 Sort your beads out and label each with a code letter so that you can follow the pattern sequence. Main colour (M) light gold iris, 1st colour G (green), 2nd colour T (teal), 3rd colour A (aubergine) and 4th colour B (blue)

6 **Row 2:** *Pick up three M and go through the middle bead in the next loop. Pick up one M, one G, one M and go through the middle bead in the next loop. Repeat from * all the way round and then follow the sequence from row 3.

Base row: 32 light gold iris (M)
Row 1: MMM MMM
Row 2: MMM MGM
Row 3: MGG GGM
Row 4: GGG MTM
Row 5: MTT TTM
Row 6: TTT MAM
Row 7: MAA AAM
Row 8: AAA MBM
Row 9: MBB BBM
Row 10: BBB MMM
Row 11: MMM MMM
Row 12: MMM

7 Go back through all the beads in the last row and secure the thread with a half hitch (see page 17). Pass the needle through a few beads and trim the thread end. Trim the tassel to the length required.

CHAPTER 5:
Threading and Stringing

Wax Cotton Bracelet (page 96)

Waxed cotton is now available in such pretty pastel shades so no piece of jewellery need have that ethnic look again. There are several thicknesses of waxed cotton so do check that the bead holes are big enough to thread through. If slightly too small you can use a bead reamer to enlarge the holes.

YOU WILL NEED:

- 76cm (30in) in two toning colours of 1mm waxed cotton
- Five decorative beads – a single large bead and two pairs of beads
- Four small ring beads

1 Thread the largest bead on to one strand of waxed cotton. Hold the second strand over the top of the bead and tie an overhand knot, using both strands at each end close to the bead.

2 Thread the first pair of beads onto the other strand of waxed cotton, one on each side, and then tie the strands together again. Thread on the second pair of beads on the first strand and tie the threads together.

3 Overlap the two sets of cords so that the beads and cord form a bracelet sized oval. Tie one end with an overhand knot over the cords and then repeat with the other end in the opposite direction (see page 96).

4 Adjust the position of the knots so that the bracelet can go over your hand. Thread a small ring bead on the end of each cord, tie an overhand knot (see page 17) and trim neatly.

Tigertail Necklace (page 101)

Bead mixes are a wonderfully inspiring way to buy beads, especially if you handpick the ones you really like! This stunning necklace has several strands with one type of bead on each. Space the beads equally on each strand, but make the starting point slightly different so that the beads don't sit side by side.

YOU WILL NEED:

- Beadalon bead stringing wire, 0.45mm
- From the Planet bead mix select five different sets of beads, seven of larger, nine of smaller e.g. seven 13mm round beads, seven 15 × 10mm droplets, 16 10mm flower beads, nine 6mm decorative ceramic beads, seven 12 × 10mm octagonal ceramic beads
- Size 1 crimps or size 2 tubes
- Crimp pliers
- Snipe- (chain-) nose pliers
- Wire cutters
- Beading mat
- Measuring tape
- Pins
- Tubular crimp necklace fastening

1 Cut five 60cm (24in) lengths of bead stringing wire. Feed a crimp, a large round bead and a crimp on to one length of bead stringing wire. Centre the bead and secure a crimp on either side.

2 Pick up a crimp, a large round bead and a crimp on one end. Insert two pins 4.5cm (1¾in) apart into the beading mat. Use the pins as a guide to space the beads and secure with the crimps. Space the remaining round beads along the wire, three on each side.

3 Pick up the next set of beads with a crimp on either side on another wire. Secure the middle bead in a slightly different place so that the beads don't all hang together at the bottom. Vary the spacing, depending on the number and size of beads on each wire. The flower beads are secured in pairs back to back.

4 Once all five strings are complete, hold the wires together and check that the necklace strands hang attractively. Adjust the length of one or two if necessary and trim so that all ends are level.

5 Fit one end of the wires into a tube crimp fastening. You can open out the end slightly by pushing a nail or fine snipe-nose pliers gently into the hole. Push all the wires as far as they will go.

6 Hold the tubular crimp fastening with the curve upwards and press the end of the fastening with flat-nose pliers so that you are flattening it horizontally. Arrange the necklace wires and insert the ends in the other side of the clasp. Crimp the other end at the same angle as before.

Multistrand Necklace (page 103)

When beads are all the same colour you can really enjoy combining all sorts of shapes and sizes to make this stunning necklace. Pick interesting beads like the delightful little fish shapes or hexagon cylinders and then finish with a few semi-precious stones to give it a really classy look.

YOU WILL NEED:

- Mix of black beads – approximately: eight 20 x 15mm oval beads, nine 12mm round, nine 1cm faceted, nine 6 x 7mm tubular beads, 18 3 x 8mm cylinder beads, 40 6mm round beads, 40 6mm faceted beads, 23 8m flat discs, five 6 x 15mm fish beads, four 8mm bugles.
- Black bead thread
- Silver-plated calottes, two
- Silver-plated necklace fastening
- Bead mat
- Measuring tape
- Pins
- Big eye beading needle
- Bead glue
- Flat-nose pliers

1 The multi-strand section of the necklace is about 36cm (14in) long. Mark a beading mat with pins that width apart. Position a large oval bead about 7cm (3in) from each pin and one in the middle. Arrange some of the middle-sized beads individually in between and then fill with small beads.

2 Arrange two more lines of beads on the mat about the same length. Position the largest beads first so that they are staggered and no two large beads are in the same position. Add the medium-sized beads to create an attractive arrangement and then fill with small beads.

3 Cut six, 76cm (36in) lengths of beading thread and arrange in pairs. Pick up each line of beads on separate pairs of threads. To allow the beads strands to hang together at the ends pick up a bugle bead at each end of two strands and a cylinder bead at each end of the other strand.

4 Hold the three strands up to check that the beads hang nicely and adjust if necessary. Pick up all six threads at one side on a big eye needle. Pick up a medium round faceted bead and a tubular bead and then about 9cm (3½in) of mixed round and faceted 6mm beads. Repeat with the six threads at the other end.

5 Check the length of the necklace and adjust as required. Feed the six threads at one side through the hole in a calotte (knot cover) and tie several reef (square) knots (see page 17), one after the other. Apply a little glue and trim the ends. Close the calotte with pliers.

6 Attach a calotte to the other end, checking that the threads are tight and there are no gaps between the beads before tying the knots. Attach a necklace fastening to each calotte.

Macramé Necklace (page 105)

Look for a really big focus bead to set off this gorgeous macramé necklace. The contemporary style of the beads, with their pretty mottled appearance transforms a traditional technique into a thoroughly modern design. If you can't find paper jewellery cord, fine wax cotton or cord is ideal.

YOU WILL NEED:

- 3m each of 1mm paper jewellery cord in cream, beige and brown
- Large rectangular brown and gold accent bead, 4 x 2.5cm
- Brown and gold round beads, two 15mm and four 12mm
- Gold-plated heishi beads, 24
- Leather crimps, two gold-plated
- Gold plated toggle fastening
- Low tack tape
- Scissors
- Flat-nosed pliers

1 Feed the large rectangle bead onto all three cords and position in the middle. Tape the bead to the work surface so that the cords are vertical and secure the cords above the bead with a second piece of tape.

2 Work three half knots (see page 104) around the cream core thread, with the dark brown and beige cords. Pick up a heishi bead and tie a further three half knots. Pick up a second heishi bead and work another set of three half knots. Allow the knots to twist naturally.

3 Pick up a large round bead on all three cords. Repeat step 2. Pick up a small round bead and repeat step 2. Pick up a second small round bead.

4 Repeat step 2 until you have added six heishi beads after the last small round bead. Work about 8cm (3in) of plain half knots, letting the cords twist naturally.

5 Remove the tape from the centre bead and turn it around so that the other set of cords are facing towards you. Repeat from step 2 to complete the other side of the necklace. Try the necklace on for size and work more half knots if required. The finished length should be about 48cm (19in) but could be worked as a longer necklace.

6 Trim the cord ends to 6mm (¼in). Secure the ends in leather crimp ends. Attach a toggle fastening to each end using gold-plated jump rings.

CHAPTER 6:

Wire Work and Jewellery Techniques

Tiara (page 112)

This simple twisting technique can be used with lots of different beads and other colours of wire. You could work a smaller sample and attach to hair combs for the bridesmaid or make a similar tiara in really funky colours for a hen night or special birthday.

YOU WILL NEED:

- Clear AB Swarovski round crystals, one 10mm, seven 8mm and nine 6mm
- Clear AB Swarovski bicone crystals, 35, 4mm
- Ivory round pearls, three 8mm, seven 6mm and 45, 4mm
- Silver-plated tiara band
- Silver-plated wire, 8m (8yd) of 0.4mm (27swg) and 1m (1yd) of 0.2mm (36swg)
- Wire cutters

1 Pick up the 10mm crystal on a long length of 0.4mm (27swg) wire and drop down to the middle. Hold the crystal between your finger and thumb and twist the wire to create a 4cm (1⅝in) stem. The amount of twist is crucial to the look.

TIP IF YOU WANT THE STEMS TO BE STRAIGHT ONLY TWIST UNTIL THE WIRE IF EVENLY TWISTED AND BEGINS TO LOOK LIKE TINY SEEDS. **F**OR SLIGHTLY CROOKED STEMS, AS SHOWN IN THE FINISHED DESIGN, TWIST A FEW MORE TIMES AND THE WIRE BEGINS TO TWIST IN ON ITSELF.

2 Hold the twisted wire by the bead end and tuck the tiara band between the wires at the other end. Wrap each wire around the tiara band once so that the wire is sticking up towards the crystal again. The wire is wrapped spaced out so that the initial row of stems are all about 6mm (¼in) apart.

3 Pick up an 8mm pearl on one wire and fold the wire over to the other side of the tiara from where it emerged. Hold the bead just above the pre-twisted stem and twist to create the stem. Repeat with a 6mm pearl on the other side.

4 Continue adding alternate round crystals and the two larger pearls for about 9cm (3½in) on each side to make a total tiara beading length of 18cm (7in). Vary the heights from stem to stem and taper down to the outer edges. When you get to the end of the wire, wrap it once around the tiara band and trim so that the cut end is facing up towards the beads otherwise it will scratch whoever is wearing the tiara.

5 Using a 6mm round crystal, twist a long length of wire to make a 3cm (1¼in) stem. Tuck the beaded tiara band between the wires so that the stem is in the middle and wrap to secure as before.

6 Work out from the centre as before, adding 4mm pearls and 4mm bicone crystals alternately, to create shorter stems that sit in front of the main stems. Add the occasional 6mm crystal to add variety as you go.

7 Pick up alternate 4mm pearls and 4mm bicone crystals until there are 21 pearls on a 30cm (12in) length of 0.4mm (27swg) wire. Fold over the ends of the wire to prevent the beads falling off.

8 Hold the wire across the tiara band so that the centre pearl is in the middle. Beginning in the middle of the 0.2mm (36swg) wire, secure the beaded wire to the band, wrapping between the stems and each pearl and crystal in turn. Add or remove a few beads if required till you reach the end of the stems on either side.

9 Wrap the wires neatly a few times at each end to secure, remembering to keep the cut ends facing up towards the beads. Arrange the stems and if necessary, bend each a little more, bringing some slightly to the front to create the effect you desire.

Keyring Charm (page 115)

Spiral beads are quite easy to make and you don't need any special equipment. If you don't have these fine knitting needles cut a short length of 1.5mm (16swg) wire and make the spirals on that instead. Round doughnut-shaped beads would look equally good with spiral beads in the middle or simply alternate spiral beads with chunky beads for a different design.

YOU WILL NEED:

- Turquoise square beads, three 3cm (1¼in) with a 12mm (½in) aperture
- Silver-plated wire, 0.5mm (25swg)
- Bright blue craft wire, 0.7mm (22swg)
- Fine knitting needle (size 0000)
- Spring hook
- Wire cutters

1 Wrap 0.5mm (25swg) silver-plated wire around a fine knitting needle to make three 7mm (⅜in) lengths of spring. Trim the ends straight and put to one side.

2 Using 0.7mm (22swg) bright blue wire, make four 2cm (¾in) lengths of spring, trim the ends and put to one side.

3 Wrap silver-plated wire to make a 6mm (¼in) spring. Slide one of the bright blue springs on to the silver-plated wire and then wrap the wire and spring together around the needle to make the spiral bead shape. Wrap only the silver wire around the needle again for 6mm (¼in).

4 Repeat to make two more spiral beads. For the last spiral bead, wrap a longer 7mm (⅜in) spring with the silver-plated wire to begin. Once the bright blue spiral is formed, wrap the silver wire to make a 2cm (¾in) spring.

5 Cut a 40cm (16in) length of silver-plated wire and wrap around the 'D' ring of the spring hook twice. *Feed the ends through a piece of silver spring. Trim one end of the wire close to the end of the spring. Take the remaining wire through one side of a square turquoise bead and pick up a spiral bead. Feed the wire through the other side of the bead.

6 Repeat from * to add another two square turquoise beads. Thread on the last spiral bead with the shorter spring first. Bend the longer spring around to make a loop. Coil the end of the wire around the bright blue spiral and trim neatly.

Earrings (page 117)

These earrings can be made with any similar size and shape of beads so you can have a whole range of different designs ready to wear with all your outfits. Try using silver headpins and wire instead or use one of the other metallic colours.

YOU WILL NEED:

- Headpins, two, gold with decorative end
- Gold-plated wire, 0.5mm (25swg)
- Glass multicolour beads, two 12mm and two 15mm
- Gold metal-effect cylinder beads, four, 3 × 7mm
- Earring wires, two gold
- Round-nosed pliers
- Flat-nosed pliers
- Wire cutters

1 Pick up a large multicolour bead on the headpin and then a gold metal effect cylinder bead. Bend the end of the wire over at about 90 degrees close to the top of the cylinder bead. Trim the end to 7mm (⅜in). Use round-nose pliers to bend the wire around to make a loop on the end of the headpin (see page 117).

2 Make an eyepin loop on the end of the gold-plated wire. Pick up small multicolour bead and then a gold metal effect cylinder bead. Make a loop at the other end of the link and trim the wire (see page 117).

3 Open the loop below the small multicolour bead and attach the headpin dangle made earlier. Attach an earring wire to the top end of the bead link. Make a second earring to match.

TIP IF YOU CAN'T FIND DECORATIVE HEADPINS, ADD ONE OR TWO TINY DOUGHNUT-SHAPED GOLD METAL EFFECT BEADS TO A PLAIN HEADPIN BEFORE ADDING THE LARGE BEAD.

Chain Maille Bracelet (p119)

When making the jump rings for this bracelet, remember to cut the end of the spring with the flat side of the wire cutters each time so that the ends butt together neatly. You will work more quickly if you prepare some open rings and leave others closed.

YOU WILL NEED:

- Knitting needle or metal rod
- Silver-plated wire, 1.2mm (18swg)
- Silver-plated wire, 0.6mm (24swg)
- Crushed ice bead: four 8mm cubes in wine
- Crushed ice bead: four 10mm round in wine
- Round-nose pliers
- Flat-nose pliers
- Wire cutters
- Toggle clasp, silver-plated

1 Choose a knitting needle or metal rod about 7mm (⅜in) in diameter. Using the 1.2mm (18swg) silver-plated wire, make a tightly wrapped spring with about 25 coils. Trim 21 individual rings from the spring, cutting a flat end on the spring before cutting the next ring (see page 118).

2 Tension all the rings to make closed jump rings and then open two out of every three. Make seven flower shapes using the flower chain technique on page 119 and arrange on the work surface.

3 Using round-nosed pliers, make a large eye pin loop with 0.6mm (24swg) silver-plated wire. Pick up a cube bead. Make a loop at the other end and trim the end (see page 116). Make four cube bead links and four round bead links in total.

4 Open one loop of a bead link and pick up a flower shape, then close the loop. Attach a different bead link to the other side. Continue joining flower shapes and bead links until the chain is complete. Attach a toggle fastening to the end bead link loops to finish the bracelet.

Bead Corsage (page 123)

As this flower is not in realistic colours you can change it to suit any outfit or occasion. Although the main flower is all one colour, there are subtle differences that add interest and liveliness to the design. Use matt beads for the loops in the flower centre and mixed alabaster and colour-lined beads for the main petals.

YOU WILL NEED:

- Turquoise matt seed beads, size 11, 10g
- Jade alabaster and silver-lined seed beads, size 8 (2.6mm), 15g each
- Pewter gloss and transparent seed beads, size 12, 5g each
- Pewter colour-lined seed beads, size 9, 5g
- Silver-plated wire, 0.315mm (30swg) 5m (5yd)
- Silver-plated wire, 0.45mm (26swg) 10m, (10yd)
- Brooch back or hatpin
- Wire cutters

1 To make the stamens in the centre, mix the pewter gloss and transparent size 12 (2mm) seed beads. Using 0.315mm (30swg) silver-plated wire, pick up five beads in a random order. Miss the last bead added, then take the wire back through the other four beads to leave a 5cm (2in) tail. Repeat to make a row of 15 continuous stamens (see page 122).

2 Pick up at least 38cm (15in) of size 11 matt turquoise beads on 0.45mm (26swg) silver-plated wire, straight off the reel. Make a small loop on the end to stop the beads falling off. Measure 2.5cm (1in) of beads and make a loop about 5cm (2in) from the end of the wire. Repeat to make a row of 15 continuous loops.

3 Pick up at least 56cm (22½in) of size II matt turquoise beads on the 0.45mm (26swg) wire as before. Measure 4cm (1½in) of beads for each of 15 medium continuous loops. For the larger loops pick up at least 75cm (30in) of the same beads and measure 5cm (2in) of beads for each loop. Make 15 large continuous loops.

4 To make the petals, mix the size 8 (2.6mm) jade alabaster and silver-lined seed beads and pick up about 25cm (10in) on 0.45mm (26swg) wire straight off the reel for each petal. Make a loop at the end to prevent the beads falling off. Make a basic frame (see page 122) leaving 4cm (1½in) of beads on the centre wire. Make a five-row petal with a rounded top end. Make 11 petals in total.

5 To begin assembling the flower, coil the stamens into a bundle and take one tail through between the stamens to hold them together. Twist the wire underneath. Join on the small loop centre using one tail. Wrap the loops tightly around the stamen bundle and then wrap the tail around a few times to secure. Repeat with the medium and then the large loop centres.

6 Join on a piece of fine wire (0.315mm, 30swg). Pick up one petal at a time and position under the flower centre, then wrap with the fine wire to secure before adding the next petal. Once all the petals are added twist the wires together to make the stem.

7 To make the leaves, pick up about 30cm (12in) of the size 12 (2mm) mixed pewter and grey beads on 0.45mm (26swg) silver-plated wire straight off the reel, then pick up 3cm (1¼in) of size 9 (2.6mm) pewter seed beads. Make a loop on the end of the wire. Make a basic frame (see page 122), leaving the larger beads on the centre wire. Make a seven-row leaf with a pointed top end. Make three leaves in total.

8 To assemble the leaf spray, snip one side of each loop to make a stem and trim any other wires. Pick up five size 9 seed beads on each leaf stem and push up to the base of the leaf. Lightly twist two leaf stems together and pick up three size 9 seed beads. Hold the third leaf in position and twist the three stems together. Pick up another six size 9 seed beads. You may need to trim the first stem to fit the wires through the bead holes.

9 Wrap the leaf spray around the flower stem. Coil the stem around in a loop and trim the end. Secure the loop by wrapping with a fresh piece of wire. Use the wire to attach a brooch back or hatpin.

CHAPTER 7:

Bead Embroidery

Little Bag (page 129)

Choose a richly textured fabric for this bag so that the individual beads almost merge into the fabric. Although the beads are stitched one at a time on to the fabric, the solid border is not deep so it doesn't take too long to complete. Remember to stitch twice through the beads that are spaced out to prevent them being pulled out and secure thread ends so that the beads don't fall off.

YOU WILL NEED:

- Pink tweed fabric 20 × 36cm (8 × 14in)
- Seed bead mix, size 12–6 (size 6 plum, size 9 pink and white, size 11 red, metallic rainbow, pink and white, size 12 pinky-red)
- Pale pink round crystals, 6mm, 10g
- Sewing thread
- Beading needle, size 10
- Ribbon, 30cm of 1.5mm (⅝in)
- Deep fuchsia perlé cotton thread, no 5
- Cord maker

1 Fold the fabric in half crossways and press to mark the centre line. Using single stitch, sew beads densely for the first 2cm (¾in) above the crease line, making the bead panel 15cm (6in) wide. To space the beads with an even mix, sew the crystal beads first spacing them out every 1cm (½in) and then add the size 6 plum beads.

2 Sew pink and white size 9 seeds between the larger beads and then fill any gaps with smaller white and pink beads, adding some deep red and brighter pinky-red beads to liven the mix.

3 For the next 2cm (¾in) add the same number of crystal and size 6 plum seed beads adding fewer smaller beads in between. Over the next 6cm (2½in) space the beads out further. It can help to pin the larger beads in position at this point to get an even spread before sewing them in position.

4 Fold the beaded fabric with beads inside in half and sew the side seams by hand or using a zipper foot in the machine. Zigzag the seam and trim. Turn inside out. Trim around the top edge, following the weave of the tweed to 16cm (6½in) deep. Fray the last 1cm (½in) on the front and back. Sew a mix of beads along the frayed edge every 6mm (¼in).

5 Cut the ribbon in half and pin on the inside 4cm (1½in) from the top edge. Sew along both edges with sewing thread that matches the tweed. Fold the perlé cotton in three and tie a knot in each end. Secure one end to a door handle and then twist tightly using a cord maker or pencil. Fold the tightly twisted thread in half, hold the knots and allow cord to twist from the other end. Tie the ends together.

6 Smooth out the twists between finger and thumb. Tape the centre point and cut in half. Thread one length through the tweed at the side seam and then along the ribbon to the other side. Go back along the ribbon channel on the reverse side. Repeat with the other length of cord on the opposite side.

7 Tie the cord ends together and unravel the thread ends. Sew single beads all over the knots to make beaded tassels. Trim ends neatly.

Patchwork Cushion (page 133)

Patchwork fabric makes an interesting background for bead embroidery. You can use any scraps of fabric to make the patchwork but if you are unsure where to begin choose a pretty patterned fabric with three or four colours in it and then find solid coloured fabric in three colours to match. Arrange the rectangles as shown on the picture.

YOU WILL NEED:

- Patterned quilting fabric and three toning solid colours
- Scissors
- Sewing machine
- Vanishing embroidery marker
- Pastel seed beads, size 11, three colours to match
- Variegated stranded embroidery cotton
- Sewing needle
- Polyester wadding 12cm (4¾in) thin
- Polyester stuffing for filling

1 Cut three 3 x 5cm (1⅛ x 2in) rectangles from each of the plain coloured fabrics and nine from the patterned fabric. Cut a 12cm (4¾in) square for the cushion back.

2 Arrange the rectangles in three rows as indicated in the picture. Join the rectangles together in rows using 6mm (¼in seams) along the longer sides. Press the seams open.

3 Join the rows together to make a square. Press the seams open. Draw three wavy lines across the rows of patchwork. Work a different bead embroidery stitch along each line (see page 132), missing the beads out on the outer 1cm (½in) around the edge.

4 Work lazy daisy stitches in between the rows. Lazy daisy is chain stitch worked individually and in this instance the bead is added with the stitch used to catch the loop down. Use a thread and bead colour that is not used in the fabric on either side.

5 Lay the patchwork panel right side down on the plain coloured square. Lay the piece of thin wadding on top.
Pin or tack around the edge, leaving a gap at one side for turning. Machine stitch around the edge using a zipper foot attachment so that you don't crush any beads.

6 Leaving the seam allowance intact across the gap, trim the seams and across the corners. Turn the cushion through and ease out the corners with a blunt point tool. Stuff the cushion firmly with stuffing and sew the gap.

7 To work the buttonhole stitch border, attach a thread on the side seam. Pick up one of each colour of bead and take a small stitch across the seam about 6mm (¼in) away. Take the needle through the loop and pull up so that the beads are lying along the seam. Pick up another three beads in the same order and work the buttonhole stitch. Repeat all the way round. Sew in the ends securely.

Picture Frame (page 134)

Couching is an easy way to embellish patterned fabric as the decision about where to sew the beads is all done for you. The colour of beads that you choose will depend on the colour of the fabric. In this example there are three seed beads that tone in with the fabric to create the couched lines and then contrast beads and sequins to add decoration. Use double thread couching for the longer lines of couching and single thread or backstitch for the shorter or more curved lines.

YOU WILL NEED:

- 20cm (8in) square of fabric
- 20cm (8in) square of medium iron-on interfacing
- 20cm (8in) square of thin wadding
- * Seed beads, size 11 to match fabric, 3g
- Seed beads, size 11 in three toning colours, 1g each
- Sequins, 7mm (⅜in)
- Sewing thread
- Double-sided tape, 2.5cm (1in) wide
- Stiff card, two A4 sheets
- Craft knife, safety ruler and cutting mat
- Fabric marker
- Needle

1 Cut a 15cm (6in) square of plain fabric from the stiff card and mark a 3.5cm (1⅜in) border all round. Cut out the aperture in the middle. Stick double-sided tape on the front and reverse side of the card frame, leaving the backing paper on.

2 Arrange the rectangles into three rows of six. Iron interfacing on the reverse side of the fabric. Lay the fabric flat and mark the size of the frame and aperture with a fabric marker. Tack along the lines. Couch lines of beads along the design lines on the fabric inside the tacked lines (see page 131). Pick up mainly one colour and then add the occasional alternative bead in toning colours to break the solid lines.

3 Fill areas in the background with sequins and dotted seed beads in a contrast colour. Attach the sequins by bringing the needle up in the centre, pick up a seed bead and then take the needle back through the sequin hole (see page 134).

4 Cut the excess fabric from the aperture leaving 1.5cm (⅝in) inside the tacked lines. Repeat to trim the outside edge. Trim the interfacing back a little more. Snip diagonally into the corners of the aperture stopping at the tacked lines. Remove all tacking thread.

5 Remove the backing paper from the front of the card frame and attach the wadding. Trim close to the edges of the frame and inside the aperture. Position the frame wadding side down, on the reverse side of the beaded fabric so the aperture lines up with the fabric tabs.

6 Peel off the backing paper from the rest of the double-sided tape and stretch the aperture tabs gently on to the frame so that the beads line up at the edge. Stretch two opposite sides and the remaining two sides. Check the fabric is straight and adjust if necessary.

7 Cut two 14.5cm (5¾in) squares of card and mark a 3cm (1¼in) border on one piece. Cut the aperture and stick on the reverse side with double-sided tape. Apply 1cm (½in) wide strips of double sided tape around three sides of the remaining square and stick on the back.

8 Attach a hanger on the reverse side or if you want a stand, cut a 14 x 5cm (5½ x 2in) strip of card. Score across 5cm (2in) from one end and stick the square at the top of the frame on the reverse side.

CHAPTER 8:

Knitting and Crochet

Beaded Scarf (page 143)

Although a scarf is the ideal project for beginning knitting it doesn't mean it should be dull or boring. This simple design uses a luxury yarn knitted in two different textures to create the shape. String the beads in a random order or draw a chart to work out where you want the larger beads to fall.

Quantities are for a (90cm) 36in scarf

YOU WILL NEED:

- No 12 cotton perlé colour 524 – two balls
- RYC natural silk aran colour 464 – three balls
- Size 7 knitting needles
- Light seafoam AB seed beads, size 8, (6in tube)
- Smoke grey faceted beads, 4mm, 50
- Smoke grey, transparent and matt turquoise AB faceted beads, 6mm, 15 of each

1 Using the no. 12 cotton perlé straight off the ball, pick up a seed bead, a 4mm smoke grey bead, a seed bead, a 6mm turquoise bead, a seed bead, a 6mm smoke grey bead and a seed bead. Repeat, alternating between transparent and matt turquoise beads until you have added about 20 6mm beads in total.

2 Hold the cotton perlé with the silk aran yarn together and cast on 40 stitches. Knit two rows. On the next row knit one stitch then add a bead every two stitches using bead knitting (see page 140). Knit the next row with both yarns but without adding beads.

3 On the next row knit two stitches and then add a bead. Work along the row adding a bead every two stitches. Knit a row without beads again. Repeat these four rows three times.

4 Break the perlé thread and pick up size 8 seed beads on the thread straight off the ball. Change to knit one, purl one for every row to work the main part of the scarf. Add the beads on every second knit stitch so that they are on the same side as the bead border.

5 On the next bead row, knit four stitches before beginning to add the beads. Alternate between the two bead rows to space the beads attractively.

6 Once the scarf is the length required break the cotton perlé and add the same beads for the border as before. Knit the border to match the other end and cast off.

Wire Knitting Corsage (page 144)

Although circular in shape, this corsage is knitted as a rectangle, shaped slightly by knitting two together across a few rows and then simply gathered up to create the design. You can sew the beads in the centre or knit a small panel incorporating the beads as you go.

YOU WILL NEED:

- Supablue wire, 0.315mm (30swg)
- Silver wire, 0.2mm (36swg)
- Silver-lined aqua sapphire triangle beads, size 5, 3in tube
- Light seafoam AB seed beads, size 8
- Multi-iris drop beads, 3 x 4mm
- Size 3 knitting needles
- Size 10 knitting needles
- Brooch back

1 Working off the reel, twist the ends of the wires together to make a 'needle' and pick up 50 size 8 seed beads followed by 50 size 5 triangle beads.

2 Using the half hitch technique (see page 17) and a size 3 needle, cast on the first stitch. *Bring a size 5 triangle bead up to the needle and cast on another two stitches. Repeat from * to the end of the row.

3 Using a size 10 needle, purl the next row leaving the beads sitting in every second loop along the bottom edge. Using both size 10 needles from now on, knit the next row adding a triangle bead on the reverse side every two stitches.

4 Purl one row. Knit the next row adding a size 8 bead after every stitch. On the next row purl two together. Repeat along the row to reduce the stitches from 50 to 25. On the next row knit two together for 12 stitches, then knit one and then knit two together to the end of the row to reduce the stitches from 25 to 13.

5 For the last row purl two together three times, purl one and then purl two together three times. Remove the needle and pass the tail of wire through all the loops. Pull up to make a rosette shape.

6 Thread the wire ends into a needle and sew the two edges together. Stretch the outer edge of the knitting to make it as full as possible, and then shape it over your finger to create soft waves.

7 To make the outer flower centre, pick up 25 size 5 triangle beads on both wires and cast on to size 10 needles using the half hitch method, dropping a bead between every other stitch. Knit a row and then cast off. Twist the knitted strip and then form into three loops like a cloverleaf. Secure with the tails of the wire.

8 To make the inner flower centre, pick up 37 drop beads on the supablue wire and cast on 12 stitches. Knit two rows. On the next row knit five stitches, add a bead between the next three and then knit to the end. Knit one row.

9 On the next row knit four stitches and add five beads, knit to the end. Knit a row. *On the next row knit three stitches and add seven beads knit to the end. Knit a row. Repeat from * twice and then add five beads on the next row. Knit a row and add three beads on the next row. Knit two more rows and cast off.

10 Scrumple the wire mesh behind the beaded circle and form into a dome shape. Feed the tail through the centre of the cloverleaf and then through the centre of the rosette. Twist the wires at the back and trim. Either sew or stick a brooch back to the reverse side.

Mobile Phone Pouch and Charm (page 149)

*C*otton perlé is an embroidery thread that is ideal for crochet and, as it is available in a much brighter colours than traditional crochet cotton, is just right for this funky little pouch, which can be made to fit any mobile phone or mp3 player. You can either crochet a flat rectangle and stitch the back seam or work in the round adding beads on the inside as you go and then turning it inside out once complete.

YOU WILL NEED:

- Cotton perlé in orange, blue and pink, no 5
- Iridescent plum teal Toho triangle beads, size 11
- Teal/ purple iris high metallic Toho triangle beads, size 11
- Teal/purple iris gloss seed beads, size 11
- Orange/pink glass beads, 15mm and 12mm
- Bonded nylon bead string, size 4
- Teal/purple iris gloss drop beads, 3 x 4
- Gold-plated ring, 5mm
- Gold-plated split ring, 12mm
- Crochet hooks, size 1.25 and 1.5

1 Pick up about 40 iridescent triangle beads on the blue thread then using the larger hook crochet a plain chain to fit around your mobile or mp3 player tightly. Slip stitch to join the ends into a circle. Crochet three chain and then work a treble (double) crochet into each chain on the circle. Slip stitch to join to the top of the first treble again.

2 Crochet two more rounds of treble and then two chain only and work a round of double (single) crochet, adding a bead on each stitch. The bead will be on the inside of the pouch at this stage.

3 Change to orange thread. You will know exactly how many beads to add this time as it is exactly the same each round. Crochet one round in treble (double) and a round of double (single) crochet adding beads on every stitch. Change to pink thread, working three rows of treble (double) and one of double (single).

4 Continue, changing the colour of the yarn to create different widths of stripes. Remember to add the beads each time you change thread colour and add the beads on the last round.

5 Once the pouch is the length required change to the next contrast colour, in this case pink but don't add any beads. Crochet six chain and then work a double crochet into the second stitch along. Repeat to create a decorative loop edge around the top.

6 For the base of the pouch, fold the crochet flat so that the back 'seam' is in the middle. Add a contrast colour at the bottom edge one stitch in from the fold edge. Crochet three chain and then work treble (double) along to one stitch away from the fold edge. Work a second row of treble. Sew the base flap in position and turn the pouch through.

7 To make a charm pick up metallic triangle and gloss seed beads alternately on to nylon bead string. Using the finer hook, crochet a 5cm (2in) length of crochet rope. At one end pick up a 15mm glass bead, three triangle beads and a 12mm glass bead. Add a small drop bead and then take the thread back up through the other beads just added. Sew the thread end into the crochet rope. At the other end attach a small gold ring by oversewing and secure the end in the rope. Attach to the phone with a mobile phone loop or use a large split ring to attach the charm to the side of the pouch.

Bead Charts

Bead charts for the off-loom and bead loom stitches vary because the beads are aligned differently with each stitch. The charts are ideal for planning patterns or motifs that can be incorporated in the bead work or even for working out how to make a shaped piece of bead fabric for an amulet purse, jewellery or other items. The individual graphs can be photocopied for personal use.

HERRINGBONE STITCH

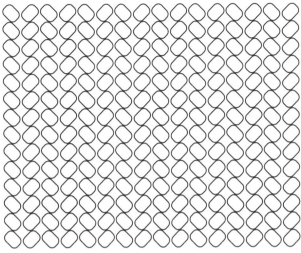

RIGHT ANGLE WEAVE

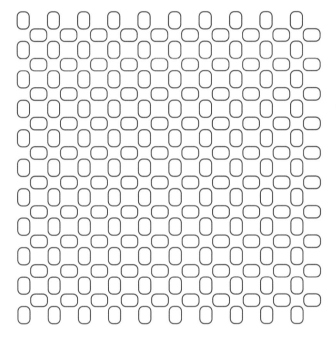

PEYOTE STITCH
Turn 90 degrees to give a chart for BRICK STITCH

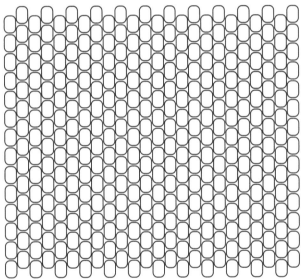

3 BEAD NETTING

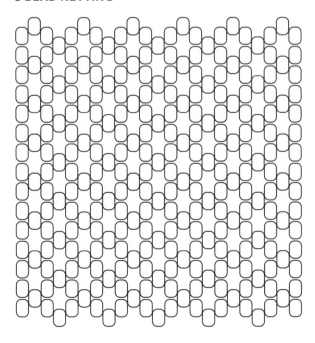

SQUARE STITCH Also use for BEAD LOOM WORK

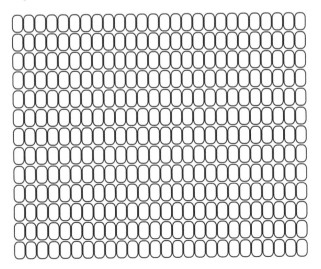

Bead Project Details

The details of specific beads used in the Bead Something Now projects are listed below. Those beads without a shop reference are either fashion beads without precise details or basic beads generally available from your local bead shop.

CHAPTER 1

BUGLE BRACELET (page 25)
Bugles, 3mm (size 1), in purple iris matt, lilac satin and white satin **(Beads Direct)**
Hex beads, 3mm, silver-lined clear **(Beads Direct)**

BEADED CANDLE BORDER WITH LOOP EDGING (page 28)
Miyuki triangle, size 10, lined ice blue 1112, deep blue AB 1831, silver-lined clear 1101 **(Stephanie Burnham Designs)**
Painted flower beads, 15mm, light blue **(Stephanie Burnham Designs)**

EVENING BAG (page 31)
Mix of seed beads, size 10, including satin bugles and Miyuki triangles **(Stephanie Burnham Designs)**
Miyuki triangle beads, size 5, lined pink 1109 and lined rose 1132 **(Stephanie Burnham Designs)**

MEDALLION BELT (page 33)
Miyuki triangle, size 10, lined lime green 1119, chartreuse AB 1153 **(Stephanie Burnham Designs)**
Cubes, 4mm, matte transparent lime green AB 143 **(Stephanie Burnham Designs)**

CHAPTER 2

SQUARE STITCH BRACELET (page 39)
Toho seed beads, size 11, rainbow metal matte F463K **(Out on a Whim)**
Toho seed beads, size 11, gold lustre green tea 457 **(Out on a Whim)**
Cube, 3mm, steel gold iris 462 **(Out on a Whim)**
Round glass beads, 12mm, in pale creamy yellow

SHOE ROSETTE (page 43)
Round crushed glass bead, 10mm, wine (colour 5505) **(Gütermann)**
Seed beads, size 11, raspberry bronze iris (460A) **(Out on a Whim)**
Swarovski bicone crystals, 4mm and 6mm rose (209) **(Rayher)**

HERRINGBONE TEA LIGHT HOLDER (page 47)
Toho triangle beads, size 10, purple teal lustre 319C, steel blue metallic 460G **(Out on a Whim)**
Toho seed beads, size 11, emerald raspberry gold lustre 318M **(Out on a Whim)**

PEYOTE STITCH RINGS (page 50)
Seed beeds, size 11, rainbow metal matte F463K, emerald raspberry gold lustre 318M **(Out on a Whim)**
Drop beads, 3 x 4mm, multi iris 455 **(Out on a Whim)**
Pale pink 4805 and dark pink 5165 bugle beads, 2mm **(Gütermann)**
Seed beads, size 9, silver-lined rose

BEADED BAUBLE (page 54)
Gold seed beads, size 10 (2mm), 14 075 06 **(Rayher)**
Gold seed beads, size 8 (2.6mm), 14 068 06 **(Rayher)**
Textured gold metal beads, 6mm and 8mm

BUTTERFLY NECKLACE (page 60)
Swarovski bicone crystals, 4mm, light peach 4 and 6mm indicolite **(Rayher)**
Seed beads, size 8, lined light sea foam AB **(Out on a Whim)**
Faceted beads, 6mm, 12 matt and 8 transparent turquoise, 26 matt peach

CHAPTER 3

SPIRAL BAG (page 66)
Seed bead, size 6, teal matte

AB **(Stephanie Burnham Designs)**
Miyuki triangle, size 10, sparkling aqua, blue-lined 1822 **(Stephanie Burnham Designs)**
Seed bead, size ll, dark brown
Washer beads, turquoise
Flat oval, 8 x 6mm, brown

CELLINI SPIRAL BEADS (page 70)
Delicas, matte gold dark gold DB322 **(Out on a Whim)**
Seed bead, size 6, gold matte silver-lined **(Out on a Whim)**
Miyuki triangle, size 10, berry red transparent rainbow **(Stephanie Burnham Designs)**
Gold ice pearls, 8mm **(Gütermann)**
Glass beads, 12mm, red/orange

HERRINGBONE EARRINGS (page 72)
Delicas, rhodium plated 032 **(The Viking Loom Ltd)**
Toho bugles, 3mm, nickel matt 451D **(The Viking Loom Ltd)**
Toho, size 6, nickel matt 451D **(The Viking Loom Ltd)**
Twisted bugles, 7mm, gun metal, bug05 **(The Viking Loom Ltd)**

CHAPTER 4

CORAL BRACELET (page 81)
Denim glass seed bead mix HOHO2
Amethyst glass seed bead mix HOHO5
Blue glass seed bead mix BMB12

NETTED SCARF (page 83)
Cube beads, 4mm, hematite 451 **(Out on a Whim)**
Pewter glass seed bead mix HOH13 **(The Viking Loom Ltd)**

BEADED TASSEL BOX (page 87)
Delica beads, light gold iris DB501, galvanised green DB426, metallic teal iris DB027,

galvanized sf aubergine 1185, silver-lined blue zircon 608 **(The Spellbound Bead Company)**

CHAPTER 5

WAX COTTON BRACELET (page 96)
Selection of beads

TIGERTAIL NECKLACE (page 101)
Planet bead mix BMB18 **(The Viking Loom Ltd)**

MULTISTRAND NECKLACE (page 103)
Selection of black semi-precious beads
Jet set bead mix BMB07 **(The Viking Loom Ltd)**

MACRAMÉ NECKLACE (page 105)
Brown and gold accent beads
Blue Moon Silver-plated heishi beads

CHAPTER 6

TIARA (page 112)
Swarovski crystals 6, 8 and 10mm round, clear AB **(Rayher)**
Swarovski crystals, 4mm bicones, clear AB **(Rayher)**
Pearls, 4, 6 and 8mm round ivory **(Rayher)**

KEYRING CHARM (page 115)
Turquoise square beads J27 \

EARRINGS (page 117)
Multicolour glass beads, 12 and 15mm, 7160 **(Gütermann)**
Blue Moon Antique gold metal cylinder beads, 3 x 7mm
Blue Moon Decorative antique gold headpins

CHAINE MAILLE BRACELET (page 119)
Crushed ice beads, 8mm cube, 10mm round 5505

Suppliers

BEAD CORSAGE (page 123)
Seed beads, size 11, opaque turquoise
matt AB F430R **(Out on a Whim)**
Seed beads, size 8 (2.6mm), jade 15,
alabaster and silver-lined **(Rayher)**
Pewter glass seed bead mix HOH07
(The Viking Loom Ltd)

CHAPTER 7

LITTLE BAG (page 129)
Seed beads, size 6, light amethyst colour-
lined fuchsia matt F399D, size 11,
metallic rainbow transparent red AB
254, emerald raspberry gold lustre 318M
(Out on a Whim)
Seed beads, size 9 and 11, pink and white,
size 12, pinky-red
Faceted glass beads, 6mm, pink 5185
(Gütermann)

PATCHWORK CUSHION (page 133)
Seed beads, size 9 (2.5mm), chalk assorted
pastel colours 6201 997 **(Knorr Prandell)**

PICTURE FRAME (page 134)
Seed beads, size 11, black, brown, golden
yellow and soft green to match fabric

CHAPTER 8

SCARF (page 143)
Seed beads, size 8, light seafoam AB 263
(StitchnCraft)
Faceted beads, 4 and 6mm, smoke grey
6975 **(Gütermann)**
Faceted beads, 6mm, transparent AB and
matt AB turquoise

WIRE KNITTING CORSAGE (page 144)
Miyuki triangles, size 5, silver-lined aqua
sapphire **(Stephanie Burnham Designs)**
Seed beads, size 8, light seafoam AB 263
(StitchnCraft)
Drop beads, 3 x 4mm, multi iris 455
(Out on a Whim)

**MOBILE PHONE POUCH AND CHARM
(page 149)**
Toho triangle, size 11, metallic
iridescent nickel-plated plum teal T515F,
teal purple high metallic T505
(Out on a Whim)
Seed bead, size 11, teal/purple iris gloss
455 **(Out on a Whim)**
Drop bead, 3 x 4 teal/ purple iris gloss 455
(Out on a Whim)
Multicolour glass beads, 12 and 15mm,
7160 **(Gütermann)**

EUROPE

Beads Direct
Tel: 01509 218028
Email: service@beaddirect.
co.uk
www.beadsdirect.co.uk

Gütermann
www.guetermann.com

Knorr Prandell
www.knorrprandell.com/en

Ilona Biggins
PO Box 600
Rickmansworth
WD3 5WR
Tel: 01923 282 998
Email: info@ilonabiggins.
co.uk
www.ilonabiggins.co.uk

Rayher
Tel: +49 (0)7392 7005-260
Email: Kundenservice@
Rayher.com
www.rayher.com

**Stephanie Burnham
Designs**
36 Graham Hill Road
The Shires
Towester Northamptonshire
NN12 7AB
Tel: 07894150240
Email: info@
stephanieburnhamdesigns.
com
stephanieburnhamdesigns.
com

StitchnCraft Beads
8 Berwick Courtyard
Berwick St Leonard
Salisbury
Wilts
SP3 5UA
Tel: 01747 830666
Email: enquiries@stitchncraft.
co.uk
www.stitchncraft.co.uk

**The Spellbound
Bead Company**
45 Tamworth Street
Lichfield
Staffs WS13 6JW
Tel 01543 417650
Email:
info@spellboundbead.co.uk
www.spellboundbead.co.uk

The Viking Loom Ltd
Wigginton Lodge,
Wigginton Road,
York,
YO32 2RH
Tel: 01904620587
Email: vikingloom@
vikingloom.co.uk
www.vikingloom.co.uk

Wires
Unit 3 Zone A, Chelmsford
Road Industrial Estate, Great
Dunmow, Essex, CM6 1HD
Tel: 01371 238013
Fax: 01371 871882
www.wires.co.uk

US

Beadworks
139 Washington Street
Norwalk
CT 06854
Tel: 203 852 9194
Email:
norwalk@beadworks.com
www.beadworks.com

**Be Dazzled /
Land of Odds**
718 Thompson Lane
Ste 123
Nashville
TN 37204
Tel: 615 292 0610
Email: oddsian@
landofodds.com
www.landofodds.com

Harlequin Beads
2833 Willamette Street
Eugene
OR 97405
Tel: 541 683 5903
www.harlequinbeads.
com

Out On A Whim
121 E. Cotati Ave
Cotati
CA 94931
Tel: 707 664 8343
www.whimbeads.com

Index

It has been a wonderful opportunity writing *The Beading Bible* and I would like to thank the companies who supplied beads and materials for many of the projects. Gutermann, Knorr Prandell, Kars and Rayher Hobby were extremely generous and I have really enjoyed creating with their beautiful beads and materials. I would also like to thank Illona Biggins who loaned the fabulous semi-precious beads for the introduction shot on page 7. Contact details for all these suppliers are on page 174-175.

Thanks to Cheryl Brown for giving me the opportunity to write this book; to the team at David and Charles for their support and expertise in putting the book together, to Jean Power for checking the technical detail and to Kim Sayer and Sarah Underhill for the gorgeous photography. Finally thanks to Sue Cleave the designer who worked so hard to fit it all in!